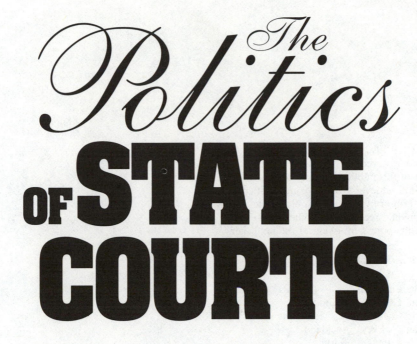

The *Politics* OF STATE COURTS

HARRY P. STUMPF

University of New Mexico

JOHN H. CULVER

California Polytechnic State University, San Luis Obispo

D0209720

Longman

New York & London

Copyright © 1992 by Longman Publishing Group.
All rights reserved.
No part of this publication may be reproduced,
stored in a retrieval system, or transmitted
in any form or by any means, electronic, mechanical,
photocopying, recording, or otherwise,
without the prior permission of the publisher.

Longman, 95 Church Street, White Plains, N.Y. 10601

Associated companies:
Longman Group Ltd., London
Longman Cheshire Pty., Melbourne
Longman Paul Pty., Auckland
Copp Clark Pitman, Toronto

Chapters 4, 5, and 7 have been drawn in part from
American Judicial Politics by Harry P. Stumpf, published
in 1988 by Harcourt Brace Jovanovich, second edition
under contract with Prentice Hall.

Senior editor: David J. Estrin
Production editor: Victoria Mifsud
Cover design: Thomas Phon Graphics
Text art: Fine Line Inc.
Production supervisor: Richard C. Bretan

Library of Congress Cataloging-in-Publication Data

Stumpf, Harry P.
    The politics of state courts / Harry P. Stumpf and John H. Culver.
        p.   cm.
    Includes bibliographical references and index.
    ISBN 0-8013-0051-7
1. Courts—United States—States.   2. Judicial process—United
States—States.   3. Political questions and judicial power—United
States—States.   4. Justice, Administration of—United States—
States.   I. Culver, John H.   II. Title.
KF8700.Z95S78   1991
347.73′3—dc20   91-27556
[347.3073]   CIP

1 2 3 4 5 6 7 8 9 10-MA-9594939291

Contents

CHAPTER 8   THE JUDICIARY IN STATE AND COMMUNITY: AN ASSESSMENT   160

Preface

This book grew out of the conviction, expressed by a number of observers over the years, that our preoccupation with federal courts in our formal teaching, research, and public education has tended to obscure the significance of state and local judicial systems. To be sure, researchers in the modern sociolegal tradition have produced a wide variety of studies revealing some of the mysteries of courthouse government in cities and towns across the nation. But especially in our academic endeavors, and particularly in political science, we tend to present the case for the importance of law and courts almost entirely within the framework of federal tribunals. And there, we join with our colleagues in law schools in the mad rush to materials with U.S. Supreme Court relevance.

As explained more fully in the first chapter, state judiciaries process the vast bulk of litigation in the United States in a given year, and they are the tribunals with which the average citizen is most likely to have contact. Citizens' experiences with courts, lawyers, and judges are strong, perhaps the dominant factors in shaping public attitudes toward things legal and governmental, which in turn bear obvious relevance for the legitimacy and stability of government as a whole. The importance of state courts was emphasized by William Brennan several years before his retirement from the U.S. Supreme Court: "Without detracting in the slightest from the work of the federal courts, it is fair to say that the decisions that affect people's day-to-day lives most fundamentally are increasingly made by state courts."*

That "the only politics is local politics" may not be completely true, but its grain of truth applies to the courthouse as well as to the state and local legislative, executive, and administrative organs of government. The traditional view of the judiciary holds that the legal system and political system are separate entities. A more realistic approach is to

---

* William J. Brennan, Jr., in his foreword to Joseph Grodin's *In Pursuit of Justice* (Los Angeles: University of California Press, 1989).

regard the judiciary as a component of the larger political system. Thus, topics such as judicial decision making, judicial selection, and judicial discretion are conceptualized as political since they involve deliberate choices that work to the advantage of some and the disadvantage of others.

We accent judicial politics along two dimensions. First, our federal system of government has created dual judicial systems, one at the national level encompassing all of the states, the other being the product of the states themselves. Second, there are distinctive aspects of politics among (and within) the states. The differences usually associated with state politics and policies are evident as well in state and community courts.

Many factors are frequently employed by scholars of state politics to help explain different patterns of political behavior among the states. Foremost among these are the traditions of the states; their historical development; and their economic bases, resources, and population patterns. These same factors, we argue, give to state judiciaries their own identities, just as they do to their executive and legislative branches of government.

The chapters of this book follow the same sequence one finds in most treatments of the federal judiciary. Chapter 1 addresses the interrelations of judicial and political systems. Essential to this topic is a discussion of several major characteristics of the American judiciary and a brief overview of three basic controversies that help focus contemporary political commentary about the law and the courts. Chapters 2 and 3 concentrate on judicial structure and judicial selection. Chapter 4 examines the role of lawyers as gatekeepers to the courts. The subsequent three chapters are concerned with process—how disputes are resolved by courts at the state level. Chapter 5 considers civil issues, Chapter 6 assesses criminal matters, and Chapter 7 analyzes the work of state appellate courts. The concluding chapter summarizes the state of the state judiciary today. This summary includes alternative means to resolve disputes to reduce the crowded civil court docket and a commentary on the dilemmas faced by the criminal courts as a result of the largely ineffective anticrime policies of the past several decades. Together, these chapters address the fundamental aspects of state courts today—how they operate, the various influences on them, the key players in the judicial process, and their role in the U.S. political system.

Debts accumulated in writing this book are many, too many and diverse to acknowledge adequately here. We are indebted to the editors at Longman for their early support of the project, for their patience in awaiting the arrival of sections of the manuscript, and for working closely and effectively with us to produce the book. Comments and criticisms of early readers of the manuscript were especially helpful. These include William K. (Sandy) Muir, Jr., University of California, Berkeley; Philip L. Dubois, University of California, Davis; Beverly B. Cook, University of Wisconsin, Milwaukee; Gregory A. Caldeira, Ohio State University; and Bradley Canon, University of Kentucky.

Finally, we would like to thank members of our families who were forced to share the birth pangs of this book: Our wives Nancy Culver and Patricia Rodgers, and our children, Mollie Culver and David, Vickie, and Kathy Stumpf. Only we, however, bear responsibility for the final product.

John H. Culver
Harry P. Stumpf

CHAPTER 1

Law, Courts, and Politics in the States

A Maryland man filed a $10 million suit against a marriage counselor alleging emotional distress because the counselor engaged in an affair with his wife while the couple was undergoing counseling. The couple divorced, and the marriage counselor married the man's ex-wife. The trial court judge agreed with the counselor that there was no basis for the suit since Maryland no longer recognized alienation of affection and extramarital sex as illegal. However, the Maryland Court of Appeals reversed the judge's ruling and sent the case back for trial, noting that the defendant was not "the milkman, the mailman, or the guy next door" but a professional who had a responsibility to help preserve the marriage, not break it up.

The New Jersey Supreme Court held that the word family *applied to 10 Glassboro State College students who were living in a single-family house. A Glassboro zoning ordinance, adopted in 1986, was designed to limit the number of unrelated persons who could live in a single-family dwelling. According to the high court, the 10 students had the "stability and permanency" of a traditional family.*

A Tennessee state court judge granted temporary custody of seven frozen embryos to the woman who produced the eggs. The embryos were produced by in vitro fertilization because of the woman's difficulty in becoming pregnant. But her marriage dissolved and the husband contested his former wife's claims that she had a right to the embryos.

A zoning ordinance in Flossmore, a wealthy suburb of Chicago, prohibits residents who own pickup trucks from parking their vehicles in their driveways or in front of their homes. The ordinance is the target of a lawsuit brought by a resident who owes $200 in fines as a result of not keeping his Mazda pickup in his garage, out of the sight of other residents.

After a 17-day trial in Reno, Nevada, a judge exonerated members of the heavy metal music group Judas Priest in the suicides of two young men. The 18-year-old died instantly from a self-inflicted gunshot. His 20-year-old friend failed to kill himself but was horribly disfigured by a shotgun blast to his head; he died three years later. Parents of the youths maintained that subliminal messages on several of the group's songs promoted self-destruction and contained the words "Do It." The judge said the plaintiffs failed to prove that the group intentionally placed the messages on the recordings and that whatever messages there were resulted in the suicides.

As these examples illustrate, courts in the United States are called on to render decisions in an almost unbelievably wide, if not wild, assortment of interpersonal disputes and public policy issues. In no other society are courts and judges given so much responsibility. The range of matters brought to the judiciary is seemingly endless, from traffic tickets to divorces, from petty crimes to death penalty cases, and from violations of obscenity laws to complex personal injury matters.

A glance at the evening television news or afternoon newspaper serves as a reminder that laws and courts are constants in our daily routines. Even in entertainment, people flock to see Hollywood movies that depict legal problems and courtroom dramas, and there are few areas in the country where a Judge Wapner or a "Superior Court" television show cannot invade the living room. In fact, according to the *New York Times,* a recent survey indicated that 54 percent of Americans knew who Judge Wapner was, but only 9 percent could identify William Rehnquist as chief justice of the U.S. Supreme Court ("For the Record," 1990: B5).

Over a century and a half ago, the French writer Alexis de Tocqueville (1954) traveled around our new republic and recorded his observations on life, politics, and culture. Of interest and puzzlement to him was our judiciary. At one point he wrote,

> The judicial organization of the United States is the institution which the stranger has the greatest difficulty in understanding. . . . The magistrates seem . . . to interfere in public affairs by chance, but by a chance which occurs every day. . . .
> The political power which the Americans have entrusted to their courts is . . . immense. (15–17)

Were Tocqueville to reappear today to traverse the political landscape, he would surely be amazed by the development of the United States; its place in international affairs; and among other things, the diversity of its population. However, his remarks about the power of the courts would be as appropriate today as they were 150 years ago. Indeed, our courts touch on peoples' lives perhaps even more now than they did at the beginning of the nation.

THE STUDY OF STATE AND LOCAL COURTS

Although Americans are accustomed to the centrality of courts in the affairs of the state, our attention is usually drawn to the federal judiciary. But the case for increased attention to state and local courts is compelling. One might begin with some raw statistics, which are themselves rather convincing.

According to data supplied by the National Center for State Courts (1990: 3), a grand total of some 98 million cases were filed in all courts, state and national, trial and appellate, in the United States in 1988. Of these, *99.7 percent* were filed in state and local courts. For every appellate case filed in federal courts there are five cases in the state courts of appeals, and for every federal trial court filing there are 100 cases initiated in state trial courts. Even if we delete the largest category of state trial court filings, those involving traffic and/or other ordinance violations, we still have a federal-state trial court filing ratio of 1:9.

Indeed, however caseloads are measured, a number of individual states exceed the total caseload for the entire federal court system by a healthy margin. Excluding minor legal matters, California still had almost 3 times as many case filings in its courts in 1988 as did *all* federal courts, and Texas had 3.7 times as many, to name only two of the larger state jurisdictions. New York's *total* case filings dwarf those of all federal courts by a ratio of more than 10:1.

For every federal trial judge there are 13 state trial judges, for every federal appellate judge there are 7 state appeals judges, and for every federal court of any type there are nearly 150 state courts of various degrees of specialization and jurisdiction. And again, a number of states by themselves far exceed the federal figures in all three of these categories.

According to the Bureau of Justice Statistics, of the $61 billion spent in fiscal year 1988 by governments at all levels for civil and criminal "justice activities," state and local governments together bore almost $54 billion, or 88 percent of the total. Local (county and municipal) governments by themselves shouldered 55.6 percent of all these expenditures. State and local governments also employed the lion's share of personnel to handle these court and court-related activities. Of some 1.6 million persons working in this area in 1988, state and local government employees accounted for 92.6 percent of the total (U.S. Department of Justice, 1990). Thus, whether we contrast judicial personnel, cases, courts, or expenditures on justice-related activities, the story is the same: Our state courts represent nine-tenths of the iceberg of the entire judicial system in the United States.

Another argument for increased attention to state courts is the role of trial courts. It is here that citizens are most likely to have their first, and perhaps only, contact with judicial institutions, and it is at this level that concepts of law and justice have meaning for most Americans. As two political scientists said, in commenting on the contrasts between federal and state caseload statistics similar to those presented above,

> These numbers serve to illustrate the statistical magnitude of local legal activity as well as the substantial importance of the local scene. They make clear that for the vast majority who in any way become involved with the law, the measure of law and justice will be a local measure—a policeman or a local judge—and not the majesty and pomp of the United States Supreme Court or even the lesser dignity of one of the higher state or federal courts. (Klonoski and Mendelsohn, 1970: xiv).

Many people perceive local trial courts in America as involved largely with enforcing community norms, as opposed to the more weighty policy-making work of appellate courts. Such a view tends to diminish the significance of trial courts, even those processing the most "petty" of disputes. In their day-in, day-out processing of thousands of seemingly trivial cases, the lowest of our courts significantly shape the contours of legal rules for the community. That so very few of these decisions are ever appealed serves to enhance their role further in shaping policy at the state and local level (Mather, 1991).

Finally, the current surge of activity of state appellate courts bolsters our plea for increased research and teaching attention to state courts. Although we cover these important policy-making bodies at length in Chapter 7, a few examples are instructive here. With the swing of the pendulum of American federalism from national to state power, which has characterized American politics in the 1970s and 1980s, has come a concomitant enhancement of state appellate judicial power. Relying on their own state constitutions, many state supreme courts have begun to enunciate judicial doctrine, which is now forming the leading edge of American constitutional law in several areas. Consider the following examples (Mosk, 1988):

- The U.S. Supreme Court ruled in 1973 that state inequalities in funding for public schools was acceptable since education was not a fundamental right under the Constitution (*San Antonio Independent School District v. Rodriguez*). However, the California Supreme Court reached the opposite conclusion in 1971 (*Serrano v. Priest*). Since 1971, state supreme courts in Arizona, Connecticut, Kentucky, Michigan, Mississippi, Texas, Washington, Wisconsin, and West Virginia have followed the precedent established in California, not that of the U.S. Supreme Court.

- In 1984, the U.S. high court said there could be "good-faith" exceptions to the exclusionary rule on the admissability of evidence seized in criminal cases (*U.S. v. Leon*). The supreme courts in Michigan, New Jersey, New York, and Wisconsin have not adopted the *Leon* ruling. Law enforcement officials in those states are bound by stricter standards imposed by their own courts on the lawful seizure of evidence than those used in federal prosecutions.

- In 1975, the Alaska Supreme Court held that the personal use and possession of marijuana by adults in their own homes fell within the meaning of Alaska's constitutional guarantee of privacy.

- In *Miller v. California* (1973), the federal high court sought to make it easier for state and local officials to prosecute obscenity and pornography cases by recognizing "community standards." The Oregon Supreme Court in 1987 avoided a conflict with *Miller* in a ruling that recognized freedom of expression "on any subject whatever" under the Oregon constitution.

Other policy thrusts at the state level could be cited in the areas of environmental regulation, consumer protection, and personal injury law, where state appellate courts have broken new legal ground (Porter and Tarr, 1982; Tarr and Porter, 1988). The point is, state courts at all levels now cry out for increased study, lest we miss the greater portion—and currently the most dynamic portion—of American judicial politics and policy development.

CONCEPTUALIZATION OF THE JUDICIAL FUNCTION

How we study courts—courts at any level—turns largely on our concept of the role or roles courts perform. At bottom, what do courts do? Traditional American jurisprudence (legal theory or legal thought) has embodied the notion of a rather sharp distinction between that which is political (and certainly social) and that which is purely legal. Such perception or stereotypes remain with us today as holdovers from the now discredited notions of the English legal philosophers John Austin and Sir William Blackstone (see

Stumpf, 1988: Ch. 1). Thus, many think of legislative, executive, and administrative business as clearly political, but the judicial arm of government we like to call "legal." Similarly, we often hear the plea that "politics" must be removed from the process of selecting judges, lest the choices be corrupted by sinister forces in society. And who has not heard the claim that courts of all kinds must render decisions in strict accordance with "the law" (or in the case of the U.S. Supreme Court, the "clear intent of the framers" of the Constitution) rather than allowing the policy values of the judge to shape judicial determinations?

Beginning in the 1930s and 1940s, though with roots going back into the nineteenth century, American legal thought moved away from these rather unrealistic conceptualizations of what courts do. The new departure began with the truism that judges are human beings. As such, their own mode of thought and policy preferences inevitably enter into the business of interpreting statutes, ordinances, and the Constitution itself. Thus, the reality is that policy-making is the unavoidable result of judging. And since political science came to a consensus that policy-making is at the core of what politics is all about, it follows that courts are political. Actually, Oliver Wendell Holmes (1881) laid the foundation for what is now called sociological-realist jurisprudence when he wrote,

> The very considerations which judges most rarely mention, and always with an apology, are the secret root from which the law draws all the juices of life. I mean, of course, considerations of what is expedient for the community concerned. Every important principle which is developed by litigation is in fact and at bottom the result of more or less definitely understood views of public policy; most generally, to be sure, under our practice and traditions, the unconscious result of instinctive preferences and inarticulate convictions, but nonetheless traceable to views of public policy in the last analysis. (35–36)

And it was only a modern restatement of this conception of the role of law and courts when Associate Justice Felix Frankfurter (1962), himself hardly a radical jurisprudent, wrote,

> The words of the Constitution . . . are so unrestricted by their intrinsic meaning or by their history or by tradition or by prior decisions that they leave the individual justice free, if indeed they do not compel him, to gather meaning, not from reading the Constitution, but from reading life. . . . Members of the Court are frequently admonished by their associates not to read their economic and social views into the neutral language of the Constitution. But the process of Constitutional interpretation compels the translation of policy into judgment. . . . (30)

It is this view of the role of courts that provides the point of departure for this book. Courts and judges are seen not in legal isolation nor as separate from politics but inevitably and inextricably part of the larger political process. Although hardly new to modern political science, this orientation still meets with resistance from some who long for a role of law above politics and society, a sort of neutral, objective, perhaps even semidivine role for the law and the courts. Appealing though this may be, it does not fit well with the findings of modern social science research, many of which are presented and discussed in the following chapters.

Thus, when we consider the historical development of state courts, their structure and jurisdiction, we find that political considerations (i.e., the policy preferences of competing individuals, groups, and political parties) provide more convincing explanations for outcomes than do such factors as efficiency, "good management," "sound administration of justice," and similar euphemisms. Moreover, "merit," even if it were possible to define that term, has had a good deal less to do with the selection of state judges throughout our history than have the policy preferences of dominant state and community interests. And so it is as we move through the various stages of the state judicial process. State court agenda setting (how cases come to courts in the first place), trial and appellate court decision making, as well as the overall impact of such decisions—these and related outcomes are better explained by sociopolitical than merely legal factors.

STUDYING COURTS IN CONTEXT

Although a political conception of law, courts, and judges constitutes our general approach to the topics that follow, politics itself encompasses an enormous array of institutions and processes, some of which are more relevant than others in understanding courts. To study courts in context requires that we understand the influences of the legal system of which the judiciary is only a part. These various systems are depicted as a series of concentric circles in Figure 1.1.

The Legal System

What is a legal system? As Friedman (1977) suggests, "The legal system brings to mind not an abstract set of norms, but a working process, a breathing, active machine. The legal system is behavior, movement, demand, and response." With Friedman, we may divide legal systems into three parts: structure, substance, and legal culture. Structure, of course,

Figure 1.1 The Judicial System in Context

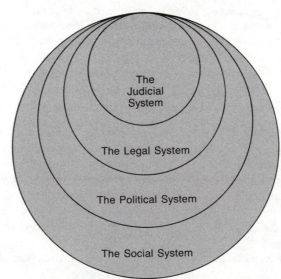

The
Judicial
System

The Legal System

The Political System

The Social System

refers to the framework of legal institutions. Hence one can diagram the way our courts are structured and police departments organized, the shape of bar associations and their relation to other elements of the system, and the structure and jurisdiction of administrative agencies. Although the salient aspects of American state court structure are discussed in Chapter 2, the *structure* of the legal system as it pertains to state courts is touched on throughout the book.

Substance refers to the rules and norms that constitute the "what" of the law in any society. For example, we have substantive rules (the city ordinance prohibiting jaywalking) as well as procedural rules, sometimes called rules about rules, such as the one requiring "Miranda" warnings to be given by the police to a criminal suspect. Also, there are rules originating in the legislature (statutes), courts (judicial decisions), and administrative agencies (administrative rulings), and these are to be found at the local, state, and national levels.

In studying legal systems we must also appreciate the point made by Roscoe Pound many years ago on the distinction between "law on the books" and "law in action." The latter refers to the norms of behavior that officials and citizens actually enforce and follow. Formal law specifies definitions of and penalties for jaywalking. "Law in action"—the "real" rule people follow—allows for numerous exceptions to the formal rule and, in fact, almost writes that rule out of existence. This is not a book that stresses substance or legal rules, formal or otherwise. The process or politics of state courts is our focus. But the student of the judiciary needs to be aware of the importance of substance (legal rules) as both dependent and independent variables, and these are discussed throughout the following chapters to illustrate important aspects of the politics of state courts.

Legal Culture

Legal culture is the third vital dimension of legal systems. In essence, legal culture refers to the "ideas, attitudes, beliefs, expectations, and opinions about law" held by the public (Friedman, 1977: 7). Thus, our attitude toward the U.S. Supreme Court (largely adulatory if not worshipful) is quite significant in understanding why that unique judicial body has so much political power. The beliefs we have about what rules we ought to obey, our attitudes toward lawyers, our propensity to use or not to use courts to solve disputes are examples that suggest the importance of legal culture in understanding how the law and courts actually function in our society.

The set of variables constituting legal culture is especially important in studying state and local courts in the United States. For example, scholars are at a loss to explain state and regional differences in legal structures and legal norms except through the variable of *localism*. Since colonial times Americans have viewed their law and their courts as local or county institutions beholden to the populace of the immediate area. Thus, one can speak of local legal culture in Chicago, Savannah, or Phoenix with the expectation that the perceptions of how the courts operate in these cities rest in large part on their different histories, politics, and traditions. The assumption is that public attitudes about the courts by residents of Chicago, a polyglot metropolitan region with a history grounded in strong partisan politics, will be distinct in many ways from views held by residents of Savannah, a southern city steeped in the traditions of the old South. In contrast, Phoenix is a fast-growing city of new wealth and conservative politics, set against the experience of the West.

Localism also implies that those who manage the judicial process, at either the state or local level, identify with the politics and traditions of the state or communities. Legal historian Lawrence Friedman's (1984: 128) comments on localism and legal cultures are instructive. As he points out, a state judge on the trial court bench in any particular city will most likely never leave that court to assume a higher post, and a lawyer in that same city is unlikely to try a case several hundred miles away in another city, much less in another state.

The makeup of the Kansas Supreme Court illustrates this point in a different fashion. As of 1988, five of the seven justices on the court were born in Kansas, and all seven obtained their law degrees from either the University of Kansas or Washburn University in Topeka, Kansas. It would not be an overstatement to say that the Kansas Supreme Court is indelibly marked with the imprint of the state. This same localism is apparent in the backgrounds of the seven members of the Louisiana Supreme Court; only one justice was born out of state (in neighboring Texas), and all received their legal education at one of three law schools in Louisiana. Although the background characteristics of justices on other state supreme courts may be more diverse, judges are often tied to the states and towns where they preside. Or as Friedman (1984: 128) puts it, "This state of affairs makes American legal culture quite parochial; it tends to keep alive aspects of local legal culture."

The linkage of judicial behavior with a city's legal culture and political tradition was evident in Levin's (1977) study of criminal court sentencing behavior in Minneapolis and Pittsburgh. These two cities are polar opposites in several respects. Minneapolis has a nonpartisan and structurally fragmented city government. Its political system emphasizes professionalism and reform. Minneapolis judges are elected on a nonpartisan ballot. In contrast, Pittsburgh city government is partisan and highly centralized. The Democratic party is the driving force in city politics. Trial court judges in Pittsburgh are elected on a partisan ballot.

Levin (1977) found that Minneapolis judges gave far more severe sentences in criminal cases than jurists in Pittsburgh. The explanation for these sentencing disparities rests with the city's political systems. Because city politics influences judicial selection, the two communities, with their divergent political styles, tend to recruit different types of judges—judges oriented to the partisan style of Pittsburgh politics and judges of a more independent and professional orientation in Minneapolis. Pittsburgh judges tend "to act as a buffer between the law and the people upon whom it is enforced. . . ." However, judges in Minneapolis are oriented toward society. This orientation means that they take a harsher view of those who commit crimes and hand down longer sentences to those who are found guilty than judges in Pittsburgh (149). Minneapolis and Pittsburgh are hardly unique cities in this respect. There is every reason to assume that the links among legal culture, political traditions, and judicial behavior exist in other metropolitan areas as well.

FEDERALISM

One can easily discern an overlapping of the three elements of legal systems. For example, structure can affect attitudes and vice versa. Similarly, we can hardly divorce the adoption of legal norms, formal or informal, from the force of public opinion, which is an important part of our legal culture. Hence, we must view the three elements of a legal system—structure, substance, and legal culture—as clearly interlocking aspects of the entire system.

A particularly prominent example of this phenomenon is that of American federalism. Federalism, as a structural element, is embedded in American history and politics as a way of thinking about government. Of course, this was the intention when it was adopted in the first place. But whether viewed as an element of structure, substance, or culture (and clearly it is all three), it is so central to the study of courts, especially state courts, that we must say something about it in this introductory chapter.

Judicial Federalism

Federalism is an arrangement of government powers with at least two centers of authority, one central and one or more regional or local, each existing, at least partially, independently of the other. The strong tradition of localism mentioned above was the force that brought into being a federal system of government in the writing of the Constitution. An important element of American federalism is judicial federalism, by which we mean the existence of two separate judicial systems, one federal and the other at the state level. The federal judiciary, of course, extends across the whole country. In contrast, the laws of the states, and the courts they create, are creatures of the individual states. State laws must fall within the umbrella of rights and powers set forth in the U.S. Constitution. That is, the separate states cannot assume authority not allowed to them, nor can they limit the rights of their citizens that are provided for in the Constitution. However, for all the similarities in the laws of the states, there are differences as well. These differences are a result of the diverse social, economic, and political experiences of the states.

Opposition to an expanded federal judiciary in the 1780s was based on the fear that a larger federal court system would encroach on legal affairs that rightly belonged to the states. Although this concern has been voiced frequently throughout our history, it assumed increased political visibility from the mid-1950s to the mid-1970s, when the federal courts took an active role in promoting equal treatment of black Americans, particularly in the South. At the time, some southern governors angrily charged that the federal courts were interfering in matters traditionally belonging to the states through the court-ordered desegregation of schools and public accommodations decisions.

This same issue is seen in the more recent example of federal courts ordering some 40 states to reduce overcrowding in their prisons. Even state social welfare policies have been affected as a result of federal court mandates. As a result of a federal district court decision, Alabama mental health expenditures soared from $14 million in 1971 to $58 million two years later (D. L. Horowitz, 1977: 6). An area in which state versus federal responsibility is murky involves environmental issues. Environmentalists who are unsuccessful at the state level in halting projects in sensitive areas often turn to the federal courts, seeking relief under a variety of congressional acts designed to minimize air and water pollution as well as the destruction of endangered species.

There is no clear-cut line that unequivocally separates the legitimate responsibility of the states from that of the federal government. Part of the reason for this is the growth in the number of federal regulatory agencies, the increase in the number of entitlement programs created by Congress since the 1940s, and Supreme Court decisions that have expanded the oversight powers of the federal government.

In any event, state courts and the exercise of state judicial power can hardly be understood without taking into consideration the constraints, as well as the opportunities, implicit in our federal system of government. As we shall see, federalism is necessary to help explain the operation of our criminal judicial system, the creativity of state appellate courts, and a number of other aspects of the politics of state courts.

Differences among the states are often mirrored in their laws. These differences are a product of our federal system of government, which enables state law-making bodies to enact legislation appropriate to their needs. In addition, state laws reflect another "context" that helps to explain why courts in the states can handle similar issues in dramatically dissimilar ways.

Influences on State Laws

Laws are passed by legislative bodies for many reasons, including the desire to regulate citizens' behavior. They can also reflect the power of various interest groups and thereby illustrate the dominant moral, economic, political, and cultural forces in the state.

For instance, laws can be more favorable to employers than to employees, and they can be sensitive to environmental concerns if the lawmakers feel this is of political significance to their constituents. Whereas many northern states adopted laws recognizing a variety of rights associated with workers, southern states did so reluctantly, and often these rights were grudgingly accepted in the South only after the adoption of federal standards made them applicable to all of the states (Friedman, 1984: 133–137). Over the past two decades, California and Oregon, among other states, have enacted stringent laws governing the discharge of toxic materials into rivers and the Pacific Ocean (although some of these laws were passed by initiatives when lawmakers did not want to antagonize business interests by passing them by statute). In contrast, in states where mining and petroleum are dominant economic forces, as in Oklahoma, Louisiana, and Kentucky, environmental protections are lax.

Another example of the influence of economics was illustrated in 1990 when the Kentucky legislature rejected a bill that would have banned smoking in all public schools, including elementary schools. Why did Kentucky lawmakers act this way in an era when other states and local governments are actively restricting areas where tobacco products can be used? One clue is that tobacco is the leading cash crop in the Bluegrass State. Kentucky is the only state in the union that has no age restriction for buying cigarettes.

Early in the twentieth century, Nevadans realized their economic fortunes would be improved by the passage of laws allowing certain types of vice activities, such as gambling and prostitution, that were prohibited in other states. Only the neophyte to state politics would be surprised to learn that neighboring Utah, with a predominately Mormon population, never shared the Nevada view of acceptable moral behavior.

The peculiarities of some state laws are based on the moral and social views, or fears, of the state residents. Until recently, for example, New York's stringent divorce laws (allowed only in the case of adultery) reflected the pressure of the Catholic church against making the dissolution of marriage easy. Southern states had miscegenation laws prohibiting interracial marriage, although these were invalidated by the federal Supreme Court in *McLaughlin v. Florida* (1964) and *Loving v. Virginia* (1967).

It was only in 1980 that Louisiana abolished a law that made husbands "heads and masters" of all property held jointly by married couples. Until 1952, aliens in California could not own land, a reflection of the historical legacy of anti-Asian prejudice in that state. In 1963, the Dallas, Texas, suburb of Plano passed an ordinance that banned pool tables in restaurants, recreation centers, and private homes to protect the city's youths from the immoral influences of those associated with the game. The ordinance was amended in 1971 and finally abolished in 1990. The prohibition against dancing in Purdy, Missouri, still stands, however, a testament to the power of the local religious forces.

THE DEVELOPMENT OF AMERICAN LAW

Just as courts and state laws are most profitably studied in context, we need to acknowledge the historical development of legal systems that transcend the bounds of the nation-state. No legal or political system is itself isolated from its history. In fact, legal history can often explain aspects of a contemporary judicial system that cannot be explained in any other way.

The foundation of American jurisprudence is the English common law. Common law is judge-made law, largely based on custom and tradition. It is not codified (written down), and the emphasis is on adherence to precedent (stare decisis). Not surprisingly, the early colonists, familiar with the common law system, brought this experience with them to Jamestown and other settlements in the New World. The royal colony of Virginia officially adopted English common law in 1660, as did several other colonies before the Revolution.

Common law worked well in England largely because it had been developed and refined over several centuries. Moreover, England was a unitary system and had a common tradition, history, and customs shared throughout the country. Yet the colonies had a limited shared experience, had few common traditions, and were a confederation of states where customs were more likely to be identified regionally than nationally. Other factors were to impose constraints on the common law in this country. Our Constitution set limits on the power of the three branches of government, and the Bill of Rights established limits on the power of the federal government itself. The federal system of government dispersed power and created a dual judiciary. All these features were foreign to European governments at the time.

Even though the common law was to survive into the early 1800s, changes were made soon after independence to mold the common law to the American experience. The existence of state legislatures and state constitutions led state lawmakers to resolve certain types of disputes by passing their own laws, measures that were written down and not judge-made. Forty years after the Constitution was ratified, the importance of common law was considerably less than what it had been:

> Law was no longer conceived of as an eternal set of principles expressed in custom and derived from natural law. Nor was it regarded primarily as a body of rules designed to achieve justice only in the individual case. Instead, judges came to think of the common law as equally responsible with legislation for governing society and promoting socially desirable conduct (M. J. Horwitz, 1977: 30).

The common law is not dead, but our laws today are more likely to emanate from the federal and state constitutions; legislative bodies; and in a number of states, from the people themselves by means of the initiative process. The initiative gives state voters the opportunity to enact laws as long as they do not conflict with the state and the U.S. Constitution. Precedent is still followed by jurists when appropriate and discarded when inappropriate. Adherence to precedent provides a welcome stability to judicial rulings, yet changing social, political, and economic conditions necessitate the abandonment of precedents that bind us too closely to outdated principles.

In sum, the development of American law has been influenced by several factors— the creation of a constitutional federal system, the modification of common law, the growth in the authority of the federal courts, and an emphasis on the rights of the individual. As the country grew in population, geographical size, and complexity, the judiciary responded. These changes have meant that judges have assumed legislative-type roles and that adherence to precedent is less predictable. As one historian puts it, "Our legal history reflects back to us generations of pragmatic decision making rather than a quest for ideological purity and consistency. Personal and group interests have always ordered the course of legal developments; instrumentalism has been the way of the law" (Hall, 1989: 335).

CONCLUSION

The central point of these introductory comments should be clear: that courts, as with any other subject, are most usefully viewed as creatures of their environment. It is true that state courts are to some extent separate and distinct entitites, with characteristics of their own, and their uniqueness must be appreciated. But they are so very much the products of their legal and political contexts, locally, nationally, and historically, that these contextual factors should be kept in mind as we begin our exploration of the politics of these institutions.

REFERENCES

Frankfurter, Felix. 1962. In Archibald McLeish and E. F. Prichard, Jr., eds., *Law and Politics*. New York: Capricorn Book.
Friedman, Lawrence M. 1977. *Law and Society: An Introduction*. Englewood Cliffs, NJ: Prentice Hall.
Friedman, Lawrence M. 1984. *American Law: An Introduction*. New York: W. W. Norton.
"For the Record." 1990, January 5. *New York Times*, p. B9.
Hall, Kermit L. 1989. *The Magic Mirror: Law in American History*. New York: Oxford University Press.
Holmes, Oliver W. 1881. *The Common Law*. Boston: Little, Brown.
Horowitz, Donald L. 1977. *The Courts and Social Policies*. Washington, DC: Brookings Institution.
Horwitz, Morton J. 1977. *The Transformation of American Law, 1780–1860*. Cambridge, MA: Harvard University Press.
Klonoski, James R., and Robert I. Mendelsohn, eds. 1970. *The Politics of Local Justice*. Boston: Little, Brown.

Levin, Martin A. 1977. *Urban Politics and the Criminal Courts.* Chicago: University of Chicago Press.

Mather, Lynn. 1991. "Policy Making in State Trial Courts." In John B. Gates and Charles A. Johnson, eds., *The American Courts: A Critical Assessment,* pp. 119–157. Washington, DC: Congressional Quarterly Press.

Mosk, Stanley. 1988, March. "The Emerging Agenda in State Constitutional Rights Law." 496 *The Annals* 54–64.

National Center for State Courts. 1990. *State Court Caseload Statistics: Annual Report 1988.* Williamsburg, VA: National Center for State Courts.

Porter, Mary C., and G. Alan Tarr, eds. 1982. *State Supreme Courts: Policymakers in the Federal System.* Westport, CN: Greenwood Press.

Stumpf, Harry P. 1988. *American Judicial Politics.* San Diego: Harcourt Brace Jovanovich.

Tarr, G. Alan, and Mary C. A. Porter. 1988. *State Supreme Courts in State and Nation.* New Haven, CT: Yale University Press.

Tocqueville, Alexis de. 1954. *Democracy in America.* New York: Vintage Books.

U.S. Department of Justice, Bureau of Justice Statistics. 1990, July. *Justice Expenditure and Employment, 1988.* Washington, DC: U.S. Government Printing Office.

CHAPTER 2

Judicial Organization, Jurisdiction, and Administration

The nature of the judiciary in the 50 states is a result of each state's history, geography, population, constitution, and traditions. As we shall see, the judicial structure in some states is relatively explicit, whereas in others it appears overly cumbersome. The *structure of the judiciary* refers to the hierarchy and relationships between courts, and *jurisdiction* connotes the level at which cases are heard or reviewed in the courts. As reformers have long experienced, proposals to change the structure or jurisdiction of the courts to make them more efficient produce heated political battles. This chapter examines how the courts are organized, the differences in their responsibilities, and some of the changes that have occurred in judicial operations and administration in this century.

Only six states (Idaho, Illinois, Iowa, Massachusetts, Minnesota, and South Dakota) have the three-tiered structure that corresponds to that of the federal judiciary. All the states have a court of last resort, usually called a supreme court, although Oklahoma and Texas have two separate supreme courts, one for civil matters and the other for criminal appeals. The states differ when it comes to intermediate appellate courts as well as the number of trial courts and lower courts with specialized jurisdiction. The majority of states (37) have an intermediate court of appeals, and two of these, Alabama and Tennessee, have separate intermediate appellate courts for civil and criminal appeals. Forty-four of the states differentiate between trial courts of general and limited jurisdiction. Those with general jurisdiction handle the bulk of criminal and civil cases in the states, whereas as the label suggests, those with limited jurisdiction handle only certain types of cases.

The jurisdiction and caseloads of the courts are influenced by several factors. The state legislatures affect the courts through the passage of laws that designate new criminal offenses and by any expansion of the courts' supervisory duties on the civil side of the law. For example, after the 1986 Connecticut legislature passed a law that *required* arrests in situations of family violence, an estimated 600 new cases were added to the court dockets each month (Peters, 1987: 20). In an anticrime effort, the states have passed mandatory sentencing laws. As a result, more suspects will choose a trial rather than plead guilty on the assumption that they have nothing to lose.

Changes in social attitudes affect the courts as well. Prior to the Lee Marvin "palimony" case in the 1970s, the courts did not have to contend with domestic relations matters when the individuals were not married. Today, that precedent, which recognized the rights of a woman who lived with a man outside of marriage, and a turn in the public's attitude toward more tolerance of unmarried couples living together have resulted in the courts handling these disputes with increased frequency.

A downturn in the economy brings more cases to the courts, such as bankruptcies, divorces, wage garnishments, and foreclosures. The farm belt states were particularly hard hit by adverse economic and weather conditions in the 1980s. As the chief justice of the South Dakota supreme court said in his address to the state legislature, "My generation of lawyers, until recently, seldom, if ever, prepared and completed a foreclosure case. As a matter of fact, most of us did not know how. Economic stress has changed all of that. Unfortunately, foreclosures are becoming increasingly common" (Wuest, 1987: 28).

Actions by the federal government can change the jurisdiction of the state courts. In 1988, Congress sought to lighten the civil caseload in the federal courts by changing the rules on "diversity jurisdiction" suits. These lawsuits involve litigants from one state who sue others in different states. Historically, such cases were filed in the federal courts because of the fear that state judges and juries might be biased for one side or the other. Under the new procedures, these cases are now handled at the state level if the disputes involve less than $50,000.

THE DEVELOPMENT OF STATE COURTS

The colonists brought their English legal tradition with them but made significant modifications appropriate to their experience in the New World. Whereas eighteenth-century England had numerous courts, the colonies did not have the complexity of commercial activities and the political motive to make such courts a necessity until the nineteenth century. As one legal historian notes, informality and local authority characterized the handling of legal issues at this time: "In the beginning, judicial business in the colonies was not separated from public business in general. The same people made laws, enforced them, decided cases, and ran the colony. A special court system grew, and divided into parts, only when there were enough people, and territory to make this sensible" (Friedman, 1985: 37–38).

The early courts were county courts, which played a dual role (judicial and legislative) in the resolution of legal issues and in colony governance. Justices of the peace were also created in many of the new states. Then, as now, their role was confined to relatively minor legal disputes, although they had nonlegal functions as well. At the time of independence, several states had both trial and appellate courts, but the distinctions between them were often blurred as appellate judges conducted trials in addition to hearing appeals. Some of these courts were called circuit courts because judges traveled a circuit from one village to another to hear cases.

Efforts to provide structure to the courts did not come easily. The so-called radicals (antifederalists who embraced an extreme view of Jeffersonianism) opposed efforts to establish appellate courts and worried about a judiciary that would not be under the control of, and responsive to, the common people. The moderates agreed with the federalists on the need for a judiciary to provide a check on the popular will. There was an underlying economic aspect to this dispute. A judiciary, which was independent, was structured, and could invoke judicial review if necessary, could resist potential legislative efforts to undermine property rights (Hall, 1989: 79).

The judiciary expanded in response to population growth, the increase in legal business, and the acquisition of new federal territory in the West. As economic interests developed, so, too, was there a need for a judiciary that could resolve more complicated questions of law. However, this growth was accompanied by administrative problems and a lack of coordination among the courts. As Friedman (1985) has noted, political leaders were not responsive to the need for reform: "Lay politicians did not want a czar for the courts of their states. Muddled and overlapping jurisdiction was perfectably acceptable; the alternative—a strong chief justice with power to run his system—was not" (387). By the turn of the century, little had changed to suggest that a modern judiciary would soon be on the horizon: "In 1900, most trial courts could best be described as judge-centered, semiautonomous entities that rendered legal decisions with little regard for public access or productivity" (Henderson et al., 1984: 3).

A fascinating chapter in the development of state courts, which has received only scant attention, is the judiciary in the territories before they became states. In their territorial stage, Washington, Colorado, Montana, and Wyoming, among other soon-to-be states, depended on Congress to appoint judges to handle their legal business. Although federal judges have always had the security of lifetime appointment, the territorial federal judges could be removed by Congress for any reason, as some were, usually for political purposes (Sheldon, 1988).

Each state has added its own unique characteristics to the history and development of its courts. In general, however, the state judiciaries today reflect their colonial and postcolonial heritage. Localism is still a prominent characteristic of the court structure, some courts are administered in a manner reminiscent of the past century, and the multiplicity of local courts suggests that the reorganization that reformers advocate to promote efficiency may not arrive until the next century. Despite the diversity of the courts and the lack of a common label for each, one can identify a hierarchy common to their structure across the states—the appellate courts, the trial courts of general jurisdiction, and courts of limited jurisdiction.

THE HIERARCHY OF STATE COURTS

Courts of Limited Jurisdiction

The courts at this level in the judiciary go by a variety of names—traffic court, probate court, magistrates court, justice court, municipal court, and city court. According to the most recent data, illustrated in Figure 2.4, traffic violations constitute some three-fourths of the business in these courts; the remainder of the docket is made up of misdemeanor criminal cases (11.9 percent), civil cases (11.9 percent), and juvenile matters (.6 percent). Altogether, over 71 million filings were made in these courts in 1988 (Conference of State Court Administrators, 1990: 5).

Courts of limited jurisdiction are found in 44 states, and in the others (Idaho, Illinois, Massachusetts, Minnesota, and South Dakota) the legal matters are handled by the trial courts of general jurisdiction. Georgia and New York both have a complex network of courts of limited jurisdiction. In Georgia there are seven separate courts at this level, including a municipal court for Atlanta, magistrate courts in the counties, county probate courts that handle mental health and estate matters, and one municipal court in Columbus (see Figure 2.1). In New York, there are eight separate courts of limited jurisdiction, as illustrated in Figure 2.2. In contrast, a number of states have only one or two of these lower courts (see Figure 2.3).

Mention needs to be made of the justice courts (or justice of the peace courts) if for no other reason than that they were created early in our country's history, have been glorified (and vilified) in western folklore and motion pictures, and have survived numerous attempts at abolition in some but not all the states. The judges of these courts are usually "lay" judges—ordinary citizens whose backgrounds in law range from some training to none. Today, some 1,300 nonlawyer judges preside over traffic and minor misdemeanor cases in 43 states. Most frequently, they are located in rural communities. Lay judges are often ridiculed because of their lack of legal training in particular and general education in general. California has restricted the types of cases lay judges can hear after a law suit in 1973 successfully challenged the right of non-law-trained lay judges to sentence defendants to jail, even for short periods. The following anecdotes are from that lawsuit (*Gordon v. Justice Court of Yuba City et al.*, 1973):

- Lay judge "D" in Kern County states that in his court a defendant is presumed guilty until proved innocent;
- Courtroom practice for one non-attorney judge was to conduct an informal poll for the "verdict" of the courtroom audience prior to announcing his own decision in a case;
- One lay judge stated that he always practiced "sniffing" each witness from the bench because he believed he could tell the witnesses' veracity by the witness's scent;
- Lay judge A stated, "If a nigger comes in here and doesn't have any money for a $10 fine, that doesn't bother me just because he's black. I'm not prejudiced. . . . I don't have anything against the black bastards even though they lie and steal all the time." (*Monthly Report*, 1973: 4)

At the time of the lawsuit, there were 156 nonattorney judges in California; today there are about 90, and reform proposals would have the municipal courts assume the duties of the justice courts. New Mexico abolished its justice of the peace (JP) system in the early 1960s after a critical report was submitted to the legislature that cast considerable doubt on the general competency of the state's JPs. According to the report, the JPs would hold court in their places of business—a coffee shop, gas station, and coal mine, among others. The report also documented kickbacks to law enforcement officers by the JPs in traffic cases. The JPs used to perform the function of a coroner, which is to establish the cause of death in questionable circumstances. "A JP headed an inquest in which a man was shot 'three times in the heart and once in the head' and the verdict of 'suicide' was rendered" (*The Courts in New Mexico*, 1961).

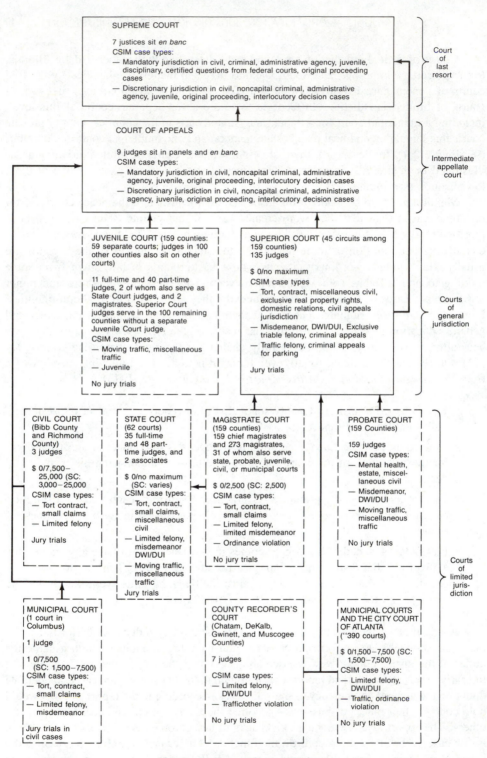

Figure 2.1 Georgia Court System

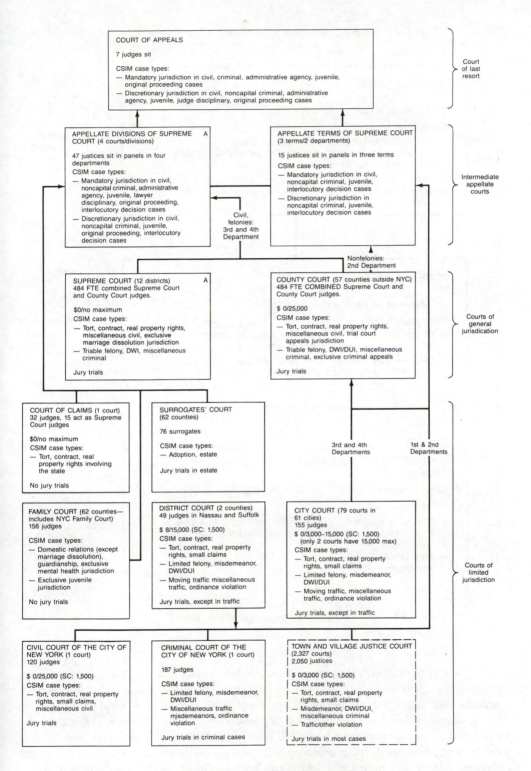

Figure 2.2 New York State Court System

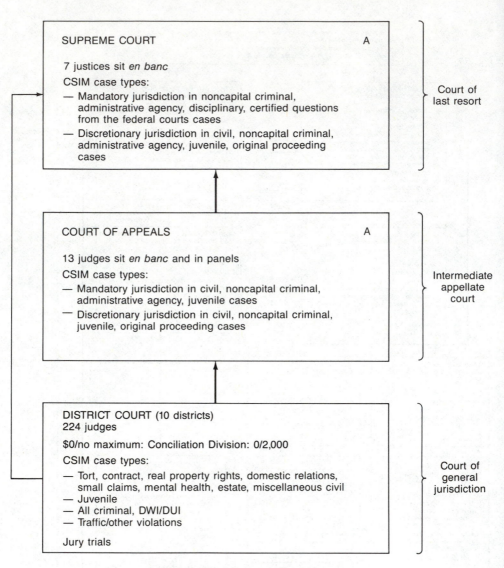

Figure 2.3 Minnesota Court System

It would be inaccurate to portray all lay judges as incompetent, and negative examples, such as the above, appear to generate more publicity than those of lay judges who perform their duties conscientiously. Many, if not most, receive some legal training in the fundamentals of law and administration and resolve minor legal problems equitably. As one scholar, once a lay judge herself, has pointed out, the organized bar has been one of the leading advocates of the elimination of lay judges on the grounds that their duties are too important to be handled by nonlawyers. Yet these judges perform a valuable service, connect the people to the legal system, and dispose of relatively minor matters that otherwise would add to the burden of our already clogged courts (Provine, 1986).

Other Specialized Courts of Limited Jurisdiction

Since the states are responsible for their own judicial system, they can have different types of legal disputes heard in one court or they can create separate courts to deal with specific disputes. Sometimes these specialized courts reflect issues unique to the states, as the water courts in Colorado and Montana, which adjudicate water rights conflicts. Maine has a separate administrative court to handle the appeals of administrative agency cases. Family courts, found in Mississippi, Rhode Island, and South Carolina, hear matters involving delinquency, child neglect, and some adult crimes against juveniles. Montana and Nebraska have a workers' compensation court with jurisdiction over workers' compensation disputes. New Jersey and Oregon have tax courts, where state and local tax matters are heard. And New York City has a housing court that handles disputes over public housing and rent-controlled apartment buildings.

The existence of specialized courts is advantageous since they have specific rather than general expertise over legal issues. A typical trial court judge whose caseload largely involves divorce matters will rarely have familiarity with the intricacies of the law in water rights disputes. The argument against most specialized courts is that they simply add another layer to the judicial bureaucracy and to the administrative problems that already plague the courts. One way to achieve the benefits of special legal expertise without creating a separate court is to create divisions within the state's main trial court. These divisions handle certain issues such as cases involving children. Indeed, most of the states have opted for this arrangement rather than the creation of specialized courts.

All of the states have either a separate court or judges assigned to hear "small claims." These courts represent a forum for the resolution of relatively minor civil matters without the use of attorneys or juries. Typical small-claims actions include landlord-tenant disputes, hospitals seeking to obtain fees from patients, and retailers suing to recover payment or merchandise bought on credit. Usually, small-claims actions involve less than $2,000. The maximum amounts range from a low of $300 in Arkansas to $10,000 in Pennsylvania. The process is quite straightforward. The individual (or business) who wants to sue another party pays a small fee to the court, whereupon the party being sued is notified to appear in court and told the nature of the dispute. The judge listens to both sides and then issues the decision immediately or within a few days.

Small-claims courts are appealing in that they serve to resolve disputes quickly, informally, and inexpensively. However, they are not the "common man's" court as originally intended. The problems identified with small-claims courts are discussed in Chapter 7.

Trial Courts of General Jurisdiction

Trial courts of general jurisdiction are the courts most Americans associate with the judiciary, in part no doubt because of their depiction by the visual and print media (Stumpf, 1988: 86). As discussed throughout this book, trial court judges are immersed in the political thicket of municipal problems that affect the local courts. In most states, these judges are selected locally, not statewide as with appellate court jurists. As one veteran observer of the judiciary said, "State trial courts occupy an uneasy position between the rhetoric of judicial independence and the reality of political and administrative vulnerability" (Church, quoted in Cook and Johnson, 1982: 188).

TABLE 2.1 State Trial Courts of General Jurisdiction

State	Name of Court	Number of Judges	Terms (Years)
Alabama	Circuit Court	124	6
Alaska	Superior Court	29	6
Arizona	Superior Court	101	4
Arkansas	Circuit Court	41	4
	Chancery & Probate Court	30	6
California	Superior Court	724	6
Colorado	District Court	110	6
Connecticut	Superior Court	139	8
Delaware	Superior Court	13	12
	Chancery Court	4	12
Florida	Circuit Court	362	6
Georgia	Superior Court	135	6
Hawaii	Circuit Court	24	10
Idaho	District Court	33	4
Illinois	Circuit Court	780	6
Indiana	Superior Court	117	6
	Circuit Court	89	6
Iowa	District Court	159	6
Kansas	District Court	155	4
Kentucky	Circuit Court	91	8
Louisiana	District Court	192	6
Maine	Superior Court	16	7
Maryland	Circuit Court	109	15
Massachusetts	Superior Court	61	life
Michigan	Circuit Court/Recorders Court	196	6
Minnesota	District Court	224	6
Mississippi	Circuit Court	40	4
	Chancery Court	39	4
Missouri	Circuit Court	303	6
Montana	District Court	36	6
Nebraska	District Court	48	6
Nevada	District Court	35	6
New Hampshire	Superior Court	25	until age 70
New Jersey	Superior Court	321	7
New Mexico	District Court	59	6
New York	Supreme Court	269	14
	County Court	118	10
North Carolina	Superior Court	72	8
North Dakota	District Court	26	6
Ohio	Court of Common Pleas	339	6
Oklahoma	District Court	148	4
Oregon	Circuit Court	84	6
Pennsylvania	Court of Common Pleas	330	10
Rhode Island	Superior Court	19	life
South Carolina	Circuit Court	31	6
South Dakota	Circuit Court	35	8
Tennessee	Circuit Court	69	8
	Chancery Court	33	8
	Criminal Court	26	8

TABLE 2.1   (*continued*)

State	Name of Court	Number of Judges	Terms (Years)
Texas	District Court	375	4
Utah	District Court	29	6
Vermont	Superior Court	10	6
	District Court	15	6
Virginia	Circuit Court	122	8
Washington	Superior Court	133	4
West Virginia	Circuit Court	60	8
Wisconsin	Circuit Court	197	6
Wyoming	District Court	17	6

SOURCE: National Center for State Courts, *State Court Organization, 1987* (Williamsburg, VA: National Center for State Courts, 1988), pp. 198–207. Reprinted with permission.

All of the states have at least one trial court of general jurisdiction, which goes by the name of superior court, circuit court, district court, or county court. These courts are listed in Table 2.1. However, the terminology can be misleading, as in New York, where one of the main trial courts is called the supreme court (and its state court of last resort is called the court of appeals). Only six states (Arkansas, Georgia, Indiana, Mississippi, New York, and Vermont) have more than one trial court of general jurisdiction (see Figures 2.1 and 2.2 for this arrangement in two of these states). Collectively, there are some 2,250 trial courts of general jurisdiction in the 50 states.

These courts handle the serious criminal and civil cases and are the level in which juries are used most frequently. The criminal cases are felonies, for which a sentence of imprisonment for more than one year can be imposed. Typical felony filings include burglary, assault and battery, drug violations, fraud, forgery, and rape. The civil cases, including divorce and real estate matters, involve sums of money above a certain minimum amount, as indicated in the several figures that illustrate examples of state judicial structures in this chapter. In the popular image of these courts, this is where the adversary process is employed, with skilled counsel for both sides articulating their arguments for the judge and/or jury. Yet as discussed in Chapters 5 and 6, upward of 90 percent of all criminal and civil cases are resolved prior to trial by means of plea bargaining in criminal cases and out-of-court settlements in civil matters.

As the pie diagram in Figure 2.4 illustrates, traffic cases make up half the caseload in these courts, civil cases constitute about one-third of the work, criminal cases represent only about 13 percent of the legal matters, and juvenile cases are 4 percent of the workload. Although not indicated in the figure, appeals from the trial courts of limited jurisdiction are often heard by these courts of general jurisdiction. In 1987, there were some 25 million matters filed in these courts. Even with plea bargaining and out-of-court settlements, there is a phenomenal number of cases to be filed, scheduled for hearings, and moved from one calendar to another to accommodate delays and conflicts among the parties, as well as conferences between lawyers and litigants with judges (especially in child custody and divorce cases). As James Eisenstein (1973: 119–120) remarked, the business of the trial courts is to process large numbers of cases quickly and with an

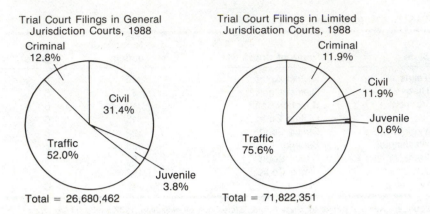

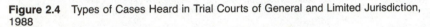

Figure 2.4 Types of Cases Heard in Trial Courts of General and Limited Jurisdiction, 1988

SOURCE: National Center for State Courts, *State Court Caseload Statistics: Annual Report, 1988* (Williamsburg, VA: 1990), National Center for State Courts, p. 5. Reprinted with permission.

element of bureaucratic efficiency. In this regard their operation is similar to that of a Social Security office or motor vehicle license bureau. Another characteristic of these courts is that much of the work occurs in private—meetings between opposing counsel, conferences with the judges in chambers, and so on. The relative lack of litigants' involvement in how their disputes are resolved is a source of frustration to some. This issue is discussed in Chapter 8.

State Appellate Courts

The state appellate courts, similar to their counterparts in the federal judiciary, consist of an intermediate court of appeals and a state court of last resort, commonly called the state supreme court. The majority of states (34) have one court of appeals, 5 states have two separate courts of appeal, and 11 predominately rural states have none. Because of the large populations in 14 states, the legislatures have carved their states into two or more geographical districts for the courts of appeal. For example, although Florida has one court of appeal, the appellate justices serve in one of five different geographical settings. Illinois also has 5 appellate districts and neighboring Ohio has 12. All of the states have a court of last resort.

The main purpose of the court of appeals is, as the name implies, to hear appeals from the lower courts. The appellate courts serve to correct errors that may have occurred in the trial courts and to clarify any ambiguities in the laws. As such, appellate court decisions are of interest not only to the party appealing a decision but also to others who may be affected in similar cases. Hence, appellate court judges have an opportunity to engage in policy-making, perhaps even more than their colleagues on the lower courts. Although all litigants are entitled to one appeal, most do not do so because they have resolved their legal matters through plea bargaining or out-of-court settlements. As the data in Table 2.2 demonstrate, there is a considerable fall off in the number of cases reviewed by the appellate courts in contrast to cases filed in the trial courts.

TABLE 2.2   Caseload Filings in State Courts, 1988

Supreme courts	67,203	(.07%)
Intermediate appellate courts	154,590	(.16%)
Trial courts: general jurisdiction	26,680,462	(27%)
Trial courts: limited jurisdiction	71,822,351	(72.8%)
Total	98,724,606	(100.03%)

SOURCE: National Center for State Courts, *State Court Caseload Statistics: Annual Report, 1988* (Williamsburg, VA: National Center for State Courts, 1990), pp. 5, 18.

In most states that have intermediate courts of appeal, the line of appeal is from the lower court, the trial court, to this appellate level. But in five states (Hawaii, Idaho, Iowa, Oklahoma, and South Carolina) appeals go from the trial courts to the state supreme court, which then decides which appeals should be heard by the intermediate appellate court.

Unlike trial court judges, appellate judges do not hear testimony. In most instances, judges on the courts of appeal read the transcripts of the case at hand and uphold the lower court's decision. The often monotonous processing of these cases prompted this candid response from one state appellate jurist about his job:

> Once in a while I cheat a little bit to get an interesting case out of there, but generally I try
> to give the more interesting cases to judges who have more time to devote to them. My job
> is to get rid of the garbage, because I get rid of the garbage faster than anyone else. . . .
> (Wold and Caldeira, 1980: 339)

When an appeal is successfully upheld by the courts of appeal, the case is sent back to the trial court for a new hearing consistent with the ruling of the appellate court. In a criminal case, this may mean that a trial judge's instructions to the jury were improper or that some evidence should not have been considered. When an appeal is upheld, it is left to the prosecuting attorney to decide whether to retry the case, engage in a new plea bargain, or simply dismiss it.

Because the term *supreme court* is associated with the highest-level court in a state, we use it to refer to these state courts of last resort although we recognize that they are called the court of appeals in both Maryland and New York and the supreme judicial court in Maine and Massachusetts. The characteristics of these courts of last resort are shown in Table 2.3. The number of justices range from a low of three (on one of Oklahoma's two supreme courts) to nine in a number of states. The average size is seven. Two states, Oklahoma and Texas, have two courts of last resort. Nine justices sit on Oklahoma's supreme court and three others on that state's court of criminal appeals. The situation is the same in neighboring Texas, except that nine justices serve on both the supreme court and the separate court of criminal appeals.

The state supreme courts have jurisdiction on all issues relating to state law and state constitutions. Most of their caseload is discretionary; if a majority of the justices want to hear an appeal, it will be heard. However, these courts may also have mandatory jurisdiction when the state constitution or statutes require that certain cases must be reviewed by the supreme court. Capital cases, for example, must be reviewed by the state supreme court in the majority of states that have the death penalty. Another example of mandatory

TABLE 2.3 State Courts of Last Resort

State	Name of Court	Number of Judges	Terms (Years)
Alabama	Supreme Court	9	6
Alaska	Supreme Court	5	10
Arizona	Supreme Court	5	6
Arkansas	Supreme Court	7	8
California	Supreme Court	7	12
Colorado	Supreme Court	7	10
Connecticut	Supreme Court	7	8
Delaware	Supreme Court	5	12
Florida	Supreme Court	7	6
Georgia	Supreme Court	7	6
Hawaii	Supreme Court	5	10
Idaho	Supreme Court	5	6
Illinois	Supreme Court	7	10
Indiana	Supreme Court	5	10
Iowa	Supreme Court	9	8
Kansas	Supreme Court	7	6
Kentucky	Supreme Court	7	8
Louisiana	Supreme Court	7	10
Maine	Supreme Judicial Court	7	7
Maryland	Court of Appeals	7	10
Massachusetts	Supreme Judicial Court	7	to age 70
Michigan	Supreme Court	7	8
Minnesota	Supreme Court	7	6
Mississippi	Supreme Court	9	8
Missouri	Supreme Court	7	12
Montana	Supreme Court	7	8
Nebraska	Supreme Court	7	6
Nevada	Supreme Court	5	6
New Hampshire	Supreme Court	5	to age 70
New Jersey	Supreme Court	7	7
New Mexico	Supreme Court	5	8
New York	Court of Appeals	7	14
North Carolina	Supreme Court	7	8
North Dakota	Supreme Court	5	10
Ohio	Supreme Court	7	6
Oklahoma	Supreme Court	9	6
	Court of Criminal Appeals	3	6
Oregon	Supreme Court	7	6
Pennsylvania	Supreme Court	7	10
Rhode Island	Supreme Court	5	Life
South Carolina	Supreme Court	5	10
South Dakota	Supreme Court	5	8
Tennessee	Supreme Court	5	8
Texas	Supreme Court	9	6
	Court of Criminal Appeals	9	6
Utah	Supreme Court	5	10
Vermont	Supreme Court	5	6
Virginia	Supreme Court	5	12
Washington	Supreme Court	9	6
West Virginia	Supreme Court of Appeals	5	12
Wisconsin	Supreme Court	7	10
Wyoming	Supreme Court	5	8

SOURCE: National Center for State Courts, *State Court Organization 1987* (Williamsburg, VA: National Center for State Courts, 1988), pp. 127–141.

jurisdiction arises when two appellate courts in a state disagree on an interpretation of state law. Again, the case will be heard by the supreme court to provide clarification for the lower courts in subsequent cases of a similar nature. Lower court appeals in states without an intermediate court of appeals usually are heard by the state supreme court.

Most of the discretionary petitions for high court review are not granted, in which case the decision of the lower court prevails. There is considerable variation among the state supreme courts and their caseloads. In 1987, the California Supreme Court was faced with over 4,500 discretionary petitions, but it granted review in only 224, or in just 5 percent. The Illinois Supreme Court had over 1,600 requests for review, but the justices heard only 138 appeals. The Wisconsin Supreme Court accepted 30 percent of the discretionary appeals in 1987, whereas the justices on the Washington Supreme Court accepted just 6 percent (Conference of State Court Administrators, 1989: 54–59). The dissatisfied litigant whose appeal is not accepted by the state supreme court can petition the U.S. Supreme Court for review, but the cause for appeal must then hinge on a federal issue, not an interpretation of state law. Even then, it is unlikely that this route of appeal will be successful given the relatively few appeals that the federal high court agrees to review annually. It is an unusual circumstance when the court agrees to hear an appeal based on an interpretation of a state constitution.

ADMINISTRATION AND REFORM IN STATE COURTS

The state courts do not run themselves. Indeed, much of what the judiciary does is dependent on other political decision makers. The state legislatures determine whether new judgeships will be authorized, how the courts will be funded, the jurisdiction of the various courts, and how judges are to be selected, and they allocate the budgets necessary for those who function in a support capacity in the courts. In some of these decisions, the role of county and municipal politicians is important, especially in the operations of the trial and specialized courts. In addition to the clerks and bailiffs who work in the courts, all of the states have various agencies that are part of the judicial bureaucracy.

Court Structure

State courts have not kept pace with the tremendous social, political, and economic changes that have occurred in the country since independence. All too often, the courts have engaged in battles with state legislatures over jurisdictional boundaries, methods for the selection of judges, funding, and political independence. As one political scientist summarizes the situation, the state courts "are outmoded organizations attempting to deal with increasingly complex issues. The problems are many, from insufficient and unstable funding to antiquated and inefficient procedures leading to chronic delays" (Stumpf, 1988: 98). Reformers have sought to professionalize and modernize the courts over the years, particularly from the 1930s on. Some of their efforts have been successful, whereas others have been disappointing. One of their major goals has been to bring about court unification, which would give the judiciary a coherent organization and economic base.

In essence, the structure of a state court falls into one of two categories, unified and nonunified. The distinction between them hinges on the existence of simple structure and central administration. The American Bar Association (1974) characterizes a unified court system as follows:

> The trial court should have jurisdiction of all cases and proceedings. It should have specialized procedures and divisions to accommodate the various types of criminal and civil matters within its jurisdiction. The judicial functions of the trial court should be performed by a single class of judges, assisted by legally trained judicial officers. The appellate court should have general appellate jurisdiction and should be divided into levels or tiers when a single appellate court level cannot adequately handle the appellate caseload. (2)

In addition to consolidation and simplification of the court structure, centralized management, rule making, and budgeting, unification proponents also advocate state financing of the judiciary (Henderson et al. 1984: 5).

An obvious question raised in the debate over unification is why anyone would oppose it if it results in increased efficiency, better administrative organization, and more accountability? The answers to this are practical and political. As with many reform proposals, the reality of their operations sometimes falls short of the expectations. Quite simply, the experience of court unification is mixed, and there appear to be some advantages as well as disadvantages to unification (Tarr, 1981). Second, any reform change alters the status quo. For example, as Glick (1982: 684–686) has noted, high-status, Republican lawyers favor reform because it would give them more power, whereas urban, Democratic lawyers fear losing control of the local judiciary. Additionally, some judges oppose unification since it would mean that they would have to operate under new procedures and rules that would lessen their independence.

An example of the problems encountered trying to move to unification is illustrated in New York. Governor Mario Cuomo (D) has supported the consolidation of the courts in New York City with the expectation that the lengthy backlog in the processing of cases would be reduced if not eliminated as a result of increased efficiency. Under the proposal, the county and family courts, New York City civil and criminal courts, and the Long Island district courts would be merged into a single, statewide supreme court (the main trial court of general jurisdiction). Yet the legislature has been in no rush to put the reform initiative before the voters. Unions and worker associations have raised questions about pay and working conditions, some local judges prefer to retain their local control of the courts, and both Republican and Democratic leaders are worried about the diminution of their influence (Lynn, 1987).

Proposals to realign the New York judiciary are not new. Indeed, the existence of eight separate courts of limited jurisdiction have troubled reformers for years (see Figure 2.2). The situation in the civil court in one of New York City's boroughs, the Bronx, aptly demonstrates the case for major reform. Most of these judges are selected by the political party leaders, who largely determine which candidates will appear on the ballot. But 80 percent of the judges are reassigned to relieve pressure on the city's *criminal* courts ("For Civil Court in the Bronx," 1989). According to reformers, a change in the method of judical selection and trial court unification would result in more efficient and less political courts.

Budgets and State Courts

A common problem facing all state courts across the country is inadequate funding. Appellate courts usually are funded by the state, and the lower courts are financed by a combination of state and local governments. In six states (Alaska, Hawaii, Kentucky, Massachusetts, New Hampshire, and New York), the state funds all trial courts, and in three states (Arizona, Texas, and Washington), the trial courts are financed entirely from local revenues (Conference of State Court Administrators, 1989: 8–9).

Historically, local courts were financed by local governments. However, this type of arrangement has been criticized on the grounds that it is unstable and can lead to undue influence in the courts from local political interests. There is no geographical pattern to the extent of state financing of trial courts. State support is high (over 80 percent) in Alaska, Colorado, Hawaii, Kentucky, New Hampshire, and Oregon. In contrast, local courts receive only 20 percent or less of their funding from the state in California, Oklahoma, and Washington (Lim, 1987: 14–17). The call for centralized budgeting in the 1980s has run into a fiscal roadblock. The elimination of federal revenue-sharing grants in 1985, increased fiscal demands for other programs in the states, and the reluctance of legislators to increase taxes to pay for state courts have stalled the momentum of the previous decade.

Budgeting, of course, involves political as well as economic decisions. County budget officials may want the state to finance local courts, but they are hesitant to turn the revenues from court-levied fines over to state coffers in return. Local political leaders would like to retain their influence on the municipal judiciary; yet they would like to have the state absorb the costs of judges' salaries. At times, the responsibility for court finance is uncertain. This was the situation in Philadelphia in 1989 when a Pennsylvania Supreme Court decision that year held that the state, rather than local governments, had to provide full funding for the county courts. Estimates of the costs to the state to do so ranged between $300 and $500 million that year alone. However, the high court did not say when the state had to begin allocating money for the 67 county courts. Philadelphia Mayor Wilson Goode cut $30 million from his city budget that would have gone to the county courts, yet the legislature refused to make up the difference. Ultimately, the presiding judge of the county court sued both the state and Philadelphia on the grounds that someone had to pay for the courts. The state supreme court ruled that Philadelphia had to pay court costs in 1989 but the legislature would have to absorb the costs in subsequent years. However, the legislature has balked at this prospect since it does not want to increase taxes or reduce funding for other programs in order to do so (Caba, 1989).

California has recognized the need to provide state financial assistance to local courts when the costs of certain trials threaten to exhaust county revenues. The trial in the McMartin preschool molestation case in Los Angeles County set records for both longevity and expense. The cost of the trial, which lasted two and one-half years, was a staggering $15 million. In the end, one defendant was acquitted and another was freed after the jury deadlocked on its verdict in the second retrial. In rural Sierra County, there were 10 murder trials over a three-year period, although only one of the victims was a county resident. The costs of the trials were such that one local official hired a land surveyor to determine whether one body was actually dumped just inside or outside the county boundary (Guccione, 1987).

The high costs of some sensational trials aside, the operating expenses of the courts are not a major financial drain on state and local budgets. The median salary for a state supreme court justice is about $83,000; court of appeals justices' salaries average $80,000, and the salary of the average trial court judge is $70,000. For years, judges associations have pleaded with legislators to increase salaries in order to attract more qualified individuals for the bench.

The operating budgets for the judiciaries reflect the number of judges and courts in the states. The 1988 Alaska court system budget was almost $39 million, an expenditure that represented only 1.5 percent of the general fund budget. In states such as Idaho, Montana, Vermont, and Wyoming, the courts operate on budgets of less than $10 million or so, a sum that constitutes less than 1 percent of the general fund budgets in these states. In contrast, large-population states require significantly higher budgets. The costs of running the New York judiciary in 1987 was $735 million, or about 2 percent of the state budget. In midrange is the Colorado judicial budget in 1989 at $90 million, or slightly more than 1 percent of the general fund. The expenses of operating just the trial courts in California was over $1 billion in fiscal year (FY) 1988–1989.

The point illustrated by these figures is that the operational costs of the state courts are not a significant aspect of state budgets. The public is disturbed by various aspects of how the courts work, but citizens appear disinterested in the relationship between adequate funding for the courts and court performance. There is no public outcry to increase the financial base for the judiciary, and those who work within the judiciary do not constitute a major political force that can effectively cajole additional revenues from state legislators. Indeed, the opposite situation may hold in some states. In Vermont, for instance, the courts were forced to suspend jury trials in some civil matters in 1990 to comply with state-mandated budget cuts. The cutbacks affected mediation and judge training programs as well as building renovations and a new program on drunk driving. Although such restrictive measures may forestall reductions in other worthwhile social and educational programs, they certainly do not improve the efficiency of the judiciary and they raise constitutional questions as well.

The courts also produce revenues for state and local governments through the fines and penalties assessed on litigants. In California, the trial courts collected over $900 million in assessed costs from litigants. About half of these revenues were kept in the counties and the remainder divided between the state and the cities. In 1988, operating expenses for the Arizona judiciary amounted to about $175 million, but the state recovered almost $72 million in fines, fees, and sanctions (*The Arizona Courts*, 1988: 14–15). All states require court-levied fines resulting from conviction of certain offenses to be allocated to special programs. Thus, for example, individuals convicted of violating fish and game statutes in Colorado have half of their fines earmarked for fish, game, and parks programs. In 1987–1988, these fines amounted to more than $160,000 (*Annual Report, Colorado Judiciary*, 1987–1988: 65). In many jurisdictions, a portion of the fines collected from convicted drunk drivers is allocated to highway programs and anti-drunk-driving educational programs.

Judicial Administration

Professional management of the state courts was not widespread until the early 1970s. Up to then, the trial courts in particular were beset by a number of common problems. All too often lawyers were able to manipulate the court calendar, judges lacked the administrative resources to keep track of trials in an efficient manner, record keeping was haphazard, clients and witnesses got lost in the system, and case backlogs were routine (Rubin, 1984: 209–210). These are not new issues. Over a half century earlier, in 1906, Roscoe Pound mentioned them in his famous assessment on the public's dissatisfaction with the American legal system to the American Bar Association.

Since the early 1970s, all of the states have initiated administrative measures to improve the case management, record keeping, budgeting, and processing of legal matters in the courts. In some states, a centralized system is used to coordinate these tasks at the appellate level. Most states, however, employ localized procedures at the trial court level. At the top of the judicial administrative hierarchy is the *state court administrator*, whose job is to maintain statistical information on the cases filed in the courts. All of the states publish the administrator's annual judicial report, which presents data on caseloads, dispositions of cases, appeals, and other information on the business of the judiciary. The state court administrator is often the chair of the state judicial council or similarly named agency, which suggests reform legislation to lawmakers and recommends improvements in the state courts. The judicial councils, on their own initiative or with the approval of the state supreme court, can reassign judges to handle unexpected matters in other jurisdictions statewide. Another component in the state judicial bureaucracy is the commission on judicial conduct, the agency that handles complaints of judges' misconduct (as discussed in Chapter 3).

The degree of innovation employed in addressing the problems in the courts is a result of how active the state bar, legislature, governor, and judges are in calling attention to the problems. The issue of managing the courts involves more than simply making sure that the right litigants show up in court at the scheduled times. In the state of Washington, for example, the supreme court established a Court Interpreter Task Force in 1985 to recommend changes in making interpreter services available for non-English-speaking persons. Two years later, a Gender and Justice Task Force was appointed by the chief justice to suggest ways to prevent gender bias in the courts. Similarly, a Minority Task Force was authorized by the legislature to assess the situation of minority litigants, attorneys, and judges in the judiciary. Other specific programs and concerns include improved methods for indigent defense; jury management; and a Bench-Bar-Press Committee, which meets annually to focus on the real and potential conflicts between the freedom of the press and a defendant's right to a fair trial (*Annual Report, Courts of Washington,* 1988: 1.7–1.11).

In 1987, the Montana Supreme Court established an 11-member commission to advise the state judiciary on the use of appropriate technology in its courtrooms. Some of the court services provided by the Office of the State Court Administrator in Colorado include a mediation program for some domestic cases, mandatory arbitration for civil cases involving less than $50,000 in damages, an alcohol and drug driving safety program, and a child-support enforcement program to collect child support from divorced parents who have left the state.

Several different organizations have initiated nationwide reform programs in the states and have sponsored studies to improve the administration of justice in state courts. The American Judicature Society has played a leading role in promoting judicial reform. Other organizations such as the State Court Administrators, the National Center for State Courts, and the Institute for Court Management in Denver have been influential in the court reform movement. Moreover, some state and private universities now offer advanced degrees in judicial administration to students seeking to acquire the professional expertise to serve as court administrators.

One courtroom innovation that has been used in California is sure to be adopted in other urban areas across the country. Video technology was introduced in 1990 to enable municipal court judges to hear arraignments for individuals arrested in misdemeanor cases. The closed-circuit television system connects the courtroom with a county jail. Interviews with judges, probation officers, public defenders, and inmates are conducted with television. Although this arrangement is not appropriate for more serious offenders, it saves time and the expense of transporting prisoners to the courthouse. An interesting side effect was noticed by one public defender: "Some inmates seem to regard advice they get from their lawyers more seriously when they're on television." He referred to this as "television conditioning—if it's not on t.v., it's not reality" (Gonzales, 1990).

Technological advances are bound to bring labor and time-saving measures to the courts in this decade. At the 1990 National Conference on Court Technology, judges and judicial administrators were exposed to courtroom computer terminals, which would speed the flow of case information to judges and enable them to use data bases for legal research. Even the now-popular compact disks in the music recording industry can be retooled for the courts. Optical disks in the future will be able to store information on one disk, which previously would have been kept on 20,000 printed pages. Also in the development stage is electronic communication between courts and law offices (Nejelski, 1990: 136).

The Politics of Court Reform

As noted previously, proposals for judicial reform can face considerable political and financial obstacles. For instance, in 1989 a Commission on the Courts recommended sweeping changes for the Arizona judiciary. Among the proposals endorsed by the 14-member body were (1) a program to resolve some disputes by arbitration, (2) the merging of several lower courts into the existing superior courts, (3) a central computer system for the state's entire judicial system, (4) increases in both the salary and qualifications for judges, (5) state funding for all of Arizona's courts, and (6) a change in the selection systems (from elective to appointive) in the state's two largest counties. Originally the commission endorsed a wholly appointive judiciary but relented on this in the wake of opposition from judges in a number of rural counties. Should these recommendations be adopted, court rules will have to be changed, legislation will have to be approved by state lawmakers, and changes in the state constitution must be agreed to by the voters (Manson, 1989). Although the counties and cities will welcome state funding for the courts, legislators can be expected to balk at assuming such a financial burden when more politically attractive programs for voters are put forth.

The goals of judicial reformers over the years have remained much the same. In general, reform efforts seek to modernize judicial institutions, make the process more efficient, and ensure that judges are nonpolitical professionals. The targets of reforms have been selection systems, court structures, judicial rules and procedures, and centralized planning and budgeting. These are broad goals that provoke controversy over how they can best be accomplished. Yet at different times in the states, efforts to achieve them have been met with opposition by some groups and indifference by governors and legislators.

The reform movements in Alabama and New Jersey illustrate how the efforts of key players can bolster the independence and reputations of state courts. Until the 1970s, the Alabama court system functioned under outdated rules and procedures. The courts, especially the supreme court, deferred to the legislature and the governor and appeared content with their racist reputation. The state high court legitimized the segregationist cause when it had the opportunity to do so. In one advisory opinion to the governor, the court said it was appropriate to close public schools rather than comply with federal integration orders. In another instance, the justices helped draft a list of questions that local clerks could ask of black residents seeking to register to vote. The questions were deliberately designed so that they could not be answered correctly. In speeches before public groups, the justices would indicate their opposition to civil rights organizations and to the efforts of the federal government to achieve racial equality (Tarr and Porter, 1988: 81).

The changes that resulted in the transformation of the Alabama court system began with the civil rights movement. Although many of the old-guard jurists opposed the changes advocated by civil rights leaders, Howell Heflin initiated the judicial reform movement in the mid-1960s when he became president of the state bar association. He organized a broadly based Citizens' Conference on State Courts that drafted reform legislation, which was later adopted. In 1971 he was elected chief justice of the Alabama Supreme Court. His efforts to increase the visibility and role of the state bar in the reform movement, to change the rules of procedures, and to encourage younger lawyers to become active in judicial politics were largely successful. In speaking of the state supreme court, Tarr and Porter (1988) note that by the mid-1970s,

> . . . the court's role changed dramatically. Where the old court performed a legitimating, supportive, even sycophantic function vis-a-vis the other branches of government and the dominant political, social, and economic forces within the state, the new court is far more independent, far more willing to take initiatives, far more mindful and respectful of the federal judiciary, more interested in utilizing precedent from other states, and certainly more sympathetic to civil liberties claims. (103)

Whereas the emphasis in Alabama was to bring new faces to the state courts and to instill a spirit of political independence in the judiciary, the target of Arthur Vanderbilt's reform efforts in New Jersey was to revamp the antiquated structure and process common to the state courts. Before 1947, when New Jersey adopted a new constitution, there were 17 separate classes of courts. The old supreme court had 16 members, making it, as the saying went, "a little larger than a jury, a little smaller than a mob." The rules and procedures for the courts had changed little since the early 1800s, and up until about 1950 judges were appointed almost exclusively on a partisan basis. Vanderbilt was appointed chair of the New Jersey Judicial Council in 1930. Although this body was only advisory, it issued numerous recommendations that were included in the 1947 constitution. The new document consolidated the judicial structure, created a seven-member supreme court, and centralized managerial authority in the hands of the chief justice.

Vanderbilt, appointed chief justice in 1948, sought to standardize the rule and procedures in the state judiciary. Previously, each of the various courts functioned autonomously and created its own operating guidelines. Vanderbilt attacked delays in the processing of cases by requiring all judges to submit weekly reports on their caseloads, matters heard, and cases awaiting disposition. Recalcitrant jurists were phoned to ask why cases were not handled in a more expeditious manner.

By the time of Vanderbilt's unexpected death in 1957, the state judiciary had been modernized. The reforms that he initiated proceeded in large part because of the respect that he had generated. A state's supreme court is the flagship in the state court system, and it is generally easier for reforms to filter down the judicial structure than rise from the lower courts to the top. Vanderbilt's mark on the New Jersey Supreme Court was evident. As Tarr and Porter (1988) write, "by raising the reputation of the state's courts, Vanderbilt's reforms increased the attractiveness of serving on the state's high court, a fact reflected in the caliber of judges recruited in the post-1947 era" (196).

Judicial reform does not occur by itself, nor does it come quickly or easily. Obstacles to reform abound. Heflin (now a U.S. senator) had to abandon his fight for merit selection of Alabama judges in the face of political opposition, and many of Vanderbilt's proposals in the 1930s were discarded for the same reason. Judges may resist reform efforts that would undercut their authority; lawyers may oppose reforms because of the uncertainty that follows. Moreover, according to one scholar of the reform movement, "Neither state nor local legislators march to the beat of the court drummer; other constituencies may well exceed the importance of the court system in the eyes and ears of elected lawmakers" (Rubin, 1984: 241).

Finally, it should be remembered that judicial reforms, like those reform measures for other political institutions, may not accomplish their goals. One of the main points stressed by reformers who advocated the "merit plan" selection of judges over the elective system was that the merit plan would result in better-qualified judges. As discussed in Chapter 3, this has not been the case. In fact, the empirical evidence shows that there are few, if any, significant differences in the "quality" of judges selected by elections or the merit system (Dubois, 1980). Throughout our history, the courts have had to adapt to procedural innovations and structural changes, some imposed from within and others from external sources. Such changes were, and continue to be, made in an effort to improve judicial performance. Yet it would be erroneous to think that all of the problems associated in the public's mind with the judiciary today can be resolved simply by structural reforms and more judges (Sarat, 1982). The courts are reactive bodies. The processing of cases can and should be more efficient, but nonjudicial reforms are necessary to ameliorate some of the conditions that have resulted in the higher caseloads over the past 20 years.

CONCLUSION

The courts in the 50 states today bear little resemblance to the informal, local legal bodies that existed at the eve of the American Revolution. Our judicial heritage is English, but the state courts and their federal counterparts evolved with their own unique identities and at different times over the decades. Then, as today, however, it is in the state courts that most people have their encounters with the judiciary. Whereas the federal courts may hand down the headline-making decisions, the state courts are where divorces are granted, auto accident liability disputes are resolved, traffic offenses are heard, and the vast majority of criminal actions are adjudicated.

Judicial structure and jurisdiction are essential to understanding the types of cases heard in the different courts, at what level they are filed, and the lines of appeal available to litigants dissatisfied with the decision of the trial court. Efforts over the years to streamline the courts, to eliminate overlapping jurisdictions, and to bring about modern organizational and administrative reforms have met with mixed success.

REFERENCES

American Bar Association. 1974. *Standards Relating to Court Organization*. Chicago: American Bar Association.

Annual Report, Colorado Judiciary. 1987–1988. Denver.

Annual Report, Courts of Washington. 1988. Olympia, WA: Office of the Administrator for the Courts.

The Arizona Courts. 1988. Judicial Report.

Caba, Susan. 1989, January 23. "Court Mobius Strip, Philadelphia-Style." *National Law Journal*, p. 3.

Conference of State Court Administrators. 1989. *State Court Organization, 1987*. Williamsburg, VA: National Center for State Courts.

Conference of State Court Administrators and the National Center for State Courts. 1990. *State Court Caseload Statistics: Annual Report, 1988*. Williamsburg, VA: National Center for State Courts.

Cook, Thomas J., Ronald W. Johnson. 1982. *Basic Issues in Courts Performance*. U.S. Department of Justice, National Institute of Justice.. Washington, DC: U.S. Government Printing Office.

The Courts in New Mexico. 1961, January. Santa Fe: A Report to the Twenty-Fifth Legislature in New Mexico by the State Judicial System Study Committee.

Dubois, Philip L. 1980. *From Ballot to Bench: Judicial Elections and the Quest for Accountability*. Austin: University of Texas.

Eisenstein, James. 1973. *Politics and the Legal Process*. New York: Harper & Row.

"For Civil Court in the Bronx." 1989, September 2. *New York Times*, p. 22.

Friedman, Lawrence M. 1985. *A History of American Law*, 2nd ed. New York: Simon & Schuster.

Glick, Henry R. 1982, June. "The Politics of Reform: In a Nutshell." 10 *Policy Studies Journal* 680–689.

Gonzales, Sandra. 1990, December 30. "Now on Video: The Judge." *San Jose Mercury News*, p. 1A.

Guccione, Jean. 1987, August 17. "Big Cases Strain Small Counties' Court Finances." *Los Angeles Daily Journal*, p. 1.

Hall, Kermit L. 1989. *The Magic Mirror: Law in American History*. New York: Oxford University Press.

Henderson, Thomas A., et al. 1984. *The Significance of Judicial Structure: The Effect of Unification on Trial Court Operations*. U.S. Department of Justice, National Institute of Justice. Washington, DC: U.S. Government Printing Office.

Lim, Marcia J. 1987, Summer. "A Status Report on State Court Financing." 11 *State Court Journal* 13–17.

Lynn, Frank. 1987, June 8. "Court Unity Plan Falters in Albany." *New York Times*, p. 14.

Manson, Pamela. 1989, October 19. "Justices Endorse Court Reform." (Phoenix) *Arizona Republic*.

Monthly Report, Migrant Legal Action Program, Inc. 1973.

Nejelski, Paul. 1990, August-September. "Technology Comes to the Courts." 72 *Judicature* 136.

Peters, Ellen Ash. 1987, Summer. "State Judiciary News: Connecticut." 11 *State Court Journal* 19–21.

Roscoe Pound. 1962, August. "The Causes of Public Popular Dissatisfaction with Administration of Justice." 46 Reprinted in *The Journal of the American Judicature Society* (3): 55–56.

Provine, Doris M. 1986. *Judging Credentials: Nonlawyer Judges and the Politics of Professionalism.* Chicago: University of Chicago Press.

Rubin, H. Ted. 1984. *The Courts: Fulcrum of the Justice System,* 2nd ed. New York: Random House.

Sarat, Austin. 1982. "Judicial Capacity: Courts, Court Reform, and the Limits of the Judicial Process." In Philip L. Dubois, ed., *The Analysis of Judicial Reform.* Lexington, KY: Lexington Books.

Sheldon, Charles H. 1988. *A Century of Judging: A Political History of the Washington Supreme Court.* Seattle: University of Washington Press.

Stumpf, Harry P. 1988. *American Judicial Politics.* San Diego: Harcourt Brace Jovanovich.

Tarr, G. Alan. 1981, March. "Court Unification and Court Performance: A Preliminary Assessment." 64 *Judicature* 356–368.

Tarr, G. Alan, and Mary C. A. Porter. 1988. *State Supreme Courts in State and Nation.* New Haven, CN: Yale University Press.

Wold, John T., and Gregory Caldeira. 1980, Winter. "Perceptions of 'Routine' Decision-Making in Five California Courts of Appeal." 13 *Polity* 334–347.

Wuest, George W. 1987, Summer. "State Judiciary News: South Dakota." 11 *State Court Journal* 28–29.

CHAPTER 3

The Politics of Judicial Selection

The states employ several different mechanisms—appointive, elective, or a combination of the two—to staff their courts. For far too many years the myth that candidates are selected for judicial positions simply because of their legal qualifications has endured, particularly in secondary education civic books. The chief executive announces his or her nominee as "one who has the best legal qualifications and an individual who will adhere to the spirit of the Constitution." It would be more accurate were the governor to say, "This individual has the appropriate legal credentials and is expected to interpret the Constitution the way I do, and this appointment will be to my advantage politically."

It is easy to note the characteristics one expects of judges. They should be neutral, be fair-minded, possess personal integrity, be of sound physical and mental health, be articulate, and be respectful of the judicial power they wield, and as the saying goes, it does not hurt if they know a little law as well. However, other considerations play a dominant role in determining which judges serve on the bench in the federal and state judiciaries. Foremost among these is the judicial philosophy of a prospective judge.

This does not mean that chief executives are always satisfied with the decisions made by their judicial appointees, for judges sometimes modify their views once on the bench. But it is the rare governor or president who knowingly elevates someone with dramatically different views to the prestigious and powerful position of a judge. Because those who are tapped to serve as judges can make policies through judicial decisions, and because they usually serve longer than the executive who appointed them, considerable political energy is spent to influence their selection (Stumpf, 1988: 154).

The purpose of this chapter is to examine the politics and different methods of judicial selection in the state judicial systems. At the outset however, we need to acknowledge a fundamental philosophical issue that affects the selection of judges but that does not apply to how the electorate or chief executives choose other government policymakers. Elective politicians are expected to have a general political philosophy, which the voters weigh when their fate is decided at the polls. In contrast, most voters intuitively expect judges to be politically neutral, not to be advocates for one group or another in their role on the bench. Moreover, we do not want judges to be the pawns of politicians. It is this concept of political independence that serves as a cornerstone for the judiciary. Yet democratic theory requires that policymakers (e.g., presidents, governors, legislators, and mayors) be held accountable to the public. Hence a dilemma: Should judges be given complete independence to decide cases consistent with their interpretations of the Constitution, or should there be some element of judicial accountability that ensures the voters an opportunity to decide on the fitness of judges at various times? The federal model of judicial selection tends to emphasize judicial independence since federal judges serve for life. The situation is different in the states, where with several exceptions, the judges must face the electorate at some time during their tenure on the bench. Because of these periodic elections, state judicial selection systems lean more toward accountability.

METHODS

In contrast to the relatively uncomplicated system for the selection of federal court judges (the president nominates and the Senate decides confirmation), the system of judicial recruitment and selection in the states is made complex by three major factors. First, the states employ some five different selection mechanisms. Second, many states utilize two different systems, one for the appellate courts and another for the lower courts. Third, some states ostensibly follow one method for judicial selection yet in reality employ another, an ambiguity that is illustrated later in this chapter.

The five judicial selection models utilized in the states are illustrated in Tables 3.1 and 3.2. As the footnotes in both tables explain, some states have deviated from the general model by adding their own individual features to the selection and confirmation process. The existence of five rather distinct selection systems highlights the fact that no one method seems best in terms of (1) recruiting the best legal talent available, (2) deemphasizing politics in the process, and (3) achieving the optimum balance between judicial accountability and independence.

Judicial Elections

From the founding of the Republic until the 1830s, state judges were selected either by the governors with confirmation by the legislature or by the legislature itself. The election of Andrew Jackson as president in 1828 and the subsequent rise of "Jacksonian democracy" encouraged the states to democraticize judicial selection. In 1832, Mississippi became the first state to have a popularly elected judiciary. Other states quickly followed suit.

The use of *partisan elections* was not designed to improve the quality of the bench but instead to insert populist ideology into the staffing of the courts. However, by 1870 the vote of the citizenry became captive to the political machines. According to one group of scholars, judges in this period "were often perceived as corrupt and incompetent. The notion of a judiciary uncontrolled by special interests had simply not been realized" (Berkson et al., 1980: 4). In response to the problems with partisan elections, the *nonpartisan election* of judges was introduced. The electoral process is the same, but the candidates are not identified on the ballot as Republicans or Democrats.

TABLE 3.1   Methods of Judicial Selection to the State Appellate Bench

Partisan Election	Nonpartisan Election	Merit Plan	Gubernatorial Appointment	Legislative Appointment
Alabama	Georgia	Alaska	California	Rhode Island
Arkansas	Idaho	Arizona	Maine	South Carolina
Illinois	Kentucky	Colorado	New	Virginia
Mississippi	Louisiana	Connecticut[1]	Hampshire[3]	
Pennsylvania	Michigan	Delaware[2]	New Jersey[2]	
Tennessee	Minnesota	Florida		
Texas	Montana	Hawaii		
West Virginia	Nevada	Indiana		
	North Carolina	Iowa		
	North Dakota	Kansas		
	Ohio	Maryland		
	Oklahoma	Massachusetts		
	Oregon	Missouri		
	Washington	Nebraska		
	Wisconsin	New Mexico		
		New York[2]		
		South Dakota		
		Utah[2]		
		Vermont[2]		
		Wyoming		

SOURCE: *State Court Organization,* 1987, National Center for State Courts. Williamsburg, VA. Table 7.
1. The legislature makes appointment upon recommendation of the governor from nominees submitted by merit selection panel.
2. The consent of the senate is also required.
3. The approval of popularly elected executive council is needed.

The vast majority of trial and appellate court judges must face the electorate at regular intervals during their careers on the bench. Judges in Massachusetts, New Hampshire, and Rhode Island, who are appointed for life, do not have to worry about reelection contests. And judges who are appointed by the legislature do not appear on the ballot; they are reappointed or denied reappointment by that same body. Jurists in all of the other states face the electorate when they are voted onto the bench initially or in confirmation balloting when they become eligible for a full term.

In some states that use partisan judicial elections, the real selection is made by key members of the political parties, not the voters. In New York, for example, Democrat and Republican party leaders decide which of their candidates will appear on the ballot. Recently the two major parties carried this process a step further by agreeing to endorse each other's nominees, thus ensuring the election of the candidates to the trial courts. If there are three judicial seats open, for instance, only three candidates will be put forth by mutual agreement. Party officials claim that this arrangement works to the benefit of the public since both Republicans and Democrats will be elected and that both parties tap only candidates of experience and excellence. However, as critics have pointed out, what this process actually means is that the voters will have no way to express their preference for whom they want to serve as judges. Judicial reformers have advocated an appointive system of judicial selection to replace the state's partisan elective mechanism. But these

TABLE 3.2 Methods of Judicial Selection for State Trial Courts of General Jurisdiction

Partisan Election	Nonpartisan Election	Merit Plan	Gubernatorial Appointment	Legislative Appointment
Alabama	California	Alaska	Maine	South Carolina
Arizona[1]	Florida	Arizona[1]	New Hampshire[5]	Virginia
Arkansas	Georgia	Colorado	New Jersey[3]	
Illinois	Idaho	Connecticut[2]	Rhode Island	
Indiana	Kentucky	Delaware[3]		
Kansas[4]	Louisiana	Hawaii[3]		
Mississippi	Michigan	Iowa		
New York	Minnesota	Kansas[4]		
North Carolina	Montana	Maryland[3]		
Pennsylvania	Nevada	Massachusetts		
Tennessee	North Dakota	Missouri		
Texas	Ohio	Nebraska		
West Virginia	Oklahoma	New Mexico		
	Oregon	Utah[3]		
	South Dakota	Vermont[3]		
	Washington	Wyoming		
	Wisconsin			

SOURCE: *State Court Organization,* 1987, National Center for State Courts. Williamsburg, VA. Table 20.
1. There is merit selection in the two most populous counties and partisan elections in the others.
2. The legislature makes the actual appointment from recommendations by the govenor from a list prepared by a judicial nominating commission.
3. The consent of the senate is required.
4. There is merit selection in 17 districts and partisan elections in 14 districts.
5. The approval of a popularly elected council is required.

pleas for reform have gone unheeded because the legislature does not want to upset the political parties by reducing their say in who will become a judge (Melvin, 1989).

Another illustration of the power of political parties is seen in Tennessee, where judges for the supreme court and the general trial court are selected on a partisan ballot (although intermediate appellate court jurists are selected by the merit plan). Democrats control state politics, and party leaders decide who the candidates will be for any judicial vacancies on the state supreme court. Although Republicans also offer their own slate of candidates for the high court, no Republican has been elected to the high court in this century. Instead of judicial contestants campaigning before the public for votes, candidates woo state and local party leaders for their endorsement. Once a nominee to the supreme court has been endorsed by the Democratic party in Tennessee, that individual is assured of being elected (Wade, 1990). As in New York, the vote of the Tennessee public is little more than a ratification of what the party has decided is best for it.

The Canons of Judicial Ethics restrict what judges can discuss in a campaign. In part because of this restriction, the vast majority of judicial elections are devoid of issues or controversy. As a result, these contests are usually characterized by low voter turnout. In nonpartisan, issueless judicial elections, voters simply have nothing to consider other than the sex, race, or ethnicity of the contestants, and it is not surprising that many simply leave their ballots unmarked when they come to the judicial candidates. Alternatively, they routinely vote for the incumbent on the assumption that not knowing anything about the individual probably indicates that a good job has been done!

The advantage is with the incumbent in judicial elections. In 1986, only 3 of 27 superior court judges who were challenged in California were defeated. However, the rate of defeat has been higher in Texas in recent years as Republicans have mounted opposition to Democrats. Because Texas judicial contests are partisan affairs, it is not unusual for a judge who was initially elected as a Democrat simply to change his or her registration to Republican so that the appropriate party label appears by the jurist's name (Champagne, 1986: 80–83). What this suggests, of course, is that Texans decide judicial contests in large part on the party affiliation of the contestants, not informed knowledge of their qualifications.

In partisan contests, the voters do have "cues" to guide their votes. The most obvious cue is the judge's party affiliation. The uncertain voter will probably mark the ballot according to his or her own party identification. However, in judicial election, there are other guidemarks as well that can reveal the sex, race, and ethnicity of the contestants.

The Missouri Plan

In 1914, the director of research of the American Judicature Society (AJS), Albert Kales, proposed an elective-appointive system. Under the Kales proposal, judicial nominating commissions, comprising judges, lawyers, and citizens, would screen potential judges and then recommend several worthy candidates, one of whom the governor would appoint to a bench vacancy. Once a candidate had been appointed, that person would be subject to a popular vote at a regularly scheduled election. The election would not be competitive. Rather, the nonpartisan "retention ballot" poses this yes-or-no question to the voters: "Shall Judge X be retained in office?" The Kales plan is now known as the merit plan or Missouri plan because of its introduction in Missouri in 1940.

In theory, voters consider the record of the incumbent when deciding whether the jurist should remain on the bench. Once again, voters most often mark their ballots in favor of retaining the incumbent judge. For example, according to one study of 1,864 retention elections at the trial court level in 10 states over a 20-year period, there were just 22 instances in which the incumbent was defeated (Hall and Aspin, 1987: 344). In other words, in only about 1 percent of these retention elections is a judge defeated. There are exceptions as well, usually the result of controversy. In Wyoming, a trial court judge was defeated in 1984 because his sentencing actions in two criminal cases outraged local residents. In one case, the judge suspended all but 61 days of a one-to-five-year prison sentence for a convicted child molester. In the other, the judge sentenced a 17-year-old boy to a 5-to-15-year prison sentence for killing his abusive father (Griffin and Horan, 1986).

The primary appeal of the merit plan for judicial selection rests with the implication that it is a nonpartisan mechanism. Additionally, proponents claim that judges of a higher "quality" are more likely to reach the bench via this system than any other. However, experience with the merit plan indicates that it is a very political one, with state and local bar politics substituting for public politics. Corporate attorneys want to see one of their own on the bench, and trial attorneys advocate selection of a trial attorney. A different example of politics in the merit plan was illustrated in Arizona in 1987 when the governor refused to recommend one of the three nominees to the state supreme court vacancy because none of them was compatible with the governor's philosophy. The governor called for additional names to consider. After a month of feuding with the nominating commission, the governor relented and appointed one of the original three (Stanton, 1987).

Another criticism is that the judicial nominating bodies have their own built-in biases and are overly representative of white males (Ashman and Alfini, 1974: 38). The judicial nomination commissions are subject to lobbying from judges and governors as well. For example, when three vacancies occurred on the Missouri Supreme Court in 1982, several justices were accused of collaborating with the Republican governor to rig the list of nominees to ensure that Republican candidates would be selected. The rancor that resulted from this episode led one group of observers to conclude that "no state bench of last resort filled by 'merit' selection has provided such overt and substantial evidence that politics remains a pervasive influence in a scheme designed to remove partisanship from the selection of judges" (Bunch et al., 1987: 1). Finally, there simply is no empirical evidence to suggest that this system results in the appointment of better-qualified judges than those produced by the other selection systems (Stumpf, 1988: 166–172).

Executive and Legislative Appointment

Judicial selection through executive or legislative appointment is rejected by reformers because of the obvious partisan overtones involved in such appointments. Both of these methods of judicial selection, formally employed only in a few states on the Atlantic seaboard, are holdovers from colonial days. In Connecticut, for example, the legislature not only makes the initial appointment but reconfirms to additional terms as well. Although these systems emphasize judicial independence, they also allow governors or legislators to appoint on a purely political basis. Indeed, legislative appointment is a convenient way for lawmakers to reward one of their own who has been defeated for reelection or to enable a legislator to retire to a judicial position (Glick and Emmert, 1987: 232). However, appointment to judicial positions as a reward for legislative service is not confined to the appointment system. As one former Massachusetts politician, a Democrat, recounts in his memoir, his effort to obtain the speakership of the Massachusetts House included the promise to appoint several of his Republican counterparts to judicial positions in return for their support (O'Neill, 1987: 63).

One of the more blatant examples of partisan political considerations affecting the gubernatorial appointment of a judge occurred in New Jersey in 1938 when the 28-year-old son of a politically powerful mayor was placed on the state's high court. This man had practiced law only briefly since he had to spend several years attempting to pass the state bar exam. The governor's explanation for the appointment? "I knew it would please his daddy" (quoted in Tarr and Porter, 1988: 189).

Dual Systems

As mentioned earlier, some states employ one method of judicial selection for the appellate courts and another for the trial courts. For example, California uses a modified merit plan for the appellate bench and nonpartisan elections for superior and municipal courts. Similarly, appellate court judges in Arizona are chosen by the merit plan, with confirmation by the legislature. However, the selection of lower court judges is by nonpartisan election in all but two counties, which employ merit selection. New Mexico has adopted a dual selection system in another sense by combining partisan elections with merit selection in a unique plan adopted in 1988. That approach is discussed more fully below.

SELECTION SYSTEMS IN OPERATION

The Importance of Initial Selection

Formal selection systems aside, judges in many states reach the bench initially by gubernatorial appointment. Table 3.2 indicates that trial court judges in California are selected in nonpartisan elections. Some are, but not most. About 90 percent of the state's trial court judges are appointed by the governor to fill the unexpired terms of judges who retire midterm or to staff newly created courts. The "rules" of the game go like this: If you were appointed to a trial court position by a Republican (or Democratic) governor, you plan to retire when another Republican (or Democrat) occupies the statehouse, thus giving another Republican attorney the opportunity to be appointed to the bench. When the election rolls around, that appointee will most likely be retained in office since he or she is now the incumbent.

This same situation also applies to Ohio. When appointing to a judicial vacancy, the governor solicits the recommendations of county party officials. Even though Ohio utilizes nonpartisan elections for judicial selection, interim appointments by governors are quite partisan (Baum, 1990: 108). Similarly, Washington Supreme Court justices supposedly are selected through nonpartisan elections. But as Dubois (1980: 206) has noted, some three-fourths of the justices, at least between 1948 and 1974, were originally appointed by the governor. Minnesota is a nonpartisan election state for trial court selection, yet over 90 percent of these judges were initially appointed by the governor.

Judicial Campaigns and Elections

Campaign Contributions. Once on the bench, judges can generally anticipate successful reelection, assuming their public and private behavior as well as their decisions have not created strong adverse publicity. But this does not mean that incumbents do not have to worry about campaign challengers. Traditionally, judicial campaigns have been low-budget affairs. However, the situation has been changing in some jurisdictions in recent years: Expenditures exceeded $380,000 for an incumbent on the Alabama Supreme Court in 1983, eight California municipal court candidates raised an average of about $50,000 each in 1982, and three candidates for Manhattan's surrogate court amassed some $800,000 the same year (Schotland, 1985: 59). In 1986, supporters and opponents of California Supreme Court Chief Justice Rose Bird and two of her colleagues spent more than $11 million in their efforts! In 1980, Frank Celebrezze spent $78,000 to win the chief justice's position on the Ohio Supreme Court. Six years later, he spent almost $1,800,000 in an unsuccessful effort to retain the post.

The implications of campaign costs and concern over the influence of financial contributors in judicial elections are interrelated in several ways. First, there is the actual or perceived conflict of interest when judges either actively solicit or passively accept contributions from attorneys. Lawyers, fellow judges, and in some instances political action committees are the most likely outside sources of campaign funds for judges and challengers. Attorneys who contribute to an incumbent judge may feel they will be rewarded for their largess (Schotland, 1985: 90). Conversely, attorneys who actively support the incumbent's opponent may feel they will be at a disadvantage when they appear before the judge in court. In his study of judge's attitudes on judicial selection in Florida, Atkins (1976: 182) found that judges felt they were placed in a "compromising position" when they accepted contributions from lawyers who appeared before them. Several Texas Supreme Court justices came under criticism as a result of their acceptance of almost $400,000 from lawyers representing Pennzoil Company and Texaco in an $11 billion lawsuit. Some of the justices who accepted the donations were not even up for reelection (Kaplan, 1987: 29–31).

The problems associated with contributions to judicial campaigns were illustrated in an in-depth study by the *Dallas Morning News*. According to this investigation, it was not uncommon for judges to preside at trials in which major contributors and even key fund-raisers were arguing cases. Nor was it unusual for judges in civil cases to appoint campaign workers and lawyers who had donated money to their campaigns to serve as receivers and guardians for children and mentally ill clients in personal injury lawsuits. And lawyers often contributed campaign funds to a judge days before the judge was assigned to hear cases argued by the donors. In all fairness, the reporters did not uncover a pattern linking donors to favorable judicial verdicts, but as one lawyer put it, "Anybody who makes a contribution to a candidate for public office expects some kind of a return" (Edgar and McGonigle, 1987).

However, in a two-year study of Philadelphia's municipal and common pleas courts, reporters for the *Philadelphia Inquirer* were able to link attorneys' campaign contributions to favorable judicial decisions. During one five-year period, defense lawyers who had either worked in or contributed money to judges' campaigns won 71 percent of their cases before those judges. Yet in the same municipal courts, an average of only 35 percent of the defendants won their cases (Bissinger and Biddle, 1986).

In response to the negative publicity concerning corruption and campaign improprieties by judges, all of the Philadelphia judges who faced election in 1989 agreed to have their campaigns funded by the Philadelphia Bar Association. Under this unusual and interesting arrangement, the bar allocated about $7,500 to each of the 16 jurists. The bar association raised the money primarily from attorneys, although judges were not told the names of the contributors. This method of financing municipal judicial campaigns represents the middle ground between public financing, on the one hand, which is opposed by a majority of citizens nationwide, and, on the other hand, judges bearing the sole responsibility for raising their own election contributions, a practice that critics claim has compromised the integrity of the Philadelphia bench.

Second, the need for campaign funds requires judges to concern themselves with fund-raising activities that could detract from the business of the courts. An example occurred in a Los Angeles municipal court, where the judge, presiding at a preliminary hearing in a murder case, admitted that he had asked the prosecution and defense counsel to distribute some of his campaign materials. The hearing was transferred to another judge. An Oregon Supreme Court justice was reprimanded by the state Judicial Fitness Commission in 1990 for violating ethical rules by personally soliciting campaign funds for his successful election two years earlier. Judicial rules in Oregon prohibit an incumbent or a challenger from personally soliciting donations on the grounds that the public "may come to believe that the judge will be influenced in the future by direct knowledge of who has contributed to his or her campaign" (Leeson, 1990).

Third, the increasing costs of judicial campaigns may mean that some potential challengers are prevented from seeking the bench because they lack the fund-raising capabilities of the incumbent. It is not uncommon for judges to hold fund-raisers before the existence of potential challengers is known. An incumbent judge with a sizeable campaign fund can effectively deter election opponents.

In Cook County, Illinois, even unopposed circuit court candidates need to raise at least $10,000 to pay an "assessment" to the Democratic party, which controls who is slated to appear on the nonpartisan retention ballot (Nicholson and Weiss, 1986). Illinois has weak campaign disclosure laws, and judges there are allowed to convert surplus campaign funds to their personal use.

Expensive judicial contests are the exception rather than the norm in most states. And even in large states such as California, New York, and Texas, where big money is spent on judicial races, the sums pale in comparison with expenditures for partisan political offices. According to the data collected on campaign spending in California by Philip Dubois (1986: 272), trial court judicial candidates spend only about a dime per vote, in contrast to $2.55 per vote spent by state assembly contestants. Nonetheless, it is difficult to avoid the conclusion that expensive judicial races might well negatively affect the public's perception of the integrity of the legal system.

Much to the dismay of reformers, judges are being forced to campaign in the manner of state politicians in some instances. When an incumbent on the Wisconsin Supreme Court was challenged in 1989, the first time this had occurred in more than two decades, the campaign featured several debates, television ads, accusations that the candidates were either too liberal or too conservative, group endorsements, and expenses of more than $215,000 each. To no one's real surprise, the incumbent retained her seat on election day. Unlike most judicial contests, this one was a highly visible race. What did this type of campaign produce? As one analyst put it, "In spite of the expenditures, the heat of the campaign and its ideological overtones, voters seemed to be largely unaffected" (Jones, 1989: 7). The point of this comment is not that voters cast aside politics to discern who was the better candidate but that they paid no attention to the contest in spite of the unusual publicity.

Judges and Controversial Decisions.   The linkage between judges and politicians extends beyond their campaign behavior in another way. The rise of single-issue voting blocs has resulted in some jurists being forced to defend themselves for having voted a particular way on controversial issues. In 1970, a veteran trial court judge in Los Angeles County was defeated because of his earlier decision that ordered school busing to desegregate the public schools in the county. Although an appeal stayed his order soon after it was made, the election became a single-issue referendum on the judge's busing decision. Similarly, the 1986 rejection of three California Supreme Court justices by the voters was attributable to their decisions in death penalty cases.

More recently, Justice Leander J. Shaw, Jr., the first black chief justice on the Florida Supreme Court, came under fire from prolife groups. This marked the first time the abortion controversy was tied to an incumbent judge's suitability to remain on the bench. Shaw wrote the majority opinion (the justices divided 4:3) that invalidated a state law requiring minor girls to obtain consent before an abortion could be performed. As the president of the Florida Right to Life Committee stated well before the November 1990 election in which Justice Shaw would be one of the court's seven justices to appear on the retention ballot, "Our goal is to unseat him and give the governor the chance to appoint his successor" (Wermiel, 1990). Shaw won confirmation with a 59 percent approval vote.

Lack of Information.   Elective judicial selection systems emphasize the public accountability of judges. However, unlike the election of other public officials, there is the troubling issue of just what it is judges can pledge to do (or not do) in their campaigns. Or looked at from the perspective of the voters, what can they evaluate when deciding whether to vote for Judge Smith or Judge Jones? Five months after Arthur Alarcon was appointed to the appellate court by California Governor Jerry Brown, his name appeared on a retention ballot. In spite of his brief tenure on the bench and the fact that none of his few opinions had been published, over 30 percent of the voters cast their ballots against him. Alarcon (1983) was mystified about how his "phantom record" had revealed anything of his judicial philosophy or fitness for the bench. Although he did hold onto his seat, one can only conclude that the negative votes against him had nothing to do with anything he had done as a judge. Rather, perhaps some voted against him because his name suggested that he was Hispanic (he is) or that he must be a Democrat since he was appointed by a Democratic governor (he is) or because of the belief that none of the judges on the ballot should be retained in office regardless of whether they were Republicans or Democrats.

In partisan races, the political party label may give most voters all the information they seek. Local newspapers also provide information in election articles and through candidate endorsements. In a number of jurisdictions, bar evaluations are publicized to increase voter awareness of the candidates. However, voters may not pay much heed to the bar ratings (Dubois, 1984: 407). In the 1988 elections for superior court candidates in Los Angeles County, three incumbents who were rated "not qualified" by the county bar association were retained in office despite the fact that their three challengers were favorably rated. The only judge who was defeated, and who was rated "qualified," attributed her loss to the use of the label "incumbent" on the ballot. All of the other judges had as their ballot labels "Judge of the Superior Court" (Reich, 1988). Given the lack of issues in those races, the only explanation for her defeat is that those who voted against her were unaware that she was, as the word *incumbent* implies, already on the bench.

Judges and political observers are still puzzled over the defeat of a Washington Supreme Court justice in 1990. Elections to the appellate bench in Washington are contested, nonpartisan affairs in which the incumbent usually wins the primary. However, the 20 percent of the voters who cast ballots in the race ousted Keith Callow, a veteran judge who was widely respected in legal circles. He had not been targeted for defeat by any organized groups. Neither candidate spent much money in the race and campaigning was almost nonexistent. Callow enjoyed bar and press endorsements; his opponent received none. Why did the voters turn a respected jurist out of office? Washington does not publish a voters' pamphlet; thus citizens were largely unaware that the incumbent had 20 years of service as a judge, whereas the challenger served as a judge only in a temporary capacity on several occasions. And since the contest did not involve any controversial rulings or accusations from the challenger, media attention was scant. Finally, some observers felt that Callow was defeated because his name did not sound as familiar as that of his challenger, Charles Johnson (Bone, 1990: 46). This was the first time in 40 years that a Washington Supreme Court justice had been defeated. The impact of Callow's loss was summarized by a Seattle television commentator: "This was a wake-up call for state Supreme Court justices, telling them they've got to get some name recognition. It's just not enough anymore to do a good job and hope that the word will get out" (London, 1990).

Number of Candidates.   At times, the sheer number of candidates may overwhelm voters to such an extent that they simply decide not to vote in these races or to let the political party label of the contestants determine their vote. In 1982, voters in Harris County, Texas, faced a total of 106 candidates in contests for the following judicial positions: supreme court, court of criminal appeals, district court, county civil court, county criminal court, and county probate court. As Champagne (1986) commented on this lengthy ballot, "Faced with such a number of choices and limited knowledge of judges, it should not be surprising that political party affiliation is often the determining factor in elections" (79). In 1990, Shelby County, Tennessee, voters were presented with 75 candidates for 63 judicial posts.

Race Bias and Judicial Elections.   The question of whether judicial elections are racially discriminatory has been raised in 8 of the 36 states that elect judges to one or more tiers in the judicial hierarchy. Because there are few, if any, judicial districts in the states where minorities constitute over 50 percent of the electorate, the minority vote for minority candidates is diluted by the larger vote of the white population. Added to this are several case studies that show that white voters are unlikely to vote for a black judicial candidate if a white candidate is also on the ballot (Engstrom, 1989: 89).

The central issue hinges on how one interprets a section of the 1965 Voting Rights Act, which was intended to ensure that voting district boundaries would not be drawn in such a way as to diminish deliberately the ethnic or racial minority vote. The act has changed at-large election outcomes in races for a variety of political positions including state legislative seats, city councils, and school boards. Contestants elected to these posts are expected to be representatives of their constituents. But, are judges "representatives" within the meaning of the Voting Rights Act? Some Hispanic and black organizations have sued to alter the boundaries in judicial elections, claiming that judges are representatives, an argument several federal courts have upheld. These boundaries, according to the plaintiffs, explain why the courts in many states are predominately white. The position of the states is that judges are not representatives in the political meaning of the word since they serve all the people, not just one constituency. Moreover, judicial district boundaries are customarily drawn on a caseload basis, not according to population, as are district lines for political races (Haydel, 1989).

Mississippi and Louisiana, two of the states where lawsuits have been filed, have made efforts to increase the number of minority judges through gubernatorial appointment and special elections. One way the states can sidestep this controversy is to move to an appointive system for judicial selection. Of course, such a change would remove the ability of citizens to assist in judges' initial selection. Another remedy, which is more politically feasible, would introduce the notion of "limited voting." Under this arrangement, voters would cast fewer votes than there are seats for election. Thus, for example, if five judicial seats are on the ballot, citizens could vote for only three contestants (McDuff, 1989). Since voters are most likely to vote for a candidate of their race, this system would make the election of black or Hispanic jurists more likely.

DOES IT MAKE ANY DIFFERENCE
WHICH SELECTION SYSTEM IS USED?

Despite the existence of the five separate selection systems for state judges, there appears to be little, if any, difference among them in terms of the professional characteristics of the judges who are recruited for the bench. Whereas judges generally favor the selection system that enabled them to reach the bench, most judicial support lies with the merit plan (Scheb, 1988). Moreover, the public's perception of the competence of the state and local judiciary does not appear to relate to the different formal selection systems (Wasmann et al., 1987).

One recent study indicated that none of the selection mechanisms appeared to work to the advantage of increasing female or minority representation on the bench (Alozie, 1988). But this finding needs to be viewed with some caution. When one compares the number of women and minority attorneys elevated to the bench by the different selection systems, the aggregate data suggest only minor deviations. Yet governors can make a significant difference on this issue depending on their own policy preferences. While Jerry Brown occupied the governor's post in California, he placed 86 blacks, 73 Hispanics, 33 Asians, and 132 women in judicial positions. Overall, minorities and women constituted about 40 percent of Brown's judicial appointees. The vast majority of these appointments were to the trial courts, although there were several notable exceptions. Brown appointed the first woman, first black, and first Hispanic to the state high court. In contrast, Governor Bill Clements (R) of Texas appointed a total of just 10 Hispanics and no blacks to the state bench during his two terms as governor (1979–1982, 1987–1990).

According to two observers, the question of which selection is best should be rephrased to "Does it make any difference?" Their answer was no (Flango and Ducat, 1979). As Stumpf (1988) has commented, the different selection systems may be more similar than dissimilar in terms of the caliber of those who reach the bench: ". . . the exaggerated claims for one system, as well as criticisms by proponents of another, are equally without foundation. If one mechanism fails to produce measurably better judges than another, it is also true that competing selection systems also fail to produce the disastrous results predicted" (176).

This finding is frustrating to many who intuitively assume that different systems must result in different types of judges (e.g., from different backgrounds), who could in turn be distinguished by the different types of decisions they would render. The minor differences that do appear are attributable to regional political distinctions rather than selection systems (Canon, 1972).

One is hard-pressed to gauge the public's attitude about judicial selection in the states largely because citizens are not particularly knowledgeable about their own or alternative selection mechanisms. In 1987, Ohio voters rejected a constitutional amendment that would have replaced that state's nonpartisan judicial selection with merit selection. The measure, which lost by a 2:1 majority, was opposed by organized labor and the state's Republican and Democratic parties. Since there is strong two-party competition in Ohio, the opposition of key Republican and Democratic party leaders was not surprising. The following year, residents in New Mexico did support a constitutional amendment that modified their system of judicial selection. Previously, all state judges were elected on a partisan ballot, and interim vacancies were filled by the governor. Under the new procedure, incumbent judges appear only on a retention ballot. Judicial vacancies now are filled initially by merit selection, and the new appointees face their first public vote on a partisan ballot. If they are reelected, future confirmations will be on a retention ballot (Dixon, 1989). It is this type of confusing selection mechanism that may help to explain why many voters simply leave their ballots blank in judicial contests.

Despite the complications of this arrangement, the key individual in the selection process is the governor. This system has come under criticism but not because of the competence of those tapped by the governor. Rather, a familiar political pattern is evident. Minority attorneys in New Mexico tend to identify with the Democratic party. If a Republican governor holds the statehouse, he or she will appoint a Republican to a bench vacancy, which in reality most likely means an Anglo and probably a male. In the first year of the new procedure in New Mexico, the governor, a Republican, was able to appoint new judges to replace 10 who had resigned that year. Although 3 of the 10 judges who stepped down were Hispanic, none of the governor's judicial appointees was Hispanic, although 1 or 2 were on the 3-person list sent to the governor by the screening committee (Yaeger, 1989: F–1). Given the strong partisan politics in New Mexico, a Democratic governor is unlikely to appoint Republicans to bench vacancies when the opportunity arises. It is difficult to comprehend how the new judicial selection mechanism is less political than the previous one, which was based on partisan elections.

The Role of the State Bar

State bar associations have a vested interest in who becomes a judge, regardless of formal selection systems. Other organizations such as environmental and consumer groups are concerned about who is elevated to the bench, as are members of ethnic and minority associations. But traditionally it has been the state and local bar associations that play a leading role in influencing judicial selection, be it by appointment or election. As one observer discovered, the formal role of the bar in judicial selection varies tremendously. In a number of states, particularly those utilizing the merit plan, the bar plays an active role. In many of the other states the bar investigates potential candidates and nominees, endorses candidates, or helps to solicit potential judicial aspirants. In a handful of states, mainly in the South, there is no formal bar activity (Sheldon, 1972). The important role of the bar in merit plan states is well documented (Watson and Downing, 1969). However, whether the activities of the bar in swaying outcomes in election systems are significant is still an open question.

Some Thoughts

Before leaving the issue of selection systems, two additional comments are in order. First, although selection systems do not disclose meaningful differences among the candidates elevated to the bench, it would be erroneous to imply that they are identical. Since so many judges, particularly at the trial court level, reach the bench initially through gubernatorial appointment, it does make a difference who the governor is. Presidents and governors, as we have already noted, appoint individuals to judicial posts who share their political and legal outlook. Hence, a liberal chief executive may look for a judicial candidate who opposes capital punishment, whereas the conservative may want a person who supports it. This situation is particularly evident in states such as California, where for the past 30 years citizens have alternated between voting for liberal and conservative governors.

Governor Jerry Brown was able to appoint a total of six justices to the seven-member California Supreme Court during his two terms in office (1975–1981). The most controversial of his appointees was Rose Bird, who joined the court as chief justice in 1977 and served until 1986, when she was rejected for an additional term by the voters. Two other Brown-appointed justices were denied new terms in 1986 as well, largely because of their votes in death penalty decisions. Between 1977 and 1986, the Bird court upheld only 4 death penalty sentences or convictions out of the 68 that were handed down by the trial courts. But the defeat of the three justices in 1986 gave George Deukmejian, a staunch capital punishment proponent and Brown's Republican successor as governor (1983–1990), the opportunity to place three of his nominees on the court. Deukmejian already had one of his nominees on the court before 1986 and added another in 1989. The "new" court has upheld 84 death penalty sentences out of the 109 submitted to it for review between 1986 and 1990. Thus, in contrast to the Bird court's support for the death penalty in only *6 percent* of the capital cases to come before it, Deukmejian's appointees upheld the death sentence *77 percent* of the time. This is the difference a governor can make with his or her judicial appointments.

Second, should voters take more of an interest in casting their ballots in judicial contests, the makeup of the state trial courts could change tremendously. If the relative security that state judges now enjoy on the bench were in jeopardy, perhaps more challengers would emerge in local contests. But potential pitfalls are associated with increased voter activism. One result could well be a situation in which judges are reluctant to make controversial decisions for fear of antagonizing voters and thus making themselves vulnerable at election time.

Summary: Politics and the State Courts

The state judiciary has come under considerable public criticism over the past two decades because of problems associated with the administration of justice in civil and criminal cases. Trial delays, lost records, prolonged trials, questionable decisions, and the errant conduct of some jurists are routine fare in the television news accounts and newspaper stories. Yet surprisingly little attention, outside of legal circles, is devoted to the fundamental question of how judges should be selected for the bench. Perhaps it is easier to acknowledge how we do *not* want judges selected rather than how we do. The five different selection systems illustrate the lack of consensus on this topic.

Although the selection mechanisms for state jurists are all political in varying degrees, an argument can be made that they appear to be working reasonably well despite the criticisms. There is, after all, a balance of judicial independence and public accountability. Moreover, the threat of impeachment, recall, and sanctions from state judicial disciplinary tribunals helps to ensure that the obvious misfit, incompetent, and corrupt judges will not be long tolerated.

JUDICIAL MISCONDUCT

If the issue of how best to select judges for the bench represents one side of the selection coin, the other side concerns how to deal with incompetent judges. Judges at all levels have always been subject to the federal and state criminal codes. Depending on the severity of their criminal offenses, offending judges could be impeached by legislative bodies or forced to leave office after conviction. For example, eight Philadelphia judges were removed from the bench by the Pennsylvania Supreme Court after it found they had "betrayed the public trust" by accepting cash gifts from a roofers' union. In Operation Greylord, a sting operation begun in Cook County, Illinois, in the 1980s, a number of judges, attorneys, and law enforcement officers were charged with criminal acts of wrong-doing, including mail fraud, tax violations, and racketeering, as a result of taking bribes to fix cases. Nine sitting or former judges were convicted of corruption. Most troubling about the corruption was that no judge or attorney who knew of its existence volunteered any information about it, even though they were not involved. According to a former U.S. attorney who began Greylord but left office before the indictments were handed down, corruption is a fact of life in Chicago: "There seems to be in Chicago a pervasive, deep-seated lack of honesty at all levels of government and business. I do not know whether it is worse here than elsewhere, but I do know that public and private corruption is commonplace in our city" (Middleton, 1987).

Impeachment does not address the situation of judges whose behavior is improper but not so offensive to warrant removal from the bench. As a result of several troublesome judges in the 1960s and 1970s, Congress passed a disciplinary act in 1980 to sanction federal judges for milder forms of misconduct.

In addition to impeachment, judges in some 20 state are also subject to recall. That is, they can be voted out of office for noncriminal behavior. Although a successful recall effort is rare, it does happen occasionally. In 1977, a county judge in Wisconsin was the target of a recall effort because of the way he handled a sexual assault by two teenage boys on a 16-year-old girl in a high school. Judge Archie Simonson sentenced the youths to a year at home under court supervision, although the prosecutor argued for their confinement in a residential treatment center. Simonson, in justifying his at-home sentence, remarked that the sexual permissiveness of the times and provocative women's clothing encouraged the sexual assault. Many residents of the community were offended by the judge's sexist attitudes, notably his failure to acknowledge rape as a crime of violence, not of sexual passion. The recall vote resulted in Simonson's departure from the court and his replacement by a female judge.

Disciplinary Commissions

However, it is not so much criminal violations of the law that cause problems for judges as complaints against them because of failing physical or mental health, alcoholism, inability to perform judicial duties, and conduct that maligns the judicial office. Since 1960, when

California created its Commission on Judicial Performance, the other 49 states and the District of Columbia have established their own disciplinary tribunals to handle complaints of judicial misconduct. In most of the states, the tribunals are made up of a combination of judges, lawyers, and laypersons. Typical misconduct complaints allege undue delays in rendering decisions or sexist or racist language and courtroom demeanor. The response of the disciplinary body is to notify the judge that a complaint has been filed and to ask for an explanation. Most often, the response is satisfactory and that is the end of the process. However, in the event that a serious charge is sustained, the commissions can censure (in public or in private), reprimand, remove, or forceably retire jurists.

Analysts with the American Judicature Society, who collect data on state judicial conduct commissions, reported that some 5,827 complaints were lodged against judges in 1987 (Lawton, 1989). However, 92 percent of these complaints were dismissed as being unfounded or frivolous. Charges disposed of this quickly are usually based on a litigant's dissatisfaction with a judge's decision in a particular case rather than the judge's behavior. Of the complaints that were investigated, 126 judges were either privately or publicly censured in 27 states. A public censure may affect a judge's reelection at the polls, and a private censure may keep a judge from being elevated to a higher position in the judiciary. The ultimate sanction, removal from office, was applied to 21 judges in 9 states in 1987. Some of these judges were ordered retired for medical reasons rather than deliberate misconduct. Given the number of judges in the states, clearly only a handful ever feel the sting of a disciplinary body's actions. But the suggestion of misconduct and a commission investigation can lead some judges to retire voluntarily from the bench, as 112 did in 1987. Voluntary retirement ends an investigation and can spare a recalcitrant judge the embarrassment that might accompany a public sanction for misdeeds.

Most complaints of judicial misconduct are levied by private citizens. Lawyers may be reluctant to file charges for fear of retaliation should the offending jurist become aware of the complainant. Not surprisingly, the great majority of judges who are sanctioned occupy the trial bench. These are the most "visible" judges. On the appellate courts, fellow judges would be in the best position to report the improper actions of one of their own. In reality, judges, like their counterparts in medicine and higher education, are reluctant to file charges against a colleague except under unusual circumstances.

Although judicial disciplinary commissions do administer sanctions and are successful in prodding some judges to resign before formal discipline may become necessary, financial self-interest is perhaps the best incentive to persuade judges to retire before old age or the stress of the position renders them unsuited to continue on the bench. Most of the states have established a desired age by which judges should retire, and pensions are highest for those who do so by that time. Should a judge want to stay on the bench beyond that age (usually 70 years old), the retirement pay is diminished proportionately according to the subsequent years the judge stays in office.

STATE JUDGES: A PORTRAIT

Forty-six percent of the some 17,000 state court judges are on the major trial courts. Forty-seven percent sit on the minor courts, and 7 percent occupy appellate positions. The traditional career path to a judgeship, at either the federal or state levels, included graduation from a respectable law school; some political activity; and commonly, prosecutorial experience. This pattern began to unravel in the 1970s as women, blacks, and ethnic minorities were appointed to the bench. White males continue to dominate the bench at all levels of the judiciary, but women and minorities are no longer viewed as oddities.

The typical state supreme court justice is a white male, Protestant, and a Democrat. He was educated at an in-state undergraduate school and received his degree from an in-state law school. He had an average of 14.5 years of prior judicial experience before reaching the state high court (Glick and Emmert, 1986: 108). The profiles of state trial judges are similar to their supreme court counterparts—white, male, in-state law school, but with fewer years, if any, of previous judicial experience.

In 1988, New York established a special commission to assess the implications of the predominantly white, male judiciary. Of particular concern are the urban courts, where white jurists and other white administrators contend with an overwhelmingly minority population. According to the interim report of the commission, the white makeup of some courts in urban areas creates "an appearance that the system is unjust because minorities seem to be barred from within" (Glaberson, 1989). Of the top 244 administrative positions in the New York State courts, only 10 were held by minorities. The report criticized the "old-boy network" among judges and administrators, which excluded minorities from entry and advancement. Overall, the New York judiciary is 92 percent white. The situation is similar in all other states. Similarly, since 1982, some 27 states have created task forces to eliminate gender bias in the courts. Concern is not just with female jurists but with how women—as defendants and attorneys—are treated in the predominately male judicial environment.

Although it is difficult to generalize about women on the federal bench given their low numbers (less than 10 percent of all federal court judges are women), studies of women in the state courts are revealing. In their survey of 14 female state supreme court justices, Allen and Wall (1987) characterized them as "outsiders" because they did not alter their voting behavior to agree with the decisions of the majority. That is, they had extreme voting patterns in comparison with male justices. Their decisional patterns were most pronounced on women's issues (in support of them), but they were either quite liberal or quite conservative on issues involving criminal rights and economic liberties.

In an earlier survey of over 500 women judges at all levels of the state courts, the focus was on their characteristics and how they reached the bench initially. A plurality of the women were appointed to the bench by governors or they were selected by the merit plan. A third of the women were elected to the bench, and the remainder were selected by other means (election by the judiciary or selection by the legislature) (Carbon et al., 1982).

Although more studies are needed before any definitive trends become apparent, one can note nonetheless that appointment appears to be a more productive means than election for women lawyers to become judges. One explanation for this may rest with the advantages males traditionally enjoy in political elections. Black judges benefit from the appointment process as well. For example, of the 11 black jurists in Alabama's history 8 were initially appointed to the bench by the governor.

At least 27 states have a woman justice on the supreme court, and Oklahoma has two. A milestone for women in the legal profession was reached in January 1991, when Sandra Gardebring was sworn in as a justice on the Minnesota Supreme Court. With her appointment, the state's high court became the first in the nation to have a majority of women justices, four out of seven. Three of the four women were appointed to the court by Governor Rudy Perpich (D). In contrast to what we have said previously about a governor's reluctance to appoint a jurist with opposing views on major issues, Governor Perpich did just that. Justice Gardebring supports a woman's right to choose abortion, whereas Governor Perpich had an antiabortion stance. Gardebring was appointed to the high court but a week before Perpich relinquished his position as governor. His reelection bid was unsuccessful in part because of his position on abortion (Margolick, 1991).

An Alternative Procedure

One path to the bench that has not been adopted in the United States is to acknowledge that the legal education lawyers receive in how to practice law is largely inconsequential to the adjudication of disputes. In some western European countries, law students early on decide whether they want to become lawyers or judges. The judicial track requires formal training beyond law school, perhaps an apprenticeship, and passage of competitive exams before being qualified for the bench. The new judge then advances up the judicial ladder as experience and expertise increase. Although it is unlikely that such a "civil service" type of approach would be adopted in this country, our judges would undoubtedly benefit from additional training on the administrative aspects of the job.

Toward More Women and Minority Judges

Women and minority group members have faced formidable legal and social barriers in becoming accepted in the legal profession and as judges. The legal barriers are gone, but social attitudes continue to inhibit the progress of women and minorities in the legal field. Others, such as the handicapped, are also adversely affected by the traditional image of the lawyer and, to a greater extent, the judge as a white male. Gone are the days when sexual discrimination received judicial legitimization, as occurred over 100 years ago when the federal Supreme Court upheld the right of the state to prohibit women from practicing law. As the paternalistic attitude of the Court was expressed in *Bradwell v. Illinois* (1872),

> The natural and proper timidity and delicacy which belongs to the female sex unfits it for many of the occupations of civil life. . . . The paramount destiny and mission of women are to fulfill the noble and benign offices of wife and mother. This is the law of the Creator.

Earlier in this century, the dean of the Columbia University School of Law announced that women would be admitted to the school only "over my dead body" (Wald, 1988: 76). The dean, Harlan Fiske Stone, was later named chief justice of the U.S. Supreme Court. More typical of social attitudes was the experience of Sandra Day O'Connor, who graduated from Stanford Law School in the 1950s but was unable to secure a job with a private law firm other than in a secretarial capacity. She persevered, however, and after a career in both law and politics, was nominated to the Supreme Court by President Reagan in 1981, thus becoming the first woman on that Court in the nation's history. When Martha

Daugherty was sworn in as the first woman justice on the Tennessee Supreme court in 1990, she recalled that two decades earlier, and fresh out of law school, she could not get a job in Nashville because of her gender.

Today, governors are careful to consider women and minorities as judges because they may think it is the right thing to do or that it would be to their political advantage. Most states have a lawyers' association for women and there is a National Association of Women Judges. Effective lobbying of governors by women's legal associations can influence the appointment of female judges. Since governors rely on recommendations by close advisors and outside legal organizations, some women's and minority legal associations seek meetings with the governor's appointments secretary to ensure full consideration.

It is unclear how closely the parallels are between women and blacks in securing judicial positions, but their experience is probably more similar than not. According to one recent study, there were 714 black judges on the state bench in 1986 (Graham, 1990). Only nine states, all small in terms of population and the number of blacks living in them, did not have any black judges. Black judges are most likely to attain the bench initially by gubernatorial appointment. Most of the black jurists were on the lower courts, and only a little more than 5 percent (39) were on the appellate bench. Certainly past discriminatory practices have prevented many qualified black lawyers from even being considered for a gubernatorial appointment to a court vacancy. At the same time, the pool of black attorneys historically has been small. This, of course, reflects the problems minorities have experienced in attempting to integrate law schools, many of which were traditionally white up to the 1960s.

There are signs of positive change, according to Graham (1990). Almost half of all sitting black state judges reached the bench in the 1980s. Given the awareness of law schools and the legal profession of the need to increase the visibility of blacks in the profession, the pool of black attorneys will be widening through the 1990s. While this occurs, one can speculate that blacks currently on the bench will increase their judicial experience and thus enlarge the pool of black judges who will be considered for appellate court positions.

At various places in these chapters, we have noted that efforts to initiate reform measures that purportedly would make the judiciary more efficient run into political obstacles that prevent their implementation. Indeed, it is difficult to change one element in a system, or relationship, without other components being affected. An example of this difficulty as it affects judicial selection in general and the elevation of women and minorities to the bench in particular can be seen in Virginia, where judges are selected by the legislature. Legislative judicial selection is scorned by reformers who feel that judges are selected on a partisan rather than professional basis. The Virginia Assembly does appoint judges, but it welcomes recommendations by bar groups. The Democratic party is the dominant party in the Virginia Assembly, a reality that makes it difficult for a Republican lawyer to be appointed to the bench. Reformers have called for a merit plan selection process, although they would settle for a nominating commission to provide names of qualified nominees. The Virginia Assembly would still make the final determination. However, the Democratic lawmakers do not want to share their power, much less relinquish it, with any other group. Moreover, black legislators are opposed to any changes as well. They reason that fewer women and blacks would be likely to be considered for judicial posts if initial screening is out of their hands (Winston, 1989). Judicial selection reform in Virginia appears some years off.

The selection of Reuben Anderson to be a justice on the Mississippi Supreme Court in 1985 is notable for two reasons. First, appellate court selection in Mississippi is formally by partisan election. But as previously mentioned, it is quite common for justices to be appointed to state supreme court posts even in elective system states. Second, Justice Anderson became the first black man to reach the Mississippi high court. Anderson was one of only five black law students when he graduated from the University of Mississippi Law School in the late 1960s at the height of the civil rights struggle. After a stint as a partner in a law firm, Anderson climbed the judicial ladder, beginning with his appointment to the municipal court, then county court, state circuit court, and eventually the state supreme court. Although Anderson's appointment was praised by black and white politicians in Mississippi, one cannot ignore the fact, as noted above, that the most coveted positions in the state judiciary, the appellate benches, continue to be the domain of whites. Females are making some gains, to be sure, but the obstacles that have to be overcome by black jurists are even more entrenched.

CONCLUSION

The old saw that a judge is an attorney who knew a governor still has validity. Individuals are not plucked from a vacuum; they must want to become judges, and more important, someone in a position of political power must want them to become judges. Historically, judicial selection in a state has moved from an appointive judiciary to an elective one and then to the merit plan. All states use one of these systems, with some modifications, to staff the trial and appellate courts. The federal bench is selected entirely by the president with Senate confirmation. None of these systems is without fault. Indeed, the best proponents of one mechanism can do is to say that their plan is better than the others, though such boasts become deflated when empirical comparisons are made of the jurists selected under each system. A major part of the problem in identifying how we should select judges is the lack of concensus on just what it is we expect the judges to do. Should they actively participate in trying to make American society more just, or should those tasks be left to other, partisan policymakers?

Three trends that affect the judiciary and judicial selection have become apparent since the 1940s. First, the judiciary is becoming more professional. The duties of lay judges are restricted to relatively minor civil and criminal actions, judges are encouraged to participate in special programs designed to familiarize them with new procedures for managing the courts, and the technological advances of the past 20 years are making their way into courtrooms across the country.

At the same time that professionalism is increasing, however, the issue of whether judicial selection is becoming more partisan at the federal and state levels is debatable. On the one hand, the move over the past 30 years has been to adopt merit plan selection. On the other hand, the divisiveness of issues such as abortion and capital punishment has made governors and voters focus on where the jurists stand. Federal and state executives have always been concerned with the political philosophies of the judges they appoint. But particularly from the 1960s on, this concern has been narrowed to how prospective appointees might decide certain cases. Voters also look to "box scores" as indications of whether local jurists are lenient or harsh when sentencing convicted felons.

The third and most visible trend has been the ascension of women and minorities to state and federal judgeships. The fact that many politicians and citizens seem to distinguish minority judges from male caucasian judges suggests there may be merit to the notion that background variables do have an influence on judicial decisions. From a symbolic standpoint, however, the sexual and racial integration of the bench is consistent with the concept of "blind justice" and a representative democracy.

REFERENCES

Alarcon, Arthur S. 1983. "Political Appointments and Judicial Independence—An Unreasonable Expectation." 16 *Loyala (L.A.) Law Review* 9–15.

Allen, David W., and Diane E. Wall. 1987, Fall. "The Behavior of Women State Supreme Court Justices: Are They Outsiders?" 12 *Justice System Journal* 232–245.

Alozie, Nicholas O. 1988, December. "Distribution of Black Judges on State Judiciaries." 69 *Social Science Quarterly* 979–986.

Ashman, Allan, and James J. Alfini. 1974. *The Key to Judicial Merit Selection: The Nominating Process*. Chicago: American Judicature Society.

Atkins, Burton. 1976, Summer. "Judges' Perspectives on Judicial Selection." 44 *State Government* 180–186.

Baum, Lawrence. 1990. *American Courts: Process and Policy*. Boston: Houghton Mifflin.

Berkson, Larry, Scott Beller, and Michele Grimaldi. 1980. *Judicial Selection in the United States: A Compendium of Provisions*. Chicago: American Judicature Society.

Bissinger, H.G., and Daniel R. Biddle. 1986, January 26. "Politics and Private Dealings Beset the City's Justice System." *Philadelphia Inquirer*.

Bone, Hugh. 1990, December. "Washington Primary: Judicial Politics." 11 *Comparative State Politics* 45–48.

Bunch, Kenyon D., Gregory Casey, and Richard J. Hardy. 1987, March 19. "Will Missouri Abandon the Missouri Plan? A Case Study of Judicial Selection and Politics." Paper presented at the annual meeting of the Southwest Social Science Association, Dallas.

Canon, Bradley. 1972, May. "The Impact of Formal Selection Processes on the Characteristics of Judges: Reconsidered." 6 *Law & Society Review* 579–593.

Carbon, Susan, Pauline Houlden, and Larry Berkson. 1982, December–January. "Women on the State Bench: Characteristics and Attitudes About Judicial Selection." 65 *Judicature* 294–305.

Champagne, Anthony. 1986, May. "The Selection and Retention of Judges in Texas." 40 *Southwestern Law Journal* 53–117.

Dixon, Eric D. 1989, June–July. "A Short History of Judicial Reform in New Mexico." 73 *Judicature* 48–50.

Dubois, Philip L. 1980. *From Ballot to Bench*. Austin: University of Texas.

Dubois, Philip L. 1984. "Voting Cues in Nonpartisan Trial Court Elections: A Multivariate Assessment." 18 *Law & Society Review* (3): 395–436.

Dubois, Philip L. 1986, June. "Penny for Your Thoughts? Campaign Spending in California Trial Court Elections, 1976–1982." 38 *Western Political Quarterly* 265–284.

Edgar, Mark, and Steve McGonigle. 1987, March 27. "Judges Routinely Hear Contributors' Cases." *Dallas Morning News*.

Engstrom, Richard L. 1989, August–September. "When Blacks Run for Judge: Racial Divisions in the Candidate Preference of Louisiana Voters." 73 *Judicature* 87–89.

Flango, Victor E., and Craig R. Ducat. 1979, Fall. "What Difference Does Method of Judicial Selection Make?" 5 *Justice System Journal* 25–44.

"For the Record." 1990, January 5. *New York Times,* p. B9.

Glaberson, William. 1989, July 12. "Panel Faults 'Overwhelmingly White Complexion' of New York's Courts." *New York Times,* p. A11.

Glick, Henry R., and Craig F. Emmert. 1986, August–September. "Stability and Change: Characteristics of State Supreme Court Justices." 70 *Judicature* 107–112.

Glick, Henry R., and Craig F. Emmert. 1987, December–January. "Selection Systems and Judicial Characteristics: the Recruitment of State Supreme Court Judges." 70 *Judicature* 228–235.

Graham, Barbara L. 1990, June–July. "Judicial Recruitment and Racial Diversity on State Courts: An Overview." 74 *Judicature* 28–34.

Griffin, Kenyon N., and Michael J. Horan. 1986. "Ousting the Judge: Campaign Politics in Judicial Elections." Paper presented at the annual meeting of the 1986 Western Political Science Association, Eugene, OR.

Hall, William K., and Larry T. Aspin. 1987, April–May. "What Twenty Years of Judicial Retention Elections Have Told Us." 70 *Judicature* 340–347.

Haydel, Judith. 1989, August–September. "Section 2 of the Voting Rights Act of 1965: A Challenge to State Judicial Election Systems." 73 *Judicature* 68–73.

Jones, David M. 1989, August. "Ideology & Judicial Elections in Wisconsin." 10 *Comparative State Politics* 6–8.

Kaplan, Sheila. 1987, May/June. "Justice for Sale." *Common Cause Magazine,* pp. 29–32.

Lawton, Anne. 1989, Fall. "AJS Surveys JCO Complaint Dispositions for 1987–88." 11 *Judicial Conduct Reporter* 1, 4.

Leeson, Fred. 1990, April 3. "Panel Urges Fadley Rebuke." *The* Portland *Oregonian.*

London, Robb. 1990, September 28. "For Want of Recognition, Chief Justice Is Ousted." *New York Times,* p. B10.

McDuff, Robert. 1989, August–September. "The Voting Rights Act and Judicial Elections Litigation: The Plaintiffs' Perspective." 73 *Judicature* 82–84.

Margolick, David. 1991, February 22. "Women's Milestone: Majority on Minnesota Court." *New York Times,* p. B11.

Melvin, Tessa. 1989, October 1. "Two Parties Agree to Endorse One Slate of Judicial Candidates." *New York Times,* section XXII, p. 8.

Middleton, Martha. 1987, March 2. "Chicago Courts Reel from Corruption Probe." *National Law Journal,* p. 1.

Nicholson, Marlene A., and Bradley S. Weiss. 1986, June–July. "Funding Judicial Campaigns in the Circuit Court of Cook County." 70 *Judicature* 17–26.

O'Neill, Tip. 1987. *Man of the House.* New York: Random House.

"Pennsylvania Supreme Court Removes 8 Judges from Bench." 1988, February 29. *Los Angeles Daily Journal,* p. 5.

Reich, Kenneth. 1988, June 9. "'Judge' Was the Winning Word on Ballots." *Los Angeles Times,* p. III1.

Scheb, John M., III. 1988, October–November. "State Appellate Judge's Attitudes Towards Judicial Merit Selection and Retention: Results of a National Survey." 72 *Judicature* 170–174.

Schotland, Roy A. 1985, Spring. "Elective Judges' Campaign Financing: Are State Judges' Robes the Emperor's Clothes of American Democracy?" 2 *The Journal of Law & Politics* 57–167.

Sheldon, Charles H. 1972, September. "Influencing the Selection of Judges: The Variety and Effectiveness of State Bar Activities." 30 *Western Political Quarterly* 397–400.

Stanton, Sam. 1987, February 14. "Non-Activist Judge Appointed to Supreme Court." (Phoenix) *Arizona Republic.*

Stumpf, Harry P. 1988. *American Judicial Politics.* San Diego: Harcourt Brace Jovanovich.

Tarr, G. Alan, and Mary C. A. Porter. 1988. *State Supreme Courts in State and Nation*. New Haven, CN: Yale University Press.

Wade, Paula. 1990, January 14. "2 High Court Justices Lose Nominations." (Memphis) *Commercial Appeal*.

Wald, Patricia M. 1988, November. "Women in the Law." *Trial*, pp. 76–80.

Wasmann, Erik, Nicholas P. Lovrich, Jr., and Charles H. Sheldon. 1986, Fall. "Perceptions of State and Local Courts: A Comparison Across Selection Systems." 11 *Justice System Journal* 168–185.

Watson, Richard A., and Rondal G. Downing. 1969. *The Politics of the Bench and the Bar*. New York: Wiley.

Wermiel, Stephen. 1990, February 26. "Florida Judge Faces a Trial by Voters on Ruling on Abortion Is Big Issue in 'Retention' Election." *Wall Street Journal*, p. A12.

Winston, Bonnie. 1989, May 5. "Court Overhaul Not Likely Soon." (Norfolk) *Virginia Pilot*.

Yaeger, John. 1989, December 10. "Critics Gear Up to Reverse Judge Selection Process." *Albuquerque Journal*, p. F1.

CHAPTER 4

Lawyers and Judicial Politics

INTRODUCTION

The legal profession intersects with the politics of state courts at several points and in a number of ways. Lawyers, of course, constitute the pool of candidates for judgeships, so that the ideology of the legal profession permeates the work of both judges and lawyers. As professionals having an active interest in the workings of courts, lawyers and their varied bar associations are heavily involved in the politics (i.e., the fashioning and application of rules and policies) touching on all aspects of courthouse government. The manner in which attorneys are trained; the rules, both formal and customary, by which they do their work; how courts are structured and how they process cases; the methods used to select judges, along with the more obvious question of *which* attorneys become judges—these and kindred issues about which lawyers are vitally concerned illustrate the close interconnectedness of the legal profession with the business of state courts. And these critical links, in turn, help to point up the importance of attorneys in our overall understanding of the judicial process at the state level.

Lawyers, of course, are important in America beyond their work in traditional practice settings. They frequently dominate the legislatures at both the state and federal level. They are also found in large numbers in national, state, and local administrative agencies and departments as well as serving as teachers, scholars, business executives, and of course judges. Indeed Alexis de Tocqueville (1945) over 150 years ago noted the central position of the legal profession in American society. This famous French philosopher observed that the American lawyer

> . . . resembles the hierophants of Egypt, for like them he is the sole interpreter of an occult science. . . . Lawyers consequently form the highest political class and the most cultivated portion of society. . . . If I were asked where I place the American aristocracy,

I should reply without hesitation that it is not among the rich, who are united by no common tie, but it occupies the judicial branch and the bar. (287–288)

Nor has the position of the legal profession in American society changed significantly since Tocqueville visited the United States in 1831. As a contemporary scholar wrote,

> Law is our national religion; lawyers constitute our priesthood. Legal ritual now, like religious ritual in the fifteenth century, provides coherence and form within a disorderly, chaotic universe. . . . The bar, like the church, relies upon mysterious language and procedures to instill reverence and to remove itself from the people. . . . The courtroom is our cathedral, where contemporary passion plays are enacted. . . . Because priests and lawyers constitute classes of certified experts who monopolize access to pivotal social institutions, they are both respected and mistrusted. As the priest mediated between man and God for the salvation of souls, so the lawyer manipulates a different form of death [through trusts and wills]. (Auerbach, 1976a: 38)

Our concern here, however, is less with the sociology, if not the theology, of the legal profession (although these orientations are useful to our understanding of lawyers) and a bit more with the political role of lawyers in the judicial process of state courts, particularly as it highlights the broader sociopolitical ramifications of the exercise of state judicial power. That lawyers, qua lawyers, are important political actors seems almost too obvious to require demonstration. But since apolitical conceptions of law (and lawyering) dominate current American jurisprudence, particularly as seen by the legal profession itself (Halpern, 1982; Stumpf, 1988: Ch. II), it may be useful to begin with the simple observation that if state courts are political, so too is the lawyer role in state court processes.

Lawyers are the *gatekeepers* to the judicial arena, and this role is crucial. Both individually and collectively (as in the guidelines of practice promulgated by bar associations) they determine *who* is to have access to the judicial arena, at what cost, under what combination of circumstances, and for what ultimate purpose. Hence, those who enjoy the privilege of legal services (usually, those in the upper socioeconomic strata) are in a decidedly advantageous position to reap the benefits that may flow from the judicial process or, alternately, to avoid the penalties of adverse judicial determinations. In short, such citizens and organizations have an extra string for their political bow by which they may enjoy additional advantages, material and otherwise, beyond those available to the ordinary citizen not so well endowed. Since politics is often defined as the process by which scarce societal resources are distributed, the rearrangement of resource distribution more favorable to those with professional legal representation constitutes politics in the most basic sense.

Lawyers work to the benefit of their clients indirectly through the political process, leading to the development of legislative and administrative policy and policy proclivities favorable to those fortunate enough to have such representation (see Wells, 1964; 167–171). Thus, it is not uncommon for attorney-lobbyists to represent insurance companies in pushing no-fault insurance legislation or real estate interests in pushing lower property taxes in the state legislature. In addition to these broad legislative and policy advantages, access to the judicial process itself carries with it further indirect benefits, which may turn out to be more important than mere judicial access alone. Clients (e.g., business organizations) having permanent legal representation are frequently advantaged through the development of broad judicial doctrine favorable to their cause over the long term.

It is this sort of continuing legal caretaking that Galanter (1974) had in mind when he described the advantages enjoyed by "Repeat Players" over "One-Shotters" in trial courts (see also Chapter 5). An example of long-term benefits of this sort accruing to corporate America through appellate litigation may be found in the classic work by Benjamin Twiss (1942), *Lawyers and the Constitution*. Here, Twiss describes the development of constitutional doctrines such as *liberty of contract* and *dual federalism* fashioned by the elite bar and sold to federal appellate courts as a means of protecting property rights from the demands of the rising laboring and farmer classes. In these and other ways, legal representation can be quite important in determining who gets what, when, and how in our society, again pointing to the obvious political nature of the business of lawyering.

Based on this political conception of the legal profession, it is important for us to understand the forces and influences at work in helping to explain the behavior of lawyers. What factors, for instance, determine the choice of a legal career? What are the socializing effects of law school? What are the implications for resource allocation of certain practice specialities and their incidence throughout the bar? What is the influence of bar associations on the practice of law? And implicit and most important in all of this, what factors explain the distribution of legal services in America? For it is ultimately in the answers to the last question that we can best gauge the political impact of the legal profession in states and communities.

To address these and other issues about American lawyers, it is useful to begin with the production of lawyers—law schools—then move to an examination of practice specialization (what lawyers do), and then to a consideration of the organization of the bar and attendant issues. Data presented on these three topics lead logically to the question of the overall distribution of lawyers in our society, telling us who gets what, when, and how in the important business of allocating the scarce and valuable sociopolitical resource of legal representation.

THE MAKING OF AMERICAN LAWYERS

Why So Many Lawyers?

Arguably, the most prominent aspect of modern American lawyers is their sheer number, swelled by the astounding rate of growth of the profession over just the last two decades. There are now some 800,000 licensed attorneys in the United States, and this figure is growing at an annual net rate of some 25,000 to 27,000 (Abel, 1989: 239).[1] Thus, in the year 2000 we may expect to find ourselves swamped with well over 1 million attorneys! As seen in Table 4.1, the number of lawyers almost doubled in the 1970s and has grown by another 50 percent or so just in the decade of the 1980s. The lawyer:population ratio is now far more than twice what it was even as late as 1970. These increases have made the American legal profession a major national growth industry, exceeding (as measured by value-added dollars) that of steel, automobiles, and publishing. Although the growth rates of all professions in our rapidly expanding service economy has been impressive these

TABLE 4.1 American Lawyers and Population 1870–1988

	No. of Lawyers & Judges	U.S. Population (000s)	Lawyers per Million Pop.
1870	41,701	39,818	1,047
1880	64,137	50,156	1,279
1890	89,630	62,948	1,423
1900	114,460	75,995	1,506
1910	114,704	91,972	1,247
1920	122,519	105,771	1,159
1930	160,605	122,775	1,308
1940	182,000	131,669	1,382
1950	184,000	151,329	1,216
1960	218,000	179,323	1,216
1970	274,000	203,302	1,348
1980	522,000	226,545	2,304
1988	757,000	244,200	3,100

SOURCE: Richard H. Sander and E. Douglass Williams, "Why Are There So Many Lawyers? Perspectives on a Turbulent Market," *Law and Social Inquiry,* Vol. 14., No. 3 (Summer 1989), 433 (footnotes deleted). Copyright © 1989 American Bar Association. All rights reserved.

past 20 years, the number of lawyers has surged ahead at three times the rate of all other professions and four times as fast as the general American work force (Sander and Williams, 1989: 432–434).

No nation has the lawyer:population ratio of that found in the United States; none even comes close. With only 5 percent of the world's population, Americans have nearly two-thirds of the worlds lawyers, giving us a ratio in 1990 of about 1:320, nearly three times that of any other industrial society. With some allowance for the questionable comparability of data, Japan in the 1980s was reported to have a lawyer:population ratio of about 1:10,000. Even if we include all the various occupations in Japan that would be comparable to lawyering in the United States, Japan still emerges with a ratio of about 1:1,240. For the same period, West Germany had a ratio of 1:2,400, Sweden 1:5,200, and the Netherlands 1:5,850. These figures would compare with a 1980 U.S. ratio of about 1:420 (Galanter, 1986: 166).

Although the Japanese graduate 30 percent more engineers each year than the United States (their population is about half of ours), they have no more than 10,000 to 15,000 lawyers. In the United States, we are graduating over 35,000 lawyers *per year!* The Japanese reportedly like to say, "Engineers make the pie grow larger; lawyers only decide how to carve it up" (Bok, 1983: 574). (A tongue-in-cheek remedy to too many lawyers in America was suggested by one critic: "Let's make a deal with Japan. Send them a lawyer for every car they send us"—Kailer, 1988: F–1).

These lawyer demographics are of course the direct result of the strong surge of American college students opting for a legal education. Beginning in the 1960s the number of law schools approved by the American Bar Association, along with the number of applications, law graduates, and admittees to the bar, expanded at a surprising rate (see Table 4.2). The precise explanations for this increase are a bit hazy. Scholars studying these developments have suggested that the baby boom itself, combined with increasing

TABLE 4.2 Legal Education and Bar Admissions 1963–1989

Academic Year	Number of Schools	First Year Enrollment	First Year Women Enrollment	Total J.D. Enrollment	Total J.D. Women Enrollment	Total Overall Enrollment	LSAT Administrations	J.D. or LL.B. Awarded	Admissions to the Bar
1963–64	135	20,776	877	46,666	1,739	49,552	30,528	9,638	10,788
1964–65	135	22,753	986	51,079	2,056	54,265	37,598	10,491	12,023
1965–66	136	24,167	1,064	56,510	2,374	59,744	39,406	11,507	13,109
1966–67	135	24,077	1,059	59,236	2,520	62,556	44,905	13,115	14,644
1967–68	136	24,267	1,179	61,084	2,769	64,406	47,110	14,738	16,007
1968–69	138	23,652	1,742	59,498	3,554	62,779	49,756	16,077	17,764
1969–70	144	29,128	2,103	64,416	4,485	68,386	59,050	16,733	19,123
1970–71	146	34,289	3,542	78,018	6,682	82,041	74,092	17,183	17,922
1971–72	147	36,171	4,326	91,225	8,567	94,468	107,479	17,006	20,485
1972–73	149	35,131	5,508	98,042	11,878	101,707	119,694	22,342	25,086
1973–74	151	37,018	7,464	101,675	16,303	106,102	121,262	27,756	30,879
1974–75	157	38,074	9,006	105,708	21,283	110,713	135,397	28,729	30,707
1975–76	163	39,038	10,472	111,047	26,020	116,991	133,546	29,961	34,930
1976–77	163	39,996	11,354	112,401	29,343	117,451	133,320	32,597	35,741
1977–78	163	39,676	11,928	113,080	31,650	118,557	128,135	33,640	37,302
1978–79	167	40,479	13,324	116,150	35,775	121,606	125,747	33,317	39,086
1979–80	169	40,717	13,490	117,297	37,534	122,860	111,235	34,590	42,756
1980–81	171	42,296	15,272	119,501	40,834	125,397	112,750	35,059	41,997
1981–82	172	42,521	15,811	120,879	43,245	127,312	111,373	35,598	42,382
1982–83	172	42,034	16,136	121,791	45,539	127,828	118,565	34,846	42,905
1983–84	173	41,159	16,049	121,201	46,361	127,195	111,620	36,389	41,684
1984–85	174	40,747	16,236	119,847	46,897	125,698	104,621	36,687	42,630
1985–86	175	40,796	16,510	118,700	47,486	124,092	95,129	36,829	42,450
1986–87	175	40,195	16,491	117,813	47,920	123,277	91,921	36,121	40,247
1987–88	175	41,055	17,506	117,997	48,920	123,198	100,751	35,478	39,918
1988–89	174	42,860	18,395	120,694	50,932	125,870	115,407	35,701	46,528
1989–90	175	43,826	18,722	124,471	53,113	129,698	136,367	35,520	47,147

SOURCE: American Bar Association, Section of Legal Education and Admission to the Bar, *A Review of Legal Education in the United States, Fall, 1989*, p. 66 (footnotes deleted). Copyright © 1990 American Bar Foundation. All rights reserved. Reprinted by permission of the American Bar Association.

national prosperity leading to a large pool of middle-class college graduates ready for law school by the 1960s, has been an important cause (Sander and Williams, 1989: 453–462). Also, the mid-1950s and the 1960s were times of considerable national excitement over the use of the law as an instrument of social change. Beginning with *Brown v. Board of Education of Topeka* in 1954 and moving into the creation of a national corps of poverty lawyers in the mid-1960s, law came to be viewed as a fascinating, progressive force for social change, highly attractive to the young people having a genuine desire to correct the wrongs of the world (Geoghegan, 1986; Hazard, 1969).

Additionally, this same period was one of rapid expansion of "rights" in sundry areas of American society, involving new legislative, administrative, and judicial policies extended into theretofore unregulated areas of our life. These developments led to a vast increase in the "legalization" of our activities, creating an increase in demand for lawyers' services. New legislative provisions protecting women, the aged, racial minorities, surrogate parents, and the like illustrate the expansion of legally protected rights in American society.

The expansion of the law student—and lawyer—pool was also given a significant boost by important changes in public attitudes toward women and their role in society. Whereas in the 1963–1964 academic year, women constituted only 3.7 percent of law students working for their juris doctor degree, this figure jumped to 40 percent in 1985 and to 43 percent in 1989 (Table 4.2). As a result, women, who for many decades constituted only 2 or 3 percent of the practicing bar, today make up about 20 percent, and the figure is rising rapidly as we approach law graduating classes of 40 to 45 percent women in the 1990s (Curran, 1986b). The contribution of this surge in women law aspirants to the overall growth in the American legal profession is suggested by Richard Able (1989):

> During the five years following 1969, law school applications increased threefold, but women's applications increased fourteen times. . . .
> Between 1967 and 1983, the enrollment of women in ABA-approved law schools increased 1650 percent. . . . Indeed, because the absolute number of male law students had not increased since 1973, *all* subsequent growth of law school enrollments is attributable to the entry of women (91).

Thus, the decreasing attractiveness of traditional areas of work for women (e.g., the well-known glut in the teaching market), combined with the impact of the feminist movement, helped to bring about this significant contribution to the growth in the legal profession.

Finally, the salaries, or in some cases, the perceived salaries for lawyers are cited as an important factor in explaining this rush to law school. Polls have revealed income potential as a major consideration of those entering the profession (46.3 percent of lawyer respondents), far ahead of reasons such as "to see justice done" (21.6 percent) or a desire to improve society (23.4 percent). The attractiveness of the prestige factor (43.1 percent) was also quite important (Reidinger, 1986: 44; Zemans and Rosenblum, 1981: 27–42). Although the *median income* of American lawyers actually dropped during the period under discussion (e.g., a decline of 23 percent from 1969 to 1979 for all lawyers and a drop of nearly *half* for solo practitioners between 1972 to 1982), incomes of elite law jobs continued to rise rapidly, and these figures were prominent in the eyes of young college graduates choosing a legal career.

Thus, *starting* salaries in the top New York law firms were in the range of $75,000 to over $90,000 per year by 1986, increasing to six figures by 1990, the higher salaries usually going to graduates of prestige law schools who had served a year or two as a court clerk, particularly in federal courts (Abel, 1989: 219; "Fiscal Rewards of the Practice," 1990). And of course the salaries of senior partners in the nation's top law firms did not go unnoticed by prospective law applicants; these figures often approach or exceed $1 million per year. These, then, constitute most of the forces explaining the explosion in law school applicants in the 1960s through the 1980s. The observable impact of legal education itself on the central issue of our inquiry, namely, the distribution of legal services, is such that we ought to understand more fully the law school experience.

Legal Education

Law schools as we know them today are a relatively recent phenomenon. In universities of medieval England, as well as for some educators even in our time, law was, and is, considered ". . . too vulgar a subject for scholarly investigation" (Halpern, 1982: 393; Vago, 1988: 256). Prior to the Civil War, and for much of the nation long after that time, apprenticeship was the chief means of becoming a lawyer. A young man (virtually no women entered the profession before the turn of the century; Stevens, 1983: 82–83) would attach himself to an individual attorney or small firm (often with a required fee paid by the neophyte), work for a period of perhaps one to five years, and then stand for the state bar exam, if any. It was a means of achieving "professional" status with little capital or no social standing. As late as 1879 only 15 of 38 states required any sort of formal schooling for entering the profession, and only 7 required even three years of apprenticeship (Abel, 1989: 41).

Beginning in the middle of the last century, especially after 1870, the replacement of the apprenticeship with formal training progressed rapidly. The appointment of Dean Christopher Columbus Langdell at Harvard Law School in 1870 is usually cited as the turning point. Langdell, closely following the Austinian model of law as a "science," introduced the case method of instruction, with an almost exclusive concentration on appellate court decisions. Langdell's focus was on a few leading legal principles, which could be best learned from the reading of actual court decisions and taught through the Socratic method. And with few exceptions, this pedagogy persists today in most law schools.

Although this newly found intellectual respectability for law gave it a place in university education as well as providing an important base for building professional power, the methodology of this sort of case study has come in for considerable criticism (e.g., Abel, 1989: 212–213; Auerbach, 1976b: 75–80; Bok, 1983: 581–584; Zemans and Rosenblum, 1981: 8–12). The chief bone of contention seems to be the alleged narrowness of the law school experience. As its own "science," law came to be viewed as an entity unto itself, divorced from politics, society, and all other nuances of community life. As legal historian James Willard Hurst (1950) put it in his classic work, *The Growth of American Law,*

The case method isolated the study of law from the living context of society. The student of law needed to be aware of the pressure of politics, the strands of class, religious, racial and national attitudes woven into the values and patterns of behavior with which law dealt;

he needed some appreciation of the balance of power within the community, the class of interests, and the contriving of economic institutions, as all these influenced and were influenced by the effort to order the society under law. But all of this . . . the student was made aware only incidentally—as he glimpsed the social context through recitals of fact and appraisal, of widely varying accuracy and imagination, in the reported opinions of appellate courts. (265–266)

Legal historian Lawrence Friedman (1985) added to the critique: "If law is at all the product of society," he wrote, "then Langdell's science of law is a geology without rocks, an astronomy without stars." If this sort of training is taken seriously, he continued, lawyers and judges would come to view law "mainly in terms of a dry, arid logic, divorced from society and life" (617).

But there are more shortcomings in modern legal education. Not only does it convey an abjectly apolitical and asocial view of the law, but also as *science* law is seen as value-free. It was into this vacuum that the modern business ethic came to dominate the legal curriculum. Examples drawn from corporate law became the raw material of classroom discussion, and subtly but powerfully, students came to see the most important sectors of law as those involving doctrines that created and supported corporate capitalism. Poverty law, consumer law, family law, environmental law, landlord-tenant relations, and the like—these may be found in the curriculum, but the heavy emphasis is on the really important courses, dubbed by one Harvard law graduate as "Making Money, Counting Money, and Keeping it From The Government" (corporations, accounting, and taxation) (VanLoon, 1970: 336). On the occasion of the 150th anniversary of the founding of Harvard Law School, Dean Erwin N. Griswold (1968) pointed to this obvious bias in modern legal education:

By methods of teaching, by subtle and often unconscious innuendo, we indicate to our students that their future success and happiness will be found in the traditional [property and business] areas of the law. . . . And . . . as the method of providing legal services in this country has been organized in the past, that has been the way in which one was most likely to be able to make a living. (151)

How true it was—and still is today—as the 1990 salary data for lawyers roll in: partner in major New York firm: $985,000; third-year associate in a similar firm in Los Angeles: $85,000; beginning salary in the Delaware County, Pennsylvania, district attorney's office: $20,000; salary range for legal services attorneys in Maine: approximately $25,000 to $38,000 ("Fiscal Rewards of the Practice," 1990). The reader should not miss the message in these data: Law schools are unquestionably important, if not crucial institutions for the political-legal socialization of their students (Halpern, 1982; Stover, 1982; VanLoon, 1970: 336–338). The central point of the law school lesson was scrawled on the walls of a library carrel where a recent law student-political scientist spent much of his time the first year:

TURN OFF—TUNE OUT—MAKE MONEY (Halpern, 1982: 383)

Law is a science, indeed, a jealous mistress; it is socially and politically neutral. That "law structures, sustains and legitimates economic relationships, [that it] preserves the gross inequities in our society . . ." are notions fostered by fuzzy-headed social scientists, and in any case are wholly irrelevant to learning to "think like a lawyer" (Bok, 1983: 581–582; Halpern, 1982: 385, 387). And finally and most important, law school is the path to money, prestige, and power—the great gateway to what Auerbach (1976b) called the secular "priesthood" of American life.

WHAT DO LAWYERS DO? THE POLITICS OF SPECIALIZATION

To suggest that we are approaching a lawyer gridlock in America is not to say that all of those lawyers are in practice and available for the ordinary walk-in client. Few professions could be found in any society that was more highly specialized and stratified than that of the American bar. The lineaments of this stratification say a great deal about the availability of legal services to American citizens. For this reason we should explore this facet of the profession in some detail.

Practice Settings

Of the nearly 700,000 lawyers licensed to practice in the United States in 1985, only about 70 percent were in private practice (Curran, 1986a: 26). These were distributed roughly as follows: 47 percent in solo practice, 28.3 percent in partnerships or small firms (2 to 10 lawyers), about 13.5 percent in medium-sized firms of 10 to 50 lawyers, and only about 11 percent in large firms of 50 or more. As these data have been analyzed by scholars of the American Bar Foundation, what seems most notable is the decline in the solo practice of law over the decades, with a concomitant rise in firm practice, and an increase not only in the number of law firms but also in their size, along with a significant increase in the number of lawyers in firm practice who are associates rather than partners (Curran, 1986b). Indeed, the attractiveness of the position of firm associate, as opposed to self-employment, is now such that we may speak of a revival of the apprenticeship system or something reminiscent of it, whereby young attorneys may work a number of years in comparatively subordinate circumstances waiting for the decision of "up or out" (Abel, 1989: 190–199).

Growth in the number and size of the larger law firms, with their increasing dominance of the practice of law, is perhaps the most important single development in recent trends in legal practice. The number of law firms with 100 or more employees has expanded from only 28 in 1947 to 726 in 1986, a 25-fold increase! Moreover, the number of employees of the larger firms is growing rapidly, the average employees for the 50 largest firms increasing from 303 to 540 in the 1972–1984 period. The receipts of the nation's 20 largest law firms (some employing as many as 400 to 500 lawyers) are also increasing, from $14.7 million in 1972 to $158 million in 1987. As a result, the largest firms have grown richer relative to the rest of American lawyers. Overall, the concentration of law practice in the big firms has increased some 50 percent in the period 1972–1989 (Sander and Williams, 1989: 433–440).

Of the 30 percent of American lawyers not in private practice in 1985, (nearly 40 percent) were in government service, including judges, with about two-thirds of these working at the state level. About a third of attorneys not in private practice were retained by private business and industry, another 19 percent were retired or inactive, and some 8 percent were about evenly divided between education and legal aid programs of various kinds (Curran, 1986b). Here, the growth in the number of lawyers working as business employees is most notable. Their proportion of the legal profession has almost doubled since 1951. Not only has the number of businesses establishing their own legal staff vastly increased in recent decades, but also the size and activities of these legal offices have grown, some now competing with the largest individual law firms (Abel, 1989: 168–169). Thus, before divestiture, AT&T had a legal staff of 909 lawyers, the largest law office in the world; General Electric's legal staff in the 1980s ran to around 400 lawyers. Clearly, the position of "house counsel" has achieved enhanced professional status and power in the last few decades.

The Bifurcation of the Bar

Although these data give us a general statistical picture of the present American bar, they are only the beginning of the story of the stratification of the profession. As we saw, the range of salaries of lawyers is vast—so extreme, in fact, as to suggest the existence of two, or perhaps more, American legal professions. As Abel (1989) remarked,

> . . . in few . . . professions do some members earn fifty times more than others or some subcategories (such as Supreme Court justices) bask in popular adulation while others (such as criminal defense, personal injury, and divorce lawyers) are ranked [in public opinion polls] with garbage collections. And there is virtually no movement between the hemispheres. (236–237)

The "hemispheres" of the American legal profession have been revealed and documented in a series of studies reaching back at least to Ladinsky's (1963) research on Detroit lawyers in 1960. It had become apparent even before the turn of the century that a rather rigid stratification of the bar was emerging, determined by such factors as the prestige of one's legal education, specialization, setting (whether solo, small firm, or large firm), and income (see, e.g., Brandeis, 1914; Llewellyn, 1933). Ladinsky documented the social background factors feeding into the creation of an elite-common bar dichotomy through an examination of the variables of religion and father's occupation. Watson and Downing (1969), in their study of the alignment of bar forces for and against the Missouri plan of judicial selection (Chapter 3), appeared to be the first to introduce the terms *defendant* and *plaintiff* lawyers as ways to describe the two *hemispheres* of practice, a term itself introduced by the authors of the massive study of the Chicago bar in the late 1970s (Heinz and Laumann, 1982).

To summarize our current knowledge of the bifurcation of the bar, it is convenient to begin with law schools. As almost any undergraduate college student is aware, there is a decided "pecking order" among American law schools. Debate rages over precisely which law schools deserve to be ranked in the "prestige" category, as opposed to what have been termed "national" law schools, as again contrasted to "other" or "local" schools ("Law," 1990: 59; Myers, 1990: 4; Van Alstyne, 1982). However, there is general agreement that schools such as Harvard, Yale, Columbia, Stanford, Chicago, and Michigan are among the "best" ("The Cartter Report," 1977: 46; Margulies and Blau, 1973:

21), whereas a slightly larger number of schools are knocking at the door, so to speak, with what could be called strong "national" rankings. Such schools often include the University of California at Berkeley (Boalt Hall), Cornell, Duke, Georgetown, New York University, Northwestern, Pennsylvania, Vanderbilt, and Virginia.

Although there is plenty of room for disagreement about the validity of such a listing (Myers, 1990; Van Alstyne, 1982), the point on which scholars tend to agree is that the prestige of legal education and the prestige of practice go hand in glove, with socioeconomic background factors also contributing to building the profile of what Edward S. Corwin called "The Great Bar," in contrast to "the bar in general" (Twiss, 1942: x). Thus, beginning with family background, leading into the privilege (and cost) of attending a national or prestige law school, the careers of defendant (usually corporate) attorneys are launched from a firm foundation. But practice speciality and practice arrangement seem to be the two key links in this golden chain.

Heinz and Laumann (1982) asked a subsample of Chicago lawyers to rate the prestige of a list of practice specialities on a 5-point scale, from "outstanding" to "poor." Findings from that survey contain few surprises. The top three areas of legal specialization, as ranked by attorneys themselves, were (1) securities law, (2) tax law, and (3) representing defendant corporations in antitrust matters (91). The next five most prestigious specialties were patent law, representing plaintiffs in antitrust matters, banking, public utilities, and general corporate law. In contrast, the least prestige is attached to the practice of poverty law, which is found at the very bottom of the Heinz and Laumann scale. Then, in ascending order, one finds divorce, landlord-tenant matters, condemnations, representing debtors in consumer actions, personal injury plaintiff practice, and criminal defense.

The strong credentialism present in the American legal profession is suggested by the Zemans and Rosenblum (1981) data, also drawn from a survey of the Chicago bar. In this research, undertaken just before the Heinz and Laumann (1982) study, these scholars illustrated the close association of prestige legal education with prestige practice. Hence, elite or national law school graduates are far more likely to be found in prestige practice specialties, with "other" or local law schools serving the needs of individual middle-class and poor clients in areas of practice found at the bottom of Heinz and Laumann's prestige scale. Similarly, practice *setting* (solo, small, or large firm) is also determined, to a large extent, by law school background. Zemans and Rosenblum show that in Chicago at least:

> Graduates of the elite law schools (Harvard, Michigan, and Chicago) are much more likely . . . to be in large firm practice . . . with the four local schools (Loyola, IIT-Chicago Kent, De Paul and John Marshall) significantly more likely to send their graduates into solo practice. . . . (101)

Summarizing their findings on these two variables—practice speciality and practice settings—Zemans and Rosenblum (1981) note that:

> . . . it is not so much, as Ladinsky says . . . that solo practitioners do the dirty work of the bar but rather, as Smigel points out in *The Wall Street Lawyer,* that members of large firms do virtually none of it. No large-firm lawyers in our sample of Chicago lawyers list any of the following as their prominent speciality: criminal law, family law, poverty law,

creditor-debtor law. To the extent that graduation from certain law schools predicts large-firm practice, it also eliminates the possibility of concentrating one's time in work rated low in prestige by the bar. (107–108)

A further factor, that of academic class standing, is also important in the bifurcation of the American bar. Again, data from the Chicago research as well as studies of Harvard and UCLA law graduates all indicate that academic performance while in law school correlates significantly with both high-prestige practice specialities and large-firm practice.

All of these findings are only refinements and extensions of earlier work linking these various factors to the political, organizational, and social behavior of American lawyers. Thus, in their study of the operation of the merit judicial selection plan in Missouri in the late 1960s, Watson and Downing (1969) pointed up the important distinction between "defendant" and "plaintiff" attorneys, these labels being based, respectively, on the legal representation of insurance companies, public utilities, banks, railroads, and other business concerns, as opposed to the representation of individuals in personal injury, divorce, and similar legal actions, perhaps including criminal defense. Building on the concept of "styles" of legal practice discussed in earlier work (Berle, 1933; Ladinsky, 1963), Watson and Downing link plaintiff attorneys with a greater likelihood of a liberal, Democrat political orientation; lower income; solo or small-firm practice; less prestigious legal education; and a greater propensity to membership in alternative local bar associations with a plaintiff emphasis (20–32). These scholars reported something akin to a two-party system developing in Kansas City and St. Louis, with rival candidates being put forth for seats on the nominating commissions of the new (1940) judicial selection plan. When one adds the elements of race, religion, and ethnic background, reported in a number of studies (Abel, 1989: 85–87, 104–105, 205; Ladinsky, 1963), one can more fully appreciate the depth and breadth of the distinction between "have" and "have-not" lawyers.

Not only do the two worlds of the American legal profession tend to divide along all of the lines noted above, but when the particulars of practice are examined more closely, they are also seen to diverge by concentration of effort (percentage of time devoted to given specialities), the number of clients served (plaintiff attorneys have many more and more diverse clients), and the duration of the lawyer-client relationship. These two types of attorneys also differ significantly in the way in which they relate to their clients (with large-firm clients more likely to dominate the relationship) as well as the functions they perform for their clients and the intellectual challenge of the work involved (Abel, 1989: 203–206). Thus, distinct though the two worlds of legal practice have been for many decades, contemporary research shows them to be more segregated than ever before.

The implications of these findings for the central question before us—access to legal services for all Americans—can hardly be missed. The increasing shift away from solo practice, with its services to individuals, has intensified the concentration of elite legal talent in medium to large law firms serving almost entirely wealthy business interests. Although Louis Brandeis (1914) wrote the following some 80 years ago, even before his appointment to the U.S. Supreme Court, it might well have been penned by a modern researcher summing up the lineaments of the current practice of law in America:

At the present time the lawyer does not hold that position with the people that he held [years] ago. . . . Instead of holding a position of independence between the wealthy and the people, prepared to curb the excesses of either, able lawyers have, to a large extent, allowed themselves to become adjuncts of great corporations and have neglected their obligation to use their powers for the protection of the people. We hear much of the "corporation lawyer" and far too little of the "people's lawyer." (337)

THE POLITICS OF BAR ASSOCIATIONS: THE DISCIPLINARY PROCESS

Such particulars of professional legal stratification, with their resultant bias in the distribution of legal services, help to explain—and are in part explained by—the politics of bar associations in America. As we learn from interest group theory (Truman, 1951), associations are not formed without reason, the most common focus of organizational concern being political, that is, the push for certain policies, along with the attempts to depreciate other policies and interests. The formation of the American Bar Association (ABA) was no exception, its origin in 1878 usually being attributed to the growing awareness of the mutual interests of elite (corporate) bar, as opposed to the demands of an increasing number of immigrants (and sons and daughters of immigrants) who pressed for access to legal education and admission to practice. In short, the purpose was to keep the "ins" in and the "outs" out and to enhance the influence of the former. The same can be said for the origin of state and local lawyer associations in this period (Auerbach, 1976b: 62–66).

The growth of the ABA was slow, never (even today) representing more than half of the total practicing bar. In part, this was purposeful. The organization was elite in origin and purpose, representing most if not all of those elements of the bar identified with "defendant" or elite practice orientations. As Abel (1989) notes, ABA leadership was, and is today,

> . . . dominated by older lawyers at the expense of younger, law firm partners at the expense of solo practitioners, graduates of elite law school, and private practitioners at the expense of lawyers employed in the public sector. In 1986, its thirty-six-member Board of Governors included *no* minority lawyers, and only one woman. (208; emphasis added)

As such, the ABA can hardly be said to be representative of the profession as a whole. The response to this unmet need has come in part in the creation of rival bar associations at the county, state, and national level. Early groupings such as the Law Club of Chicago; the New York County Lawyer's Association; and later, the American Trial Lawyer's Association, the National Bar Association (black), and the Lawyer's Guild reflect the fractures within the bar as well as the difficulties the profession has in speaking with one voice.

Although the first state and local bar associations predated the creation of the ABA (the elite Association of the Bar of the City of New York was formed in 1870), state bar associations were also slow to develop and, when launched, were sometime entities with little political clout. They, too, usually represented less than half of their possible membership. A significant boost in the state bar organization came with the unified or "integrated" bar movement, a sort of closed shop whereby entry into the practice of law required membership in the association (McKean, 1963). North Dakota was the first to integrate its bar in 1921. A scattering of states followed, with over 33 of the 50 states and the District of Columbia bars being integrated by the 1970s (Schneyer, 1983: 1–2).

The work of bar associations reflects the classic contract between society and professions: In exchange for the assured delivery of a specialized service in sufficient quality and quantity to all in need, the profession receives a rather high degree of internal autonomy over decisions affecting the nature and extent of service delivery. This autonomy usually includes professionally adopted and enforced rules for certification to practice, control over standard of quality of service, and the right and duty to adopt and enforce professional norms—self-policing, in other words. The role of professions in society is actually a form of borrowed sovereignty or extraterritoriality by which the normal powers of society over its citizens are suspended for a highly defined group setting forth a special claim to self-government (see Abel, 1989: Ch. 2; Vago, 1988: 254–255).

Perhaps no area of professional activity is more revealing of the details of professional bar politics than that of self-government, for it is here that we are given the opportunity to examine the interaction of the two contracting parties, society and the legal profession. In Llewellyn's terms (1951: 12–14), it is at this point that we can examine the "real" law, which is not so much the rule that is adopted but the regularized behavior of officials (here, practicing lawyers) in real-life settings. Moreover, the record of the American bar in this respect reveals, perhaps as well as any other data one might draw on, the impact of the internal politics of the organized bar on the distribution of legal talent in our society.

The first formal attempt to codify standards of professional conduct in the law came in the ABA's *Code of Ethics* in 1908. But there have been five, now close to six, revisions or attempted revisions of the code, now called the *Model Code of Professional Responsibility,* which is a suggested but not required standard for state and local bar associations. The frequent and continuing revisions of professional standards reflect the bar's difficulty in defining and enforcing accepted modes of practice. Although the ABA has undertaken to promulgate such codes, their administration has been left to state and local bar associations. Research on the troublesome subject of enforcement continues to demonstrate three key points: (1) the widespread lack of knowledge and acceptance by American lawyers of their own professed standards of conduct, (2) the almost shameful lack of meaningful enforcement of such standards, and (3) the strong elite bias in both the rules and their enforcement.

One scholar sees evidence that the promulgation of such codes of conduct has more to do with enhancing the image of lawyers in the eyes of the public than with meaningful change in lawyers' behavior (Abel, 1989: 143). Since Watergate (when several legal advisors to the president went to jail) courses in ethics have been required at most law schools. But there is little evidence of any beneficial effect on lawyers' ethics. In fact, it is surprising how little lawyers know about their own codes of conduct.

Although the vast majority of states prohibit fee splitting (kickbacks for one lawyer sending business to another), a national survey in 1984 revealed that between two-thirds and three-fourths (depending on the circumstances) of lawyers polled approved of such practices, and 40 percent thought such practices were legal (Reskin, 1985: 48–49). Almost half of Michigan lawyers felt no obligation to correct a false statement of a client in a deposition, and about the same percentage of lawyers in a nationwide sample believed that it was acceptable practice to cause delays in litigation to gain a more favorable settlement. In a national survey of 1,500 lawyers who regularly engage in litigation, half admitted that unfair or inadequate disclosure of information was a frequent problem, and over two-thirds testified that in complex cases they had encountered unethical practices such as "tampering with witnesses' responses and destroying evidence" (Rhode, 1985a: 598–599). In general, then, one obvious problem with ethics is that lawyers themselves have failed to absorb the spirit, if not the letter, of declared standards of conduct (Able, 1989: 143; Harris, 1981: 4).

State bar disciplinary mechanisms established for the enforcement of bar ethics have come to be (indeed, always were) so ineffectual that the professional social contract is actually being rescinded in a large number of states. A common pattern is to withdraw disciplinary power from the bar and place it in a variety of alternative agencies and offices, usually courts. The record is dismal, indeed, and touches on every aspect of the disciplinary process.

Attorneys, who are the parties most likely to possess the necessary knowledge, are almost universally reluctant to file a complaint against one of their own and very seldom do so. Indeed, lawyers file less than 10 percent of all grievances. Clients are hampered in a variety of ways in their attempt to file and pursue complaints (Steele and Nimmer, 1976: 956–965, 973–974): Hot lines to state or local bar offices to file complaints are seldom answered (Able, 1989: 149), delays of up to four or five years are not uncommon in processing complaints, and disciplinary files are typically closed to the public. As for how complaints against lawyers are handled and meaningful sanctions imposed, one commentator summarizes the evidence in this way:

> Surveys of bar procedures in major states reveal that some 90% of complaints are dismissed without investigation, and national statistics reflect that of grievances falling within disciplinary jurisdiction, less than 3% result in public sanctions and only .8% in disbarment. Even repeated instances of neglect, misrepresentation, and incompetence will rarely provoke license revocation (Rhode, 1985b: 547–548).

Illustrative of the almost meaningless disciplinary processes in the American legal profession is the case of Harry E. Claiborne, former judge of the U.S. District Court for Nevada. Claiborne, a Carter appointee, was convicted of income tax evasion (failing to report $106,000 in income) and was sentenced to two years in federal prison. He was subsequently impeached by the U.S. Congress and removed from office—the first impeachment of a federal judge up to that time in 50 years (Greenhouse, 1986). Yet the Nevada bar refused to impose sanctions, leaving him free to practice law in that state.

There can be no doubt about bias in the bar's attempts to impose rules of professional conduct. "Ambulance chasing," improper advertising, stirring up litigation—these are matters having to do with obtaining legal business and involve prohibitions limited largely to the have-nots of the legal profession. "As with priests of old," wrote one scholar, "these particular canons have little to do with those who formulate and enforce them" (Shuchman, 1968: 245). Rather, they were designed to apply to the struggling solo practitioner, often of ethnic minority stock, in the inner cities. Exorbiant fees charged by corporate attorneys, fallout from selling their professional independence to their corporate clients, and the tactics of evasion, harassment, and delay—such practices by elite lawyers are not mentioned in the ethical guidelines or, if included, are seldom enforced.

Data from a 1980–1981 study of the discipline of attorneys in California, Illinois, and the District of Columbia indicate that over 80 percent of that small percentage of attorneys receiving disbarment, suspension, and reprovals were solo practitioners. Yet for commiting perjury during his Senate confirmation hearings as President Nixon's choice for attorney-general, Richard Kleindienst was given a 30-day suspension from the practice of law. And a senior partner in a Wall Street firm who lied under oath to conceal evidence retained his license (Rhode, 1985b: 248–249).

As Karl Llewellyn (1938: 114–117) observed nearly 60 years ago, the canons were, and remain, ill suited to the realities of modern urban life. Rules against certain types of solicitation may have been appropriate in small-town and rural America, before the industrial revolution and the rise of the corporate state and the large law firm. But today, large law firms play the role of the solo practitioner in earlier times; they carry their own advertisement within the business community they serve, needing no special tactics to attract legal business. This leaves the individual practitioner and small firm at a distinct disadvantage, with virtually no effective means of building contacts to a profitable legal practice. More important, the individual client in urban America is left without the face-to-face information systems characteristic of rural life, including critical knowledge of how to obtain access to legal services. Llewellyn has argued that rules against solicitation work primarily to the benefit of elite lawyers. Actually, he reasons, the ambulance chaser brings legal advice to those who need it. If such services were made available at a reasonable cost to a public having knowledgeable access to them, the issue of unethical solicitation of business would not exist (Auerbach, 1976b: 204–205; Green, 1988).

Thus, along every dimension of the workings of the American legal profession, from legal education to practice specialization to the organization of the bar and its attempts at self-government, one finds the same, essential political game underway: the struggle of elite practitioners against the claims of what Shuchman (1968) calls the "little lawyer." From the perspective of the dispensers of legal advice, the prize is of course the client dollar, along with the prestige and power that professional "success" so measured carries. But as suggested above, the lawyer game is not confined to lawyers but rather has a decided impact on society as a whole through the distribution, or as some have said, the maldistribution of legal services (Bok, 1983: 570–571; Carter, 1978). Having examined a number of factors and forces internal to the legal profession that shape the decision of who is to receive the benefits of this important sociopolitical resource, it is now appropriate to explore briefly the contours of the actual delivery of legal services.

THE DISTRIBUTION OF LEGAL SERVICES

Nothing is so central to the socioprofessional contract as the promise of delivery of service to all citizens on the basis of need; probably nothing causes so much friction between society and its central policy-making representative, on the one hand, and the professions, on the other; and perhaps nowhere has the American legal profession more clearly fallen short of meeting its professional commitment. That professional obligation is spelled out in the current ABA Code of Professional Responsibility:

Every lawyer, regardless of professional prominence or professional workload, should find time to participate in serving the disadvantaged. The rendition of free legal service to those unable to pay reasonable fees continues to be an obligation of each lawyer. . . .

The legal profession has fallen seriously short of meeting this commitment. In fact, it is not only people of small means who are largely without access to the services of attorneys; middle-class citizens are almost equally squeezed out by the high fees and other barriers imposed by legal service delivery systems. Data from numerous research forays amply document these assertions.

Difficult to measure and quantify is the "need" for legal services among Americans. Some commentators have claimed that the apparent denial of access to legal services to the middle class and, more particularly, to the poor is not the injustice it may seem to be because it is only the propertied classes who have a real need for such service. But many studies, along with bar leaders themselves, have challenged this assumption (Silver, 1969: 217–221; Stumpf, 1975: 125–126). In 1974, for example, Orville H. Schell, Jr., then president of the Association of the Bar of the City of New York, asked rhetorically in his testimony before Congress, "What about . . . the delivery of legal services? Is it adequate? The answer is definitely *No!*" He went on:

[A] high percentage of people in this country are not receiving adequate legal services. The estimated percentages run from 60 to 90% of the population. Whatever estimate you take the numbers are staggering. Reasons given are: people do not know when a legal problem exists, they do not know how and where to get a lawyer, they fear size of legal fees or they know that legal fees are indeed high, and they have a general distaste and even fear of lawyers. (Curran and Spalding, 1974: 11)

Similarly, the president of the ABA, Chesterfield Smith, testified before the same committee of Congress that the problem was not confined to the poor but that legal services delivery systems had "left untouched the needs of the tens of millions of our citizens who may be loosely referred to as 'Middle America'." (11–12)

A recent study of the unmet legal needs of the poor in New York State, particularly on the civil side of the law, concluded that in contemporary America access to legal services has become "crucial" in dealing with the crises that are routinely encountered by the poor. Although citizens of means have the need of a lawyer only in certain defined situations, that need often being optional, it is paradoxical but true that for the poor, legal services are needed to provide access to the very "essentials of life: shelter, minimum levels of income and entitlements . . . child support, education . . . health care" and the like.

Precisely because poor persons cannot command access to these basic requirements by their own economic power in the marketplace, society has sought, through remedial legislation, to ensure their access to them by law. Thus, the poor must make legal claims to get basic goods and services that other people can obtain more readily. (New York State Bar Association, 1990: 14–15)

This study pointed to housing (landlord-tenant problems), access to public benefits, consumer issues, health care, discrimination, and family issues (divorce, custody, etc.) as areas in which there is particular need for legal services for the poor (18).

The New York bar report is only the latest in a series of studies drawing a similar conclusion. Attorney Carol Ruth Silver (1969) made the same argument and estimated that if the poor of the nation were afforded the same level of legal services as that available to those earning in excess of $10,000 per year, nearly half (47 percent) of all lawyers in practice at that time would be needed *just to serve the needs of the poor*. Legal services lawyers have estimated that with the multiple problems of the poor, perhaps five times as much time and effort is needed to serve their needs as compared to middle-class clients (218, 220). With the increases in the poor population in America in the last two decades, the legal needs of the poor are even greater today, relative to the legal services available. Thus, the New York bar study concluded that all types of legal aid to the poor in that state met "less than 4% of the civil legal problems of the poor" (New York State Bar Association, 1989: 203).

On the criminal side, the situation is both better and worse. The U.S. Supreme Court, in a series of decisions reaching back to 1932, established the right to counsel in criminal matters (Bureau of Justice Statistics, 1988: 2). However, the two chief methods states have established to satisfy that constitutional requirement—public defender offices with paid staff attorneys and assigned, paid, private counsel—seem hardly to have scratched the surface of meeting the need for indigent defense in criminal cases. Although nearly a billion dollars was spent by state and local governments to provide for such representation in 1986, the per-case expenditure is pitifully small (only $223), the quality and quantity of the representation are poor, caseloads are impossibly heavy, and state program officials are crying out for relief (Bureau of Justice Statistics, 1988; Riggs, 1988: A–15).

In California, for example, a study of the public defender program indicated that it is woefully inadequate to meet the demand, is "suffering from lack of funds, office support and even fundamental equipment . . ." (Fremont, 1980: I:2; Kirsch, 1984). It was reported that California had not increased its contribution to the program in 15 years (Ashby, 1980: I:1), and the same situation exists in Missouri (Siegel, 1982: I:1), New Mexico (Riggs, 1988: A–15), Texas ("Attorneys Sought for Capital Cases," 1987), or any other state one wishes to study. In spring 1990, public defenders in St. Louis held a bake sale to raise money for their program. On one cake was iced the Sixth Amendment's admonition: "The Accused Shall Enjoy the Right to Counsel." A total of $609.33 was collected (Kramer, 1990: B–12). To sum up, a title for one article on America's criminal defense system was this: "Did You Have a Lawyer When You Went to Court? No, I Had a Public Defender" (Casper, 1971: 4).

Assigned counsel systems are if anything less effective and in worse condition. With payments in the range of $15 to $30 per hour for criminal representation in some states, and with caps on the maximum amount allowed for defense of felonies of $800 to $1,500, one can hardly expect effective representation (Bureau of Justice Statistics, 1988: 6). Such figures are between 20 and 50 percent of the fees private attorneys would normally charge.

Poorly paid, sometimes wholly inexperienced assigned counsel can be (and sometimes are) so ineffective as to deny meaningful representation under the Sixth Amendment (Klein, 1986: 625–631). Although the U.S. Supreme Court has steadfastly refused to establish criteria for measuring the adequacy of counsel (see *Strickland v. Washington*, 466 U.S. 668 [1984] and related cases), grossly underrepresented clients continue to be shoved through our criminal justice system. Several studies have demonstrated that maintaining high rates of guilty pleas is the only way the public defender system can survive

(Klein, 1986: 672). Clearly, effective representation of the poor in criminal cases is not a high priority of budget makers in state and local governments. As one California lawyer put it, "If government has to choose between roads, schools, hospitals or indigent criminal defendants, you don't have to phone in for the results" (Kirsch, 1984: 24).

Since civil legal aid has never been a right but merely an obligation of the bar, such programs have scrimped along on meager resources throughout our history. The old-line legal aid societies, begun in New York City and Chicago before the turn of the century, had strong ethnic and immigrant orientations and relied almost entirely on private donations or community chest support. By 1964, the coverage of these organizations was limited largely to major cities, and there the type of legal service rendered was highly selective, staff attorneys were likely to be the least successful of the bar, and budgets were scanty (Carlin and Howard, 1965; Silverstein, 1967). In 1963, the national expenditure on all these programs was less than $8 million, representing only .35 percent of all expenditures for legal services in the nation. With some 34.5 million Americans in poverty that year, that works out to about 23 cents per person in contrast to the $14.50 spent for legal services for the nonpoor (Stumpf, 1975: 124–125).

Of course certain amounts of pro bono (voluntary) services were being rendered by members of the bar, but surveys have indicated that such service is slight indeed. The above New York study, for example, found that only 10 percent of some 88,000 lawyers licensed to practice in New York had enrolled in pro bono programs, a figure supported by a national ABA study in 1984 (New York State Bar Association, 1990: 207; Oliver, 1987: I–25), and other studies have found that the few lawyers who participate in pro bono work do so fewer than 30 to 50 hours per year, or only about 3 percent of their annual legal effort (Oliver, 1987: I–1). Two decades ago young law graduates sought positions in firms on the promise that they would be guaranteed a certain amount of pro bono opportunity. Today, attitudes are different. As one California civil liberties lawyer remarked, "The private bar treats *pro bono* cases as if they were third class cases, and the private bar has just not made the commitment" (I–25). The caption of a recent *New York Times* article read, "Increasingly, Pro Cash Beats Pro Bono" (Lewin, 1987: IV28).

Beginning in 1965 the nation launched a bold new experiment in civil legal aid, the Legal Services Program, as part of President Johnson's War on Poverty. Federal funds for legal services grew rapidly, most of them going into significant expansions of established legal aid societies across the nation. Also, the philosophy shifted from the timid, limited approach of old to a more aggressive, "law reform" orientation. Realizing early that resources would never be sufficient to meet the total legal needs of the poor on a case-by-case, individual basis (offices were quickly swamped with divorce, landlord-tenant, and consumer cases, for example), program strategists developed an approach that emphasized test cases in an attempt to bring about fundamental changes in the law to benefit large numbers of the poor (Stumpf, 1968: 711–712).

By 1980 the program had gone through a number of crises, which contained some valuable lessons concerning the politics of legal advice. The political opposition encountered by this effort at legal empowerment of the poor was overwhelming. From the first, local bar associations were afire with criticism, fearing the loss of business and attacking poverty lawyers on almost every conceivable aspect of their work (Kessler, 1990; Stumpf, 1971). Interestingly, defendant lawyers, because they were definitionally less threatened by more effective representation of the poor, tended to support expanded legal services, whereas plaintiff attorneys (usually seen as more liberal, small-firm or solo practitioners) were the most antagonistic. Local businesses as well as local and state government agencies also felt the sting of such novel legal representation, and they too often sought to limit program activities or kill programs outright (Stumpf, 1975: 256–258; "United Way Warns Denver Legal Aid," 1980: A13; Winchurch, 1987: 9).

State and national political pressures on the program soon mounted. In California, for example, a particularly aggressive statewide program, California Rural Legal Assistance (CRLA), was successful in winning a number of suits against established state interests—large growers, the state department of welfare, and so on—and was immediately attacked by Governor Ronald Reagan. After extensive investigation, the root of the problem was revealed. As candidly expressed by Lewis Uhler, head of California's anti-poverty program under Reagan, "What we've created in CRLA is an economic leverage equal to that existing in large corporations. Clearly, that should not be" ("California: War on the Poor?" 1971: 19). And clearly, as well as paradoxically, the program's success was its downfall. Law reform orientations were buried under a sea of rules and restrictions, and legal services in the traditional Band-Aid mode again became the order of the day. As one poverty lawyer wrote, law reform became "an idea of the past" (Kaimowitz, 1989: 12). Under intense pressure, Congress eventually placed program activities under the umbrella of a public corporation and in other ways attempted to protect it from attack by officials of the Nixon and Reagan administrations (Roberts, 1987: 22).

By 1990 the Legal Services Corporation was operating 324 programs of various structures with a budget of $316 million. It had survived incessant attacks from the Reagan-Bush White House only through the persistence of congressional leadership, backed by usually strong ABA endorsement (Champagne, 1984). But its activities had been severely circumscribed, usually through Reagan program directors or congressional limitations or both. CRLA, as well as a few other local or state programs, nonetheless remained in the spotlight.

In one recent incident, poverty attorneys from Texas, Mississippi, and California (CRLA) undertook the representation of black and Hispanic litigants in their efforts to attain political equity in legislative districting. Such litigation had been banned by national program directors, who themselves had earlier recommended that the corporation be totally abolished. Their thinking on litigation was that the program should concentrate on "providing basic, day-to-day service" rather than on "esoteric cases." Redistricting issues, they said, were examples of improper litigation "undertaken by some legal aid lawyers to achieve political and social change with the hope that such changes will eventually benefit the poor" (Pear, 1990: A14). In late June 1990 District of Columbia federal Judge Gerhard A. Gesell held the directors' ban illegal, as unauthorized by the Legal Services Corporation Act:

> At no time has Congress taken any action to bar redistricting activities. . . . In a particular circumstance, a redistricting case might, in the judgment of local attorneys, be the single most important and efficient means of assisting the poor . . . and . . . without LSC involvement, some redistricting cases of potential value to the poor would not be brought. (A1, A14)

This latest CRLA incident illustrates, as well as any might, the lessons to be learned from the nation's move to even moderately adequate systems of legal representation for have-nots. First, as we have seen in other contexts, legal representation is an important political resource, carrying the potential for significant shifts in the established pattern of "who gets what, when, and how" in our polity. As such, it is a "good" whose distribution is itself a recognized object of political struggle. Few political issues of the 1960s and 1970s were more intensely contested than that of federally funded legal services. And the battle continues today in state and nation, with important political interests vying for influence in determining who is to enjoy the advantage of adequate and aggressive legal representation (see, e.g., Corwin, 1990: A3; Winchurch, 1987: 9).

Second, it seems clear from this experience that the ideal of "Equal Justice Under Law" is just that—an ideal—whose realization is far removed from reality. The image it carries is not unimportant, but the political reality would suggest that, indeed, law *is* politics, and considerations of the latter will tend to dominate. That lawyers are admonished to "serve the disadvantaged" is a part of that ideal as well as a key element of the professional-societal contract. But what is clear from our experience with federally funded legal services programs is that representation is acceptable as long as it is not too effective. When it begins to threaten established interests, it is likely to be met with the countervailing power of the larger sociopolitical system.

Overall, the evidence points to a severe maldistribution of legal services in America, reflecting the long-standing but increasing stratification of the bar, which in turn reflects the pedagogy, politics, and sociology of legal education in our society. That these lineaments of legal power are themselves natural outcroppings of a capitalist society, with its emphasis on the material rewards of the marketplace, must be acknowledged. But let us then remove the term *profession* from the practice of law and accept the realities of the political-legal role of American lawyers as set forth by Chief Justice Harlan Fiske Stone (1934) over a half century ago:

> Steadily the best skill and capacity of the profession has been drawn into the exacting and highly specialized service of business and finance. At its best the changed system has brought to the command of the business world loyalty and a superb proficiency and technical skill. At its worst it has made the learned profession of an earlier day the obsequious servant of business, and tainted it with the morals and manners of the market place in its most anti-social manifestations. In any case we must concede that it has given us a Bar whose leaders, like its rank and file, are on the whole less likely to be well rounded professional men than their predecessors, whose energy and talent for public service and for bringing the law into harmony with changed conditions have been absorbed in the advancement of the interest of clients. (7)

CONCLUSION

The research findings in this chapter provide strong support for the proposition that lawyers are an important, if not crucial, adjunct of the judicial process and must be included in any overall assessment of the work of state courts. The monopoly enjoyed by the legal profession over access to judicial power carries with it the power to grant or withhold significant rewards or deprivations for all elements of society. This is politics in the most basic sense. For these reasons, issues of lawyer recruitment and training, how lawyers think, and how they organize themselves to deliver legal services are inextricably involved and often actually determine political outcomes of American courts.

NOTE

1. Richard L. Abel's work, *American Lawyers* (New York: Oxford University Press, 1989), is a monumental collection and synthesis of the most recent research findings on the American legal profession and is used extensively throughout this chapter. The authors also wish to acknowledge the assistance of Cheryl M. Minnick and Kenneth Gonzales, who gathered and organized a mass of materials used in the writing of this chapter.

REFERENCES

Abel, Richard. 1989. *American Lawyers*. New York: Oxford University Press.

Ashby, Alan. 1980, December 10. "Lack of Funding of Public Defenders Affecting Counsel." *Los Angeles Daily Journal*, p. I1.

"Attorneys Sought for Capital Cases." 1987, September 20. *New York Times*, p. A14.

Auerbach, Jerold S. 1976a. "A Plague of Lawyers." 253 *Harpers* 37.

Auerbach, Jerold S. 1976b. *Unequal Justice: Lawyers and Social Change in Modern America*. New York: Oxford University Press.

Berle, A. A., Jr. 1933. "The Modern Legal Profession." 9 *Encyclopedia of the Social Sciences* 340.

Bok, Derek C. 1983. "A Flawed System of Law Practice and Training." 33 *Journal of Legal Education* 570.

Brandeis, Louis D. 1914. *Business—A Profession*. Boston: Hale, Cushman & Flint.

Bureau of Justice Statistics. 1988, September. "Criminal Defense of the Poor, 1986." NCJ 112911.

"California: War on the Poor?" 1971, January 18. *Newsweek*, p. 18.

Carlin, Jerome E., and Jan Howard. 1965. "Legal Representation and Class Justice." 12 *UCLA Law Review* 381.

Carter, Jimmy. 1978, May 4. Speech before the Los Angeles County Bar Association.

"The Cartter Report on the Leading Schools of Education, Law, and Business." 1977. 9 *Change* 44.

Casper, Jonathan D. 1971. "Did You Have a Lawyer When You went to Court? No, I had a Public Defender." 1 *Yale Review of Law and Social Action* 4.

Champagne, Anthony. 1984. "Legal Services: A Program in Need of Assistance." In Anthony Champagne and Edward J. Harpham, eds., *The Attack on the Welfare State*. Prospect Heights, IL: Waveland Press.

Corwin, Miles. 1990, June 5. "Firm That Beat Governor May Lose Funds." *Los Angeles Times*, p. A3.

Curran, Barbara A. 1986a. "American Lawyers in the 1980's: A Profession in Transition." 20 *Law and Society Review* 19.

Curran, Barbara A. 1986b, May 7. "The Dynamics of Change in the Legal Profession and the Work of Lawyers." Paper presented at the National Association for Law Placement Conference, New Orleans.

Curran, Barbara A., and Francis O. Spalding. 1974. *The Legal Needs of the Public*. Chicago: American Bar Foundation.

"Fiscal Rewards of the Practice." 1990, March 26. *National Law Journal*, p. S2.

Fremont, Laura. 1980, December 17. "Defenders Cite Need for More Funds for Poor Defendants." *Los Angeles Daily Journal*, p. I2.

Friedman, Lawrence M. 1985. *A History of American Law*, 2nd ed. New York: Simon & Schuster.

Galanter, Marc. 1974. "Why the 'Haves' Come Out Ahead: Speculations on the Limits of Legal Change." 9 *Law and Society Review* 95.

Galanter, Marc. 1986. "Adjudication, Litigation, and Related Phenomena." In Leon Lipson and Stanton Wheeler, eds., *Law and the Social Sciences*. New York: Russell Sage.

Geoghegan, Thomas. 1986. "Warren Court Children." 194 *The New Republic* 17.

Green, Wayne E. 1988, September 20. "Bar Groups Take on Ambulance-Chasers." *Wall Street Journal*, p. 2:27.

Greenhouse, Linda. 1986, October 10. "Senate Convicts U.S. Judge, Ousting Him from Office." *New York Times*, p. A1.

Griswold, Erwin N. 1968. "Intellect and Spirit." In Arthur E. Sutherland, ed., *The Path of the Law from 1967*. Cambridge, MA: Harvard University Press.

Halpern, Stephen C. 1982. "On the Politics and Pathology of Legal Education." 32 *Journal of Legal Education* 383.

Harris, Richard. 1981, September 7. "The Real Danger of Lawyers' Abuse." *Los Angeles Daily Journal*, p. 7:4.

Hazard, Geoffrey C., Jr. 1969. "Social Justice Through Civil Justice." 36 *University of Chicago Law Review* 699.

Heinz, John P., and Edward O. Laumann. 1982. *Chicago Lawyers: The Social Structure of the Bar*. New York and Chicago: Russell Sage Foundation and American Bar Foundation.

Hurst, James Willard. 1950. *The Growth of American Law: The Lawmakers*. Boston: Little, Brown.

Kailer, Pat. 1988, July 10. "Setting Off in a Crowd of Shingles." *Albuquerque Journal*, p. F1.

Kaimowitz, Gabe. 1989, November 6. "Back When the Poor *Really* Had Lawyers." *National Law Journal*, p. 1.

Kessler, Mark. 1990. "Expanding Legal Services Programs to Rural America: A Case Study of Program Creation and Operations." 73 *Judicature* 273.

Kirsch, Jonathan L. 1984, April. "Rural Justice at the Crossroads." *California Lawyer*, p. 22.

Klein, Richard. 1986. "The Emperor Gideon Has No Clothes: The Empty Promise of the Constitutional Right to Effective Assistance of Counsel." 13 *Hastings Constitutional Law Quarterly* 625.

Kramer, Staci D. 1990, April 13. "Cake for Sale to Keep Legal Aid Free." *New York Times*, p. B12.

Ladinsky, Jack. 1963. "Careers of Lawyers, Law Practice, and Legal Institutions." 28 *American Sociological Review* 47.

"Law." 1990, March 13. *U.S. News and World Report*, p. 59.

Lewin, Tamar. 1987, March 22. "Increasingly, Pro Cash Beats Pro Bono." *New York Times*, p. IV28.

Llewellyn, Karl N. 1933, May 1933. "The Bar Specializes—With What Results." 167 *Annals* 177.

Llewellyn, Karl N. 1938. "The Bar's Troubles and Poultices—And Cures." 5 *Law and Contemporary Problems* 104.

Llewellyn, Karl N. 1951. *The Bramble Bush: On Law and Its Study*, rev. ed. New York: Oceana.

McKean, Dayton. 1963. *The Integrated Bar*. Boston: Houghton Mifflin.

Margulies, Rebecca Zames, and Peter M. Blau. 1973. "The Pecking Order of the Elite: America's Leading Professional Schools." 5 *Change* 21.

Myers, Ken. 1990, June 25. "Academics Continue to Debate the Relative Virtue of Ranking." *National Law Journal*, p. 4.

New York State Bar Association. 1989, October 16. *Report of the Special Committee to Review the Proposed Plan for Mandatory Pro Bono Service*.

New York State Bar Association, Committee to Improve the Availability of Legal Services. 1990. *Final Report to the Chief Judge of the State of New York*.

Oliver, Myrna. 1987, April 7. "Pro Bono: Renaissance in Legal Aid." *Los Angeles Times*, p. I1.

Pear, Robert. 1990, July 3. "Poor Given Right to Legal Aid to Fight Redistricting Plans." *New York Times*, p. A1.

Reidinger, Paul. 1986. "It's 46.5 Hours a Week in Law." 72 *American Bar Association Journal* 44.

Reskin, Lauren R. 1985. "Law Poll: Forwarding Fees Are Fine with Most Lawyers." 71 *American Bar Association Journal* 48.

Rhode, Deborah L. 1985a. "Ethical Perspectives on Legal Practice." 37 *Stanford Law Review* 589.

Rhode, Deborah L. 1985b. "Moral Character as a Professional Credential." 94 *Yale Law Journal* 49.

Riggs, Joseph N., III. 1988, September 1. "Public Defender System Heading for Crisis." *Albuquerque Journal,* p. A15.

Roberts, Charley. 1987, July 27. "After 13 Years, Clouds Mar Legal Service Corporation Horizon." *Los Angeles Daily Journal,* p. 22.

Sander, Richard H., and E. Douglass Williams. 1989. "Why Are There So Many Lawyers? Perspectives on a Turbulent Market." 14 *Law and Social Inquiry* 431.

Schneyer, Theodore J. 1983. "The Incoherence of the Unified Bar Concept: Generalizing from the Wisconsin Case, 1983." *American Bar Foundation Research Journal,* p. 1.

Shuchman, Philip. 1968. "Ethics and Legal Ethics: The Propriety of the Canons as a Group Moral Code." 37 *George Washington Law Review* 244.

Siegel, Barry. 1982, February 22. "Missouri Lawyers Get Lesson in Justice." *Los Angeles Times,* p. I1.

Silver, Carol Ruth. 1969. "The Imminent Failure of Legal Services for the Poor: Why and How to Limit Caseload." 46 *Journal of Urban Law* 217.

Silverstein, Lee. 1967. "Eligibility for Free Legal Services in Civil Cases." 44 *Journal of Urban Law* 549.

Steele, Eric H., and Raymond T. Nimmer. 1976. "Lawyers, Clients, and Professional Regulation." *American Bar Foundation Research Journal,* p. 917.

Stevens, Robert. 1983. *Law School: Legal Education in America from the 1850s to the 1980s.* Chapel Hill: University of North Carolina Press.

Stone, Harlan Fiske. 1934. "The Public Influence of the Bar." 48 *Harvard Law Review* 1.

Stover, Robert V. 1982. "Law School and Professional Responsibility: The Impact of Legal Education on Public Interest Practice." 66 *Judicature* 194.

Stumpf, Harry P. 1968. "Law and Poverty: A Political Perspective." 1968 *Wisconsin Law Review* 694.

Stumpf, Harry P. 1971. "The Legal Profession and Legal Services: Explorations in Local Bar Politics." 6 *Law and Society Review* 47.

Stumpf, Harry P. 1975. *Community Politics and Legal Services: The Other Side of the Law.* Beverly Hills, CA: Sage.

Stumpf, Harry P. 1988. *American Judicial Politics.* San Diego: Harcourt Brace Jovanovich.

Tocqueville, Alexis de. 1945. *Democracy in America,* Vol. I. New York: Vintage Books.

Truman, David B. 1951. *The Governmental Process.* New York: Knopf.

Twiss, Benjamin. 1942. *Lawyers and the Constitution.* Princeton, NJ: Princeton University Press.

"United Way Warns Denver Legal Aid." 1980, September 28. *San Francisco Examiner and Chronicle,* p. A13.

Vago, Steven. 1988. *Law and Society,* 2nd ed. Englewood Cliffs, NJ: Prentice Hall.

Van Alstyne, Scott. 1982. "Ranking the Law Schools: The Reality of Illusion." *American Bar Foundation Research Journal,* p. 649.

VanLoon, Eric E. 1970. "The Law School Response: How to Make Students Sharp by Making them Narrow." In Bruce Wasserstein and Mark J. Green, eds., *With Justice for Some: An Indictment of the Law by Young Advocates.* Boston: Beacon Press.

Watson, Richard A., and Rondal G. Downing. 1969. *The Politics of Bench and Bar: Judicial Selection Under the Missouri Nonpartisan Court Plan.* New York: Wiley.

Wells, Richard S. 1964. "The Legal Profession and Politics." 8 *Midwest Journal of Political Science* 166.

Winchurch, Susan. 1987, July 13. "Maryland Trying to Limit Legal Aid Suits Against State." *National Law Journal,* p. 9.

Zemans, Francis K., and Victor G. Rosenblum. 1981. *The Making of a Public Profession.* Chicago: American Bar Foundation.

CHAPTER 5

The Civil Judicial Process in the States

If the processing of disputes can be said to be a central function of courts, it is the civil dispute—typically a conflict between private citizens—that best exemplifies that process. To be sure, civil cases also involve contests between private organizations such as banks, insurance companies, or major manufacturing corporations; and they also frequently involve disputes between private organizations and individuals (e.g., employer-employee controversies, suits by private citizens against hospitals or insurance companies, etc.). Also, the civil disputing process in the United States extends to contests between individuals and government entities, for example, suits against police departments, schools, or agencies such as the welfare department. But the more typical civil case, as measured by numbers of cases, is between individuals.

In all, then, the civil judicial process—often called the *disputing process* in the current research literature—encompasses such a broad spectrum of social conflict as to make generalizations difficult. Relatively trivial differences between neighbors over a barking dog or the overgrowth of a neighbor's tree onto one's property; major damage cases involving millions of dollars as in automobile accident claims or medical malpractice suits; landlord-tenant disagreements; issues of allegedly unfair treatment in diverse areas of our lives such as employer discrimination or police mistreatment; private debt collection; consumer complaints; disputes over social security, welfare, or veterans's benefits; family law issues dominated by divorce and postdivorce disputes; mental commitment proceedings—all of these and more are found among the millions of civil cases filed each year in state and federal courts. As one scholar put it,

> Civil proceedings range over the entire potential for conflict in American society. Almost every dispute that does not involve a violation of the criminal code may come to a civil courtroom. Every broken agreement, every sale that leaves a dissatisfied customer, every uncollected debt, every dispute with a government agency, every libel and slander, every

accidental injury, every marital breakup, and every death may give rise to a civil proceeding (Jacob, 1984: 210).

Americans are much more attuned to the dramatics of criminal law, with its riveting murder trials, than they are to the seemingly more mundane intricacies of civil law. Yet disputes in the latter category crowd the dockets of our courts at both the state and federal level. State trial courts of all types registered nearly 17 million civil case filings in 1988, compared with only some 12 million criminal filings. In state courts of general jurisdiction, where the more serious state cases are processed, the ratio of civil to criminal cases is even greater, roughly 1:2.5. Thus, nearly a third of the caseloads of these courts are civil filings, whereas only some 13 percent are in the area of criminal law. As shown in Figures 5.1 and 5.2, the remaining caseload of these courts—the lion's share, in fact—is consumed largely by traffic cases.

Figure 5.1 State Trial Court Filings, 1988

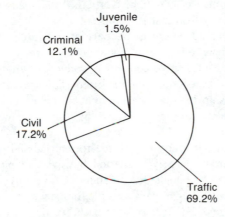

Figure 5.2 State Trial Court Filings in General Jurisdiction Courts, 1988

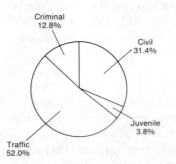

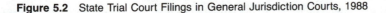

SOURCE: Data supplied by Brian J. Ostrom, staff associate, Court Statistics Project, National Center for State Courts, March 26, 1990. Reprinted with permission.

Federal trial courts are also burdened with a preponderance of civil cases, the 1988 ratio being over 5:1. Nearly 84 percent of the cases that began in federal district courts that year were civil in nature, a proportion that has been increasing for many decades (Administrative Office of the U.S. Courts, 1980, 1988).

DISPUTE PROCESSING: THE EARLY STAGES

The civil judicial process could be said to begin with a *grievance,* defined in recent research as "an individual's belief that he or she (or a group or organization) is entitled to a resource which someone else may grant or deny" (Miller and Sarat, 1980–1981: 527). Every reader will quickly identify with the feeling of anger and frustration associated with a wrong perceived to have been caused by another, along with a felt resentment and a desire to retaliate—to "even the score," to retrieve what has been lost. But we can also recall the almost instantaneous calculation we undertake in most such situations about whether an attempt to "get justice" would be worth the time, energy, and other resources required. In most cases, we reason that it would not.

Either we perceive our adversary to be beyond the reach of our efforts, or we conclude that even if recompense is won, it would not equal the costs incurred. A hit and run resulting in bent fenders; defective consumer products; "wrongs" involved in relations with one's spouse, children, neighbors, or "friends"; losses incurred through unpaid debts; defective workmanship by the local contractor; unfair treatment by one's employer—these and many more examples suggest the grievances we tend to swallow in everyday life.

The road leading from felt grievances to the formal judicial process is a long and uncertain one, with numerous, largely uncharted byways and pitfalls along the way. However, millions of citizens do pursue these matters each year by registering a *claim,* at least informally, with the party allegedly responsible for the wrong. But claims, of course, can be partially or wholly rejected. If that is the case, we may say that a *dispute* exists. And it becomes a *civil legal dispute* if it proceeds to a claim formally presented to a court (Miller and Sarat, 1980–1981: 527).

At the most elemental stage of claims adjustment it is, of course, possible to resolve the matter directly with one's codisputant, heal the potential breach in relations, and proceed more or less amicably. Although we have little systematic evidence concerning the incidence of this mode of grievance processing, it is at least the most obvious; direct; and we may suppose, well-trodden path of grievance resolution. It is when such self-help methods fail that a dispute in the legal sense comes into being.

As Mather and Yngvesson (1980–1981: 776) see it, a *dispute* is said to exist at the point in the relationship at which the conflict "is asserted publicly—that is, before a third party." But third-party dispute processing and resolution can be, and is, undertaken by a host of private, semiprivate, and public individuals, agencies, and institutions short of the formal adjudicative process. It is in this vast "landscape of disputing" that our knowledge is most deficient, for up until recently, research tended to focus almost exclusively on the formal processes for addressing disputes, particularly adjudication.

Sarat and Grossman (1975) and Sarat (1987), along with others, have attempted to map this largely unresearched world of informal dispute processing and in doing so have called to our attention the thin line between informal and formal social processes by which disputes are addressed. Sarat (450), for example, finds that techniques such as arbitration and mediation, when studied closely, often turn out to be heavily rule-bound or highly coercive and so blur the contrast between these techniques and formal adjudication in court or courtlike settings. Conversely, empirical studies of formal adjudication in real-life settings often reveal the widespread use of informal bargaining closely akin to mediation and arbitration. No approach to dispute resolution functions in a vacuum. Third-party techniques are heavily conditioned by the preceding, and continuing, bilateral efforts, just as outcomes of two-party bargainings are influenced by the shadow or threat of formal adjudication. Thus, any typology of approaches to dispute processing, such as that suggested below, must be read in the light of the persistent and inevitable fluidity of the process.

With this in mind, one might think of the world of dispute-processing institutions and techniques along two continua, the *level of formality* of the process and the *degree of publicness* of the proceeding. The former refers primarily to the extent of specialization of the third party's role, particularized rules of evidence and procedures, legally established channels of appeal, and so on (Sarat, 1987: 456). The latter is perhaps better described as the extent of the formal, coercive power of government in the process. Formal government connectedness is the variable. Using these categories Sarat and Grossman (1975) constructed a four-cell table of "ideal types" of informal adjudicative techniques. With some variation from the original, the world of informal dispute processing could be depicted as in Figure 5.3.

Private, informal dispute resolution (cell A) is common in all societies, although it appears to be a cultural norm to a greater extent in Eastern than in Western cultures (Kawashima, 1963: 44–45). Even in the United States, however, with its emphasis on the law in a formal, official, and public sense, a great deal of private, informal dispute processing—and presumably resolution—takes place. Controversies within religious organizations or ethnic communities (the Amish, e.g.) are often addressed privately and informally. Referrals to debt or marriage counselors are other examples. No one knows with any precision the extent to which Americans resort to this universal, triadic dispute-resolution technique, but the social logic of dispute settlement through the good offices of

Figure 5.3 Modes of Dispute Resolution

SOURCE: Austin Sarat and Joel B. Grossman, "Courts and Conflict Resolution: Problems in the Mobilization of Adjudication," *American Political Science Review,* Vol. 69, No. 4 (December, 1975), 1202, Table I. Reprinted with permission.

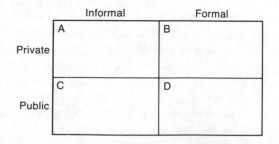

private parties in an informal setting suggests the ubiquity of this mode of dispute processing (Shapiro, 1981: 1).

Private approaches may evolve into rather *formal* processes, constituting the second mode suggested in Figure 5.3 (cell B). Ecclesiastical tribunals, as in the Roman Catholic church, which may determine issues such as marriage annulments; disciplinary proceedings in a secondary school, college, or perhaps professional association; hospital professional ethics committees—these examples suggest the technique used here. The key characteristics of this mode of dispute settlement is that although private, the lineaments of the approach established (or that which has evolved) are rather formal, courtlike in nature, following somewhat strict, prearranged procedures. Decision makers are not government officials, although their determinations may carry severe consequences for the disputants (e.g., loss of license to practice), and of course, such decisions may be subsequently contested in public forums (i.e., courts) (Sarat, 1987: 457).

In the third cell (C) one finds *public, informal* processes—dispute resolution or attempted resolution in which public officials participate but in an informal manner. Examples include police officers attempting to settle a family squabble or out-of-court settlement of formal legal claims in which court officials such as prosecutors and judges play key roles. With its long-standing focus on formal court proceedings, the law-social science research community has become familiar with this mode of settlement, for any careful study of formal disputing processes in the United States quickly points up the actual *informality* of significant aspects of the process (Blumberg, 1967; Ross, 1970).

Finally (cell D), we have *public, formal* arrangements, which are most familiar to researchers as well as the public. Officials representing the state and engaging in formal adjudicative processes, characterized by elaborate rules of procedure, are key ingredients of formal, public adjudication. A high degree of legal specialization and professional, publicly scrutinized proceedings looking to carefully crafted outcomes are also leading characteristics. Generally, access to these forums is much more circumscribed, limiting disputants to a select few (Sarat, 1987: 458). Actually, formal adjudicative processes represent only the tip of the iceberg of our entire world of dispute processing.

In sum, one may speak of unilateral action (as in withdrawal); bilateral approaches; and as suggested by the Sarat-Grossman typology, three types of informal triadic processes, which together suggest in a rough way the landscape of informal disputing in the United States. To repeat, the vast majority of disputes in our society are handled through these various informal processes; only a very small percentage seeps through to the formal adjudicative mode.

Until recently, little has been known about this so-called *transformation process*— the process whereby grievances become disputes, which in turn end up in court as civil legal filings. But through a major research venture, the Civil Litigation Research Project, undertaken jointly by the University of Wisconsin and the University of Southern California, rich empirical data has been gathered to help answer many of our questions.[1]

Approximately 1,000 households in each of five federal judicial districts (South Carolina, Eastern Pennsylvania, Eastern Wisconsin, New Mexico, and Central California) were surveyed in early 1980. Respondents were asked if anyone in the home had experienced any of a long list of problems within the last three years and how the problems were handled. This predetermined list included the usual range of grievances that ultimately leads to civil judicial claims, usually in state courts. To qualify for the research, the problem had to involve $1,000 or more, the threshold for what the researchers called "middle-range" disputes (Miller and Sarat, 1980–1981: 534–535).

About 40 percent of the households reported at least one grievance of this magnitude, and some 20 percent reported two or more grievances. Responses were elicited concerning the steps taken to pursue the grievance to the point of a claim and to the stage of a dispute (see definitions above). Questions were also asked concerning the use of lawyers or other facilitators and the success of the claim—was agreement reached. The data generated give us a rough picture of the disputing "funnel," or as we called it above, the transformation process.

The most common type of grievances reported had to do with landlord-tenant relations, representing 17.1 percent of the households (see Table 5.1). Other common griev-

TABLE 5.1 Household Grievances, Claims, and Disputes: Civil Litigation Research Project

Problem	Grievances (% of Households at Risk)	Claims (% of Grievances)	Disputes (% of Claims)
Landlord (problems with rent, eviction, repair of property, etc.)	17.1	87.2	81.7
Tort (auto accident, work or other injury)	15.6	85.7	23.5
Discrimination (employment, school, housing, etc.)	14.0	29.4	73.5
Postdivorce (property, alimony, visitation, etc.)	10.9	87.9	87.0
Government (benefits of social security, veterans, welfare, local or federal services)	9.1	84.9	82.1
Consumer (major purchases, medical or other services, home building or repair)	8.9	87.3	75.0
Property (property ownership or use, boundaries, etc.)	7.2	79.9	53.9
Debt (collections from employer, debtor, insurance company, etc.)	6.7	94.6	84.5
All grievances	41.6	71.8	62.6

SOURCE: Richard E. Miller and Austin Sarat, "Grievances, Claims, and Disputes: Assessing the Adversary Culture," *Law and Society Review*, Vol. 15, No. 3–4 (1980–1981), Table 2, Appendix. Reprinted by permission of the Law and Society Association.

ances, in descending order of reporting, are presented in the Table. The reader should note that where possible, the responses reported here are adjusted for the "at risk" variable. That is, landlord-tenant grievances, for example, are to be read as a percentage of households that are rented.

To what extent, and regarding what grievances, did respondents pursue their complaint to the stage of making a claim? In general, *claiming* was reported at a high rate, the most likely claim being the collection of a debt (94.6 percent of debt grievances). As shown in Table 5.1, other grievance categories also show a high rate of claiming, the major exception being in the area of discrimination. Here, it is supposed, the lack of availability and accessibility of dispute-processing forums may be the cause of the high incidence of withdrawal in discrimination cases. Other factors may include the difficulty of proving such claims. Also, those experiencing discrimination may be low on the assertiveness scale (Miller and Sarat, 1980–1981: 540–541).

To what extent are claims in the various categories resisted, in whole or in part, giving rise to a *dispute?* Of all claims (which, as we saw, represent nearly three-fourths of reported household grievances), almost two-thirds (62.6 percent) were resisted, resulting in some 1,100 disputes. As with the transition from grievance to claim, disputing involves a low level of problem specificity, with over 80 percent of claims in the areas of landlord-tenant, postdivorce, debts, and government ending up as disputes. One outstanding exception is in the area of torts, in which dispute resolution (often involving insurance companies) is a highly routinized and institutionalized process, resulting in a low incidence of transformation from claims to disputes (or put differently, a low incidence of resistance to claims filed) (Table 5.1).

Data gathered by the Civil Litigation Research Project give us tentative answers to two remaining questions: (1) What is the apparent role of lawyers and courts in the disputing process? and (2) What is the overall success rate of disputants? How often do they win all or at least part of what they seek? Data relative to the first question suggest a surprisingly low use of both lawyers and courts in processing middle-range disputes. Table 5.2 incorporates these findings.

Overall, lawyers were used in less than one-fourth of the disputes. And this, the reader will recall, is after a severe winnowing process, with disputes representing only a fraction of the total grievances reported. The two outstanding exceptions to this finding are in the areas of postdivorce and tort disputes, but one might say that lawyers are more or less required in resolving such issues. Postdivorce issues in fact require formal court action, which in turn all but mandates the use of a lawyer, whereas tort actions are brought largely on the basis of contingency fees, which means that lawyers are ingrained in the process (Miller and Sarat, 1980–1981: 543).

Only about 11 percent of all disputes ended up in court. If one omits postdivorce actions, for which court action is required, the figure is about 9 percent. As discussed below, this is not to say that this ends the matter of court involvement; still, the reluctance to employ the formal, public disputing forums is a bit surprising, especially in these relatively significant middle-range disputes.

As seen in Table 5.2, over two-thirds (68 percent) of those respondents who pursued their claim to a dispute won at least part of if not all that they sought. As one might expect, however, success varied with the type of dispute: Tort claimants almost always ended up with something and, indeed, won all they sought in a very high percentage of cases. At the

TABLE 5.2 Dispute Outcomes, Civil Litigation Research Project

Problem	Lawyer Use (% of Disputes)	Court Filing (% of Disputes)	Success (% of Claims)
Landlord-tenant	14.7	7.3	*(a) 55.0 (b) 10.3 (c) 34.6
Tort	57.9	18.7	(a) 2.6 (b) 11.9 (c) 85.4
Discrimination	13.3	3.9	(a) 58.0 (b) 11.3 (c) 30.7
Postdivorce	76.9	59.0	(a) 37.7 (b) 35.5 (c) 26.8
Government	12.3	11.9	(a) 40.7 (b) 18.3 (c) 41.0
Consumer	20.3	3.0	(a) 37.1 (b) 15.2 (c) 47.7
Property	19.0	13.4	(a) 32.1 (b) 9.7 (c) 58.3
Debt	19.2	7.6	(a) 23.9 (b) 23.5 (c) 52.6
All disputes	23.0	11.2	(a) 32.0 (b) 13.3 (c) 54.8

*(a) = no agreement between disputants; (b) = agreement was a compromise; (c) = obtained entire claim.
SOURCE: Richard E. Miller and Austin Sarat, "Grievances, Claims, and Disputes: Assessing the Adversary Culture," *Law and Society Review,* Vol. 15, No. 3–4 (1980–1981), Table 2, as corrected. Reprinted by permission of the Law and Society Association.

lower end of the success scale are discrimination and landlord-tenant claimants; more than half of these claims resulted in zero gains. The lineaments of the disputing process in these areas differ, with tort claims, for example, being negotiated through insurance companies. The substance of the claim thus helps us to understand at least some of this variance.

Many of these findings can be usefully displayed in pyramid or funnel fashion (Figures 5.4 and 5.5). The contrasting shapes of the pyramids in Figure 5.5 illustrate the preceding point, namely, that the disputing process is structured differently, depending in part on the types or substance of the grievances or claims.

Based on the available data, how can we explain the escalation of grievances to disputes? Researchers with the Civil Litigation Research Project (CLRP) were careful to point up the limitations of their study and the numerous questions still unanswered. But when we tie together the CLRP findings with those of other research, it is possible to set forth a number of factors that help us understand this process.

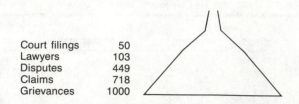

Court filings	50
Lawyers	103
Disputes	449
Claims	718
Grievances	1000

Figure 5.4   Dispute Pyramid, All Disputes Civil Litigation Research Project

SOURCE: Richard E. Miller and Austin Sarat, "Grievances, Claims, and Disputes: Assessing the Adversary Culture," *Law and Society Review,* Vol. 15, No. 3–4 (1980–1981), 544. Reprinted by permission of the Law and Society Association.

First, variables particular to the grievants can be noted. Some of us are more assertive than others, more risk-prone, and thus are more likely to have an orientation to litigation. This proclivity may, of course, vary with socioeconomic background, race, income, and other such factors. As CLRP researchers reason,

> Personality variables that may affect transformations include risk preferences, contentiousness, and feelings about personal efficacy, privacy, and independence, and attachment to justice (rule-mindedness). Both experience and personality are in turn related to social structural variables: class, ethnicity, gender, age. (Felstiner et al., 1980–1981: 640).

Second, the type of grievance weighs in rather heavily in the transformation process. This variable was discussed above. The legal system, both formal and informal, encourages some types of escalation (postdivorce, e.g.) while discouraging others (e.g., discrimination). CLRP researchers frequently returned to this factor as a major explanatory variable.

Finally, a host of external factors helps to account for the transformation of grievances to disputes. These include the relationship of the parties, the role of key representa-

Figure 5.5   Dispute Pyramids: Three Specific Patterns Civil Litigation Research Project

SOURCE: Richard E. Miller and Austin Sarat, "Grievances, Claims, and Disputes: Assessing the Adversary Culture," *Law and Society Review,* Vol. 15, No. 3–4 (1980–1981), 544. Reprinted by permission of the Law and Society Association.

	Tort	Discrimination	Postdivorce
Court filings	38	8	451
Lawyers	116	29	588
Disputes	201	216	765
Claims	857	294	879
Grievances	1000	1000	1000

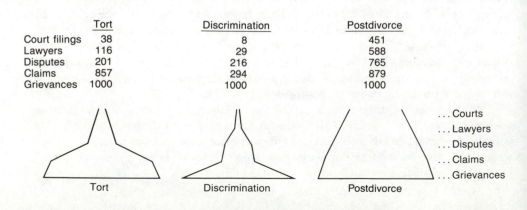

... Courts
... Lawyers
... Disputes
... Claims
... Grievances

Tort   Discrimination   Postdivorce

tives (lawyers or other counselors), and cultural norms pertinent to disputing (members of some subcultures in American society, for example, seem less likely to go to court than others).

Overall, perhaps the most striking finding emerging from recent dispute-processing research is the small number and percentage of felt grievances that ultimately end up in court: an average of only about 5 percent in the CLRP study. Thus, although most previous research has been attentive to formal modes of adjudication, the great bulk of problems experienced by Americans are processed in largely informal ways (or are forgotten), underscoring the significance of these newer research forays. If the CLRP had included grievances worth less than $1,000, the incidence of informal dispute processing might well have been much greater.

However, that courts in the formal sense appear only on the fringes of the disputing process should not be taken as a reliable measure of their importance. Scholars sensitive to the nuances of informal dispute processing have called to our attention the "shadow" phenomenon (Galanter, 1981: 6; Mnookin and Kornhauser, 1979), whereby bargaining in precourt settings is heavily influenced by the prospect of formal adjudication should informal methods fail. As one scholar suggested, this may be "the true meaning of Holmes' definition of law as a prediction of court behavior" (Shapiro, 1978).

Put a bit differently, it may be that the chief input of courts for dispute processing is the award of "bargaining chips" of sorts, which guide the disputants along legally acceptable paths of resolution. As explained by Marc Galanter (1981),

> The principle contribution of courts . . . is providing a background of norms and procedures against which negotiations and regulation in both private and governmental settings take place. The contribution includes . . . communication to prospective litigants of what might transpire if one of them sought a judicial resolution. Courts [also] communicate . . . possible remedies, and estimates of the difficulty, certainty, and costs of securing particular outcomes. (6)

Although one may grant the validity of this view—that the role of courts is still quite significant in dispute processing—it remains true that the dispute-processing research has given us a much broader and more fluid picture of their role than we have had in the past.

THE FLOW OF CIVIL LITIGATION IN THE STATES

If state courts process the great mass of civil cases filed each year, what is the nature of that caseload? What types of disputes does one find among these findings? What trends can be detected? And finally, what can be said of the apparent increases in the *level* of litigation in America?

We begin to gain some insight into the caseload simply through a quick review of the raw data provided by the National Center for State Courts (NCSC). In 1988 the 17 million civil case filings reported in state trial courts of all types were made up largely of the categories of torts (defined roughly as injuries or wrongs allegedly committed against persons or property either through commission of a wrongful act or omission of a required act) (National Center for State Courts, 1988: 8), contracts, real property rights, small claims, domestic relations, mental health, and estates. Drawing civil case filing data from 16 state trial courts—13 of general and 3 of limited jurisdiction—which reported complete data for 1988, we find that torts constituted only 7.4 percent of total civil filings, whereas contract cases made up 23 percent and real property matters another 12.7 percent (Ostrom, 1990).

In state courts of limited jurisdiction, flooded as they are with minor traffic matters, civil cases make up, on the average, only about 12 percent of their filings. However, this figure varies widely from state to state, with some states processing the bulk of civil disputes through these courts. In this case, the great majority of the civil disputes are in the broad category of small claims—debt collection (often dominant), landlord-tenant issues, consumer complaints, minor auto accident cases, and the like. Indeed, the small-claims type of dispute processing so dominates the civil caseload in these courts that we present below a more detailed description of its judicial process. In the few states in which small claims are processed in trial courts of general jurisdiction, this type of case also dominates in the civil caseload in these courts.

In state courts of general jurisdiction, where civil cases constitute, on the average, about a third of the caseload, family matters, primarily divorce and postdivorce issues, normally represent the largest portion of the dockets (Council on the Role of Courts, 1984: 38). Data supplied by the NCSC reveal that in 11 states reporting complete data on civil case filings in general jurisdiction trial courts (but excluding the three states in which small claims are processed in these courts), domestic relations cases constitute, on the average, about 52 percent of the civil caseloads (Table 5.3). Torts and contracts make up another 33 percent of the filings in these 11 states' general jurisdiction courts, and estate, mental health and administrative agency filings round out their caseloads. In sum, family-related disputes, small-claims issues of various types, commercial matters, and personal injury cases can be said to make up the bulk of the civil caseload in state trial courts.

Although banner newspaper headlines paint the civil judicial process as one involving gigantic claims of hundreds of millions of dollars (Broder, 1986), reality suggests a somewhat different picture. As already noted, the vast majority of civil cases are heard in state courts, and there it is unusual (only about 10 percent of the cases) to see awards in excess of $25,000. Indeed, in 1978, the median civil case in state courts of general jurisdiction involved amounts of about $4,500 (Kritzer, 1984: 2). Other scholars analyzing data from the CLRP have suggested that the "'modal lawsuit' involves a claim of no more than $10,000" (Council on the Role of Courts: 61).

Long-term trends in the types of civil cases handled by state trial courts are rather clear, these findings emerging from several recent studies. Overall, in the last century contract and real property cases tended to dominate state court dockets, whereas within the last 50 to 75 years there has been a decided shift to family-type issues (primarily divorce and divorce-related disputes) along with a significant, long-term rise in tort cases, largely automobile injury disputes. Of course these docket trends reflect a changing America. With the transition from a rural, land-oriented society to our present postindustrial status, along with changing lifestyles and family values, the issues Americans wished to litigate changed accordingly (Galanter, 1983: 42–43).

Of more current concern is the *level*, along with what we might call the *intensity* as well as the *novelty*, of civil litigation handled by our courts, especially at the state level. For over two decades now Americans have been bombarded with claims that our courts

TABLE 5.3 Civil Filings in Selected State Courts of General Jurisdiction, 1988

Court	Tort	Contract	Domestic Relations	Estate	Mental Health	Administrative Agency
Alaska Superior	937	1,286	7,631	1,543	959	310
Arizona Superior	20,490	25,805	35,688	10,300	811	−2
Colorado District	4,506	17,314	34,499	8,857	3,378	525
Florida Circuit	35,986	59,812	209,942	67,090	14,473	−2
Maine Superior	1,776	1,402	1,596	−2	−2	339
Montana District	1,541	1,367	7,135	3,423	661	529
Nevada District	3,855	4,794	22,819	1,148	2	1,097
New York Superior & County	53,104	20,695	68,824	−2	−2	−2
North Dakota District	552	3,653	10,192	40	−2	354
Tennessee Circuit	13,501	9,018	62,430	9,342	1,588	10,547
Washington Superior	8,746	13,970	46,974	16,431	9,138	1,244

−2: This case type does not fall within the subject matter jurisdiction of this particular court
SOURCE: Data supplied by Brian J. Ostrom, staff associate, Court Statistice Project, National Center for State Courts, March 26, 1990. Reprinted with permission.

are heavily overworked, largely because of the civil "litigation explosion" in the United States. We have been struck with the disease of "hyperlexis," notes one observer (Manning, 1977: 767), wherein we can hardly "tolerate more than five minutes of frustration without submitting to the temptation to sue" (Auerbach, 1976: 42).

Everyone sues everyone for everything, so the charges go:

- Mothers sue officials and businesses for the right to breast feed in public.
- A child sues his parents for having been improperly reared.
- A suit is brought over an alleged unfair call in a football game.
- In the wake of the Lee Marvin Palimony case, rejected mistresses now sue their former mates. (Galanter, 1983: 8–11)

This mad rush to litigate, it is charged, is hopelessly clogging our courts with trivial suits brought by greedy lawyers hoping to eke out a living. Laments *USA Today* (1986), "The greed has turned the temple of justice, long a hallowed place, into a pigsty. The time has come to clean it up!" (12A). No less a personage than Chief Justice Warren Burger (1977) joined, if he did not help to initiate, the chorus of condemnation of this generation's litigation explosion. As early as 1977 he remarked on the "inherently litigious nature of Americans," and he deplored the notion that litigation "is the cure-all for every problem that besets us." How much truth is there to these assertions? What do the data actually show?

The first place one might look for support of the hyperlexis hypothesis is in state trial court filings, where some 98 percent of America's civil litigation takes place. But although the findings are somewhat mixed, there is scant evidence here of a litigation explosion. In his study of the St. Louis courts of general jurisdiction from 1820 to 1970, McIntosh (1980–1981: 828, Fig. 1) found that the litigation rate (cases filed per capita) in 1970 was *only about half* of what it had been in the early part of the nineteenth century. And although the research revealed a steady rise in case filings in these courts since 1900, McIntosh reports that "the litigation rate has remained fairly stable during the last six decades."

Authors of a similar longitudinal study of trial court civil litigation in two Bay Area counties in California from 1890 to 1970 report similar findings: There is no evidence of a precipitious rise in litigation rates since the turn of the century, and in some instances, there are apparent declines in the rate at which citizens sue one another in state trial courts (Friedman and Percival, 1976: 292).

Although data from the more remote past—say, from American colonial times—are difficult to obtain and certainly open to varying interpretations, the available figures would suggest anything but a reluctance on the part of our forebears to go to law. Historical research unearthed by Marc Galanter (1983: 41) reveals that in Accomack County, Virginia, for example, litigation rates in the year 1639 appeared to be more than four times those found in any county for which we have contemporary data (Curtis, 1977: 287). Studies of court records in Essex County, Massachusetts, from the mid-seventeenth century reveal similarly high levels of litigation (Koenig, 1979: xi, xii). Although such rates may well constitute unreliable indicators of litigiousness, other measures or rates computed for more recent periods are no better in lending support to claims that we are an overly litigious society.

For instance, it is sometimes argued that high levels of litigiousness have come on us fairly recently, particularly in the 1970s and 1980s, and are thus not reflected in pre-1970 data. But again, this argument does not appear to be supported by the empirical evidence. National Center for State Courts' statisticians compiled court case filing figures for state trial courts of both general and limited jurisdiction for 1978 and again for 1981 and 1984. (National Center for State Courts, 1986). A summary of the data as related to the issue of American litigiousness was best stated by Marc Galanter (1986) of the University of Wisconsin School of Law:[2]

> The litigation explosion view would lead us to expect this [1978–1984] to be a period of steeply rising caseloads. But the NCSC data . . . portrays nothing that resembles the assumed explosion. Filings of civil cases surged faster than population from 1978 to 1981, but from 1981 to 1984 . . . per capita rates of filing actually declined. . . . Filings in small claims courts . . . also fell. Tort filings rose steadily, but over the six year period they grew by 9% while population grew by 8%. (6)

In addition to historical data on rates of litigation, recent or remote, foreign litigation rates are often cited in support of the hyperlexis claim. Thus, America's disputing process is often compared unfavorably with that of other nations, where, it is alleged, citizens are less contentious and much more amenable to the pacific settlement of grievances. But again, the data, such as they are, do not bear out the claim. In some roughly comparable systems, such as Germany and Sweden, available figures indeed suggest lower civil filing rates than in the United States, but similar data also indicate that Americans are about in the same litigation range as England, Australia, Denmark, and New Zealand (Galanter, 1983: 55).

Writers often look longingly to Japan as having the prototype system of dispute processing. With far fewer lawyers than we (see Chapter 4), fewer judges, and a lower litigation rate, Japan is said to be the model to which we should aspire. American-Japanese scholars who have taken a closer look at the Japanese data come away with a much more cautious set of conclusions. Although space does not permit a full discussion of these findings, two points can be noted.

First, it is argued that all recent Japanese regimes have supported a deliberate constriction of adjudicative alternatives, forcing disputants into conciliation and other quasi-private and private dispute-resolution forums. Such measures reflect "a concern on the part of the governing elite that litigation was destructive to a hierarchial social order based upon personal relationships" (Haley, 1978: 373). Thus, although it is true that the Japanese use courts less frequently than do Americans, there is every indication in their recent history that this is an artifact of artificially imposed restrictions on their effective ability to sue.

Second, the usual contrast cited between the number of American and Japanese lawyers is to some extent valid, but it is also somewhat misleading. Twelve thousand Japanese lawyers, the usual figure mentioned, is the number of *bengoshi,* who are in-court attorneys similar to the English barrister. But Japan has a number of other law occupations, such as in-house legal advisers and administrative scriveners, whose work would be performed by lawyers in the United States. One estimate has it that the true number of Japanese lawyers may be nearly 95,000, which, per capita, would mean that Japan would rank in the low or middle ranges of comparative lawyer:population ratios (Galanter, 1988: 28). Also, a severe limit on the admission of law graduates to practice artificially reduces the number of otherwise certifiable *bengoshi.* Per capita, Japan appears to graduate more than two times as many lawyers as do American law schools. But whereas nearly three-fourths of our law students pass the bar exam, in Japan the comparable figure is 1.7 percent (Haley, 1978: 386).

The point of our discussion is not that as Americans we can boast of an ideal civil judicial process free of abuse or overloading. Rather, we are merely asserting that the loud accusation of our litigation mania heard throughout the land does not appear to be supported by the bulk of the evidence and that we may be a good bit less assertive and contentious than many commentators have suggested.

Let us recall some of the data presented earlier on the disputing and transformation process. On the average, respondents in American households perceived grievances at the rate of only about 11.8 percent, with claims being pursued in about 70 percent of the cases. An Australian scholar, Jeffrey FitzGerald (1983: 24, 31), replicated the CLRP's survey in the state of Victoria. He found that his countryfolk were, on the average, more willing both to perceive a problem as a grievance (12.8 percent) and to pursue it to a claim (77 percent). Although there was a somewhat greater tendency on the part of Americans to take their claims to court, that finding, according to FitzGerald, "amounts to only 10.7 percent of disputants. . ." (35). At the very least, the Australian data, in contrast to the U.S. findings, lend little if any support to the hyperlexis hypothesis. Indeed, if Americans are litigation crazy, so are the Australians, for the central conclusion from the FitzGerald research is the striking similarity between the American and Australian transformation process.

Taking the argument a bit further, it may well be that, as in Japan, American elites recently confronted with unaccustomed legal challenges are largely responsible for the cry of alarm over current patterns of civil litigation, along with the now widespread movement toward informal modes of settling disputes (Abel, 1982). Businesses facing product liability suits, physicians and hospitals being held to account for their work, and college professors being called to task for irresponsible behavior—such are some of America's elites who have sounded the alarm: As Galanter (1988) remarked,

> The kind of litigation that once dominated the system—lawsuits to enforce market relations—has given way to tort, civil rights, and public-law cases that "correct" the market. It is litigation aimed "upwards"—by outsiders, clients, and dependents *against authorities and managers of established institutions*—that excites most of the reproach of this litigious society. (30; emphasis added).

When one soberly reflects on the CLRP data pointing up the relatively high propensity of Americans to live with wrongs, hurts, and injustices because they feel nothing much can be done, it may well be that far from being an overly litigious people, we are facing, as anthropologist Laura Nader (1980) has suggested,

> . . . a mass phenomenon in which large segments of the population, reflective of all socio-economic groups, are exposed to low-profile, undramatic, petty exploitation that is ruinous of the quality of democratic life. Despite our GNP, access to purveyors of justice is more readily available in some underdeveloped parts of the world that it is in this country. (xix)

To round out our description of the civil judicial process, we have selected two brief case studies that bring the reader closer to the everyday realities of the process. The area of small claims was chosen because by all accounts such cases numerically represent the largest single category of civil proceedings in our state courts. And we selected proceedings in medical malpractice as our second case study because aside from divorce and postdivorce litigation, tort actions in this area typify the new wave of litigation, which has been said to represent our overly litigious society.

Small Claims

For as long as we have had courts Americans have exhibited an ambivalent attitude toward small-claims cases. At times we have perceived them as troublesome issues involving petty, private disputes of no major relevance to the law, while at other times we have seen them as deep-felt grievances of the "common person" whose processing might well be taken as a barometer of the health of our sociolegal system (Steele, 1981: 295–296). Throughout American legal history reformers have periodically attempted to simplify the judicial process to realize our age-old dream of "everyone his or her own lawyer"—to create a simple and speedy dispute-resolution process understandable and workable by the ordinary citizen. The last major wave or movement in this direction before our own generation came as part of the progressive movement of about 1890–1930.

As part of the progressive agenda, legal reforms brought into being civil legal aid societies as well as small-claims and/or conciliation courts. The expense, delay, complexity, inaccessibility, and injustices of the regular courts were all to be ameliorated, if not entirely swept away, through the creation of small-claims courts, to which the average citizen could turn for easy and inexpensive resolution of grievances. The specific characteristics of this new approach were simplified procedures; lower cost; no or at least a low level of attorney participation; few appeals; an enhanced role for court clerks to guide litigants; a broader role for judges to draw out the key elements of the case; fully qualified and fully paid judges; and where possible, the use of conciliation (Steele, 1981: 330–335). Clearly, the focus of reform was to be *procedural,* to the end that ordinary citizens could benefit from enhanced access to an easy, workable mode of dispute processing. With such a procedural focus, small claims could be, and were, grafted onto existing courts, there being no need in some jurisdictions for the creation of separate tribunals.

By 1940 at least 19 states had created statewide small-claims courts of varying structures and jurisdiction, and by 1972 a survey of these courts and procedures revealed that only 9 states were without some form of small-claims processing (Yngvesson and Hennessey, 1975: 224). In a very real sense, the small-claims movement had succeeded, such a court or judicial proceeding being an ongoing part of the judicial system in virtually every state and city. But there were near-fatal flaws in their conceptualization, flaws that eventually led to the perversion of their function.

First, the assumption had always been that as "courts for the poor," the claims would be relatively simple and honest, coming from that most noble of all characters of American folklore, "the working-class poor." In practice, it meant that these courts were created with a built-in bias for the plaintiff, the claims being assumed to be valid. Second, although ordinary court proceedings were to be "informalized," the small-claims model retained the basic, though watered-down, adversarial process. And inasmuch as the adversarial model contains the assumption of the perfect equality of the litigants (ensured through the kindly interposition of the judge), there was an implicit assumption of the political neutrality of the parties to the litigation—that is, the absence of the possibility of any net social gain by one party over the other. As later researchers remarked, this faulty conceptualization meant that "the court bore within it the seeds of its gradual transformation" or, depending on one's viewpoint, one might say "destruction" (Yngvesson and Hennessey, 1975: 227).[3]

Few judicial procedures have been so widely studied as have small-claims processes. Much of this research has been empirical, providing a relatively rich collection of data useful in understanding the realities of the small-claims process. The first point usually made in reports of these field studies is that far from serving the needs of the "honest poor," the ideal litigant assumed by progressive reformers, these courts have become forums for the business community to collect debts from the working poor with ease and economy (Yngvesson and Hennessey, 1975: 235). For example, a study undertaken by Consumer's Union of 107 randomly selected complaints filed with the Hartford, Connecticut, small-claims court found *1* case involving auto damage, *1* consumer complaint against a business establishment, *1* tax matter, and *1* malicious damage claim, whereas there were *103* debt collection cases (National Institute for Consumer Justice, 1972: Appendix B, 452). Similarly, in a general review of research on 14 separate small-claims courts throughout the nation, in only 2 of these tribunals did nonbusiness claimants make up more than 42 percent of the plaintiffs, whereas individuals appeared as defendants in over three-fourths of the contests in all but 2 of these courts (Yngvesson and Hennessey, 1975: 236).

More important is the pattern of repeated use of these courts by the business community for debt collection. A 1972 study in Cambridge, Massachusetts, for example, found that the principal and recurrent users of the small-claims court were the New England Telephone Company, Macy Furniture Company, and the local hospital. In other cities the most frequent plaintiffs were a local government agency; the county; local utility companies; and quite frequently, collection agencies representing hospitals and physicians (Yngvesson and Hennessey, 1975: 236–240).

A second major finding from small-claims research is that the plaintiff almost always wins, and quite frequently by default. Research on 14 small-claims operations nationwide revealed that the plaintiff was victorious in 85 percent of the cases, and in just under half of these, the case went by default, the defendant failing to show up in court. Researchers have repeatedly pointed out that default judgments are not to be explained solely, or even primarily, because the plaintiff has an unassailable case. Sometimes summonses are not received (Caplovitz, 1971), or it may be difficult for the defendant to leave work and travel to an out-of-the-way court (Moulton, 1969: 1664). In fact, aside from the difficulty of debt collection once the plaintiff wins a court award, the most frequently mentioned complaint of litigants of small-claims courts in two Ohio counties in 1972 was the problem of getting time off from work to appear at the trial (Hollingsworth et al., 1973: 526). Some studies have suggested that the unlikelihood of defendants resisting debt claims is relied on by merchants in their selling and credit practices ("Small Claims Courts and the Poor," 1969: 493).

Marc Galanter (1974) in his now classic article entitled "Why the 'Haves' Come Out Ahead" best explained small-claims outcomes. Juxtaposing the litigants as "Repeat Players" versus "One-Shotters," Galanter posited an impressive lists of advantages enjoyed by the former. Repeat players frequently use courts and are familiar with the proceedings (if not with the judge, clerk, and other court personnel). They benefit from their superior knowledge of the law on the subject, such knowledge being a direct business concern. Like the professional gambler, repeat players can play the odds. Out of a great many cases, the loss of a few claims is no serious matter. They are thus in a position to develop a long-range strategy, wherein the rules of the litigation itself become the chief prize: If local judicial doctrine favorable to creditors can be won, that is worth many, many individual cases. In contrast, one-shotters lose all in one toss of the dice in their individual cases. Long-term strategy for them is no option (100–101). These factors, among others, help us to understand these one-sided outcomes in small-claims courts.

As for the proceeding itself, research reveals that the small-claims process is very likely to be "quick and dirty." Proceedings are rushed, often taking little more than six or seven minutes, permitting little time, indeed, to hear both sides of the case. Defendants appear to be confused and lost, playing the role of the "outsider" in a proceeding dominated by "insider" experts. Moreover, the ruling may well be little more than an endorsement of private conversations that take place on the "edges" of the court itself. Thus, whether formalized or not, the reality of court proceedings is as much conciliatory as it is adjudicatory, as that term is usually understood.

Based on such findings, which are repeated in almost lock-step fashion by most other studies, it is hardly surprising that scholars have labeled the modern small-claims process a failure, at least as measured by the intent of its progressive founders. In another sense, however, it is perhaps even less surprising that the control of these courts should fall into the hands of creditors, who use them as convenient and relatively inexpensive collection agencies. If a sociopolitical conception of courts means anything, it certainly implies the domination of the judicial process and its outcomes by established political-legal forces within the community. As we have learned in so many other contexts, the structure and process of courts means less than the sociopolitical milieu within which they operate.

Medical Malpractice: Obstetrics and Gynecology Cases

Our second case study is in the area of torts, an almost indefinable category of civil actions that in the broadest sense can be thought of as encompassing virtually all civil wrongs other than a breach of contract (Sherman, 1987: 418). From the early twentieth century, tort law has been dominated by automobile accident cases. These, together with other personal injury disputes, property damage, and wrongful death issues, make up the bulk of what we call torts. In a statistical study of 26 state courts of general jurisdiction in 1987, the National Center for State Courts (1989: 29) found torts to make up an average of 10.3 percent of the civil caseloads, and a survey of 7 state·courts of limited jurisdiction fixed the average tort figure at 5.5 percent of civil cases.

Hence, although not accounting for a larger sector of civil law, torts include a number of substantive issues (product liability and professional malpractice matters, e.g.) that represent the continuing allegations of litigation mania in our country. It is for this reason that we provide a brief glance at one of these areas: medical malpractice in obstetrics and gynecology cases (ob-gyn).

For some two decades a cry of alarm has been heard from the medical community over the malpractice crisis. Malpractice is often seen as the most serious issue facing medical practitioners, particularly in ob-gyn ("Beyond Tort Reform," 1987: 827–828). In his presidential address to the Central Association of Obstetricians and Gynecologists in Detroit in 1984, Dr. Kenneth J. Vander Kolk (1985: 140) asked his medical colleagues, will the "unlimited classes of graduating lawyers . . . increase the number involved in unbridled, insensitive, inconsiderate, and unethical litigation?" He went on to complain that "physicians are the logical scapegoats and are an easy prey for the hustling attorney who initiates a lawsuit." (142). Thus, true to form, the legal profession and legal system are blamed for the crisis; seldom the professional practitioner. Juries are said to decide cases irrationally, giving excessively large awards to undeserving patients. Advanced but unproven medical techniques, rather than physician error, are said to be the cause of much medical malpractice litigation. Driven by such beliefs, pressures are mounted to bring about major reform in our entire tort system (*National Law Journal,* 1987: 1).

Such are the claims, but what are the facts? Are aggrieved medical patients quick to name, blame, claim, and push for unconscionably high jury awards? Has litigation run wild in this area? Or does the transformation process from grievance, or potential grievance, to disputing to the filing of a civil claim more closely resemble the now familiar patterns already described?

To understand the processing of disputes in this area it is useful to begin with the same baseline used in the CLRP, namely, the universe of at-risk cases. But as with all other types of grievances, it is impossible to say just how many potential, legally action-able medical errors are committed in a given year, a given state, or a selected field of medical practice. In the absence of more empirical research, we can only estimate.

Data supplied in a recent study by the American Bar Foundation (ABF) suggest that as many as 1 in 20 medical decisions may be made erroneously, with some studies placing the figure much higher, perhaps as many as 1 in 4 (Daniels and Andrews, 1989: 165). Using the more conservative 5 percent estimate and taking the state of Texas as an example, with 295,000 live births in 1983, there would be, presumably, some 14,750 medical errors. Daniels and Andrews have suggested that no more than 10 percent of such aggrieved patients may be expected to file a claim, probably fewer. For ob-gyn cases in Texas, then, a 10 percent ratio would have been expected to produce some 1,475 civil filings for malpractice. In fact, however, there were only 219 claims filed in all ob-gyn cases in the state that year, or only about 1.5 percent of possible suits. Even if researchers have overestimated the incidence of medical error by 100 percent (giving us a ratio of only 1:40 rather than 1:20) one could still predict nearly 750 malpractice suits in ob-gyn filed in Texas in 1983, whereas less than a third of even that reduced estimate were actually filed.

Based on these estimates, then, ob-gyn cases can be represented by a pyramid with extremely flat sides, the ratio of actual court filings to possible claims being about 1 for every 150 medical errors. Such a ratio, or even half this ratio, can hardly be said to represent litigation mania on the part of aggrieved patients. Rather, what we find is a relatively timid patient population hesitant to perceive a grievance and, if perceived, highly reluctant to resort to litigation, formal or informal, to assuage their losses. As researchers Daniels and Andrews (1989) concluded, "Most patients who are injured by medical error will not pursue a claim. . . . The most common responses to patient dissat-isfaction were to 'lump it' (do nothing) or simply to change doctors" (166).

Stated differently, the transformation process here is quite similar to that seen in other areas of civil law (CLRP) and negates claims of extreme litigiousness. In fact, a com-parison of the grievance-to-court claim pyramid in tort cases in general to that just described for ob-gyn cases suggests that these medical grievants are less than half as likely to go to court as are tort victims in general.

What happens to these cases once they are filed? From our general knowledge of the civil litigation process we might expect most to be settled out of court, with few going to trial. And indeed, this is the case. Estimates of the percentage of filings of ob-gyn cases settled before trial are from 70 to 90 percent, about the same proportion as in other areas of both the civil and the criminal law. To what extent does the plaintiff win in these cases? Again, estimates vary with the particular study and jurisdiction, but in general less than half result in some payment to the patient. A study by the National Association of Insurance Commissioners in 1980 found that only 46 percent of insurance claims in malpractice cases resulted in a payment to the claimant, whereas in Texas only 20 percent of the ob-gyn claims were settled with a payment (Daniels and Andrews, 1989: 166–67).

The percentage of cases going to a jury trial, then, is quite small, usually under 10 percent. However, jury verdicts cast a long shadow over the contours of future bargaining, so it is useful to examine briefly jury outcomes in this area.

The ABF researchers tabulated the particulars of 24,625 civil jury verdicts in 46 state trial court jurisdictions in 11 states in the years 1981–1985. Of these, 7.7 percent (1,885) were medical malpractice cases, and of this group 364 cases were identified as ob-gyn cases (19.3 percent of malpractice cases and 1.5 percent of all civil jury cases).

If one defines success as the award of at least one dollar by the jury, one finds that the patients filing these cases and going to jury trials did not fare well. The success rate of plaintiffs in general malpractice was 32.4 percent; in obstetrics and gynecology cases it was slightly higher, at 36.8 percent. This rate may be contrasted with the success rate of civil jury outcomes in general, which was 57 percent (Daniels and Martin, 1986: 332). Thus, contrary to the nationwide outcry over the malpractice "crisis," juries are not overly anxious to find for the medical patient in these cases.

Researchers Daniels and Andrews (1989) dug into their data to answer at least two further questions: First, was there evidence of irrational jury verdicts, or did the jury decisions bear a logical relationship to the type and severity of the injury inflicted by the medical practitioners? Second, were these medical errors associated with, if not caused by, the newer, untested technologies, as alleged by many physicians, or were they more closely correlated with old and well-established procedures inappropriately applied? Measuring the severity of injury (from death to emotional injury only) on a four-point scale, these researchers found that the jury was somewhat more likely to find for the plaintiff if the injury were more severe. And again contrary to claims of the medical profession, juries tended to react most harshly against defendants when the injury was associated with the older, more well-established technologies.

One particularly poignant example illustrating both of these points was the use of oxytocin (usual trade name: *Pitocin*) to induce labor. The dangers of this well-known drug had been widely publicized in physicians' reference works and journals for several decades. Of the 16 jury trials involving the alleged misuse of oxytocin (when the drug was contraindicated by the medical literature), the plaintiff was successful in 14 (87.5 percent). (Daniels and Andrews, 1989: 190). This rate may be contrasted with a 45 percent success rate for all labor and delivery jury trials in the sample and the 37 percent success rate for all ob-gyn cases. Of these 16 cases, *all* led to permanent injury or death. As the ABF researchers conclude, "In the oxytocin cases . . . juries appear to have responded in no uncertain terms to the misuse of an old, established technology whose limitations and contraindications were well known and widely disseminated" (191).

Do the ABF data support the claim that monetary jury awards in medical malpractice, and particularly ob-gyn cases, have become excessive? This, of course, is similar to the question of whether the glass of water is half empty or half full. But as weighed against the background of the average or, more precisely, the median jury award in these nearly 26,000 cases, how did the medical awards compare? The median jury award in all of these civil cases was only $25,000 (1985), whereas in ob-gyn cases it was much higher, $390,000. However, in view of the seriousness of these cases, nearly 60 percent involving a permanent injury or death and in view of the tendency of juries to award the higher settlements to the more severely injured, this figure might not seem inordinately high.

In conclusion, researchers have found that patients are still highly reluctant to bring legal action against their physicians and hospitals, even when medical error seems apparent. And when they do sue, the physician usually wins the case. In the few but significant cases decided by juries, capricious or random decision making does not appear to be the rule. Rather, there is a relationship between the severity of injury (as well as the type of medical procedure) and jury awards. In the relatively infrequent cases in which the plaintiff wins, the amount of jury awards, especially in ob-gyn cases, are high but perhaps reasonable in relation to the seriousness of the injury. Thus, as with the cry of hyperlexis in general, little if any empirical evidence from medical malpractice cases thus far discovered can be said to support charges of a litigation explosion. Rather, it seems more likely that as Galanter (1983: 61–71) remarked, it is the case of entrenched elites complaining because they are being forced to the bar of public accountability.

CONCLUSION

For too long we have tended to ignore the civil judicial process, instead focusing inordinate attention on the attractions of criminal law. Research by Galanter (1974, 1983), Miller and Sarat (1980–1981), Ross (1970), and a host of others has brought new excitement to the study of civil law and has called attention to the "landscape of disputing," which heretofore had been almost unknown to students of the American judiciary. Although we have long understood the importance of pretrial bargaining in criminal cases, it is only recently that we are beginning to understand the world of private and semiprivate dispute processing and settlement in millions of civil matters in our society. Research findings presented here should help to alert readers to the importance of this fast-developing field of scholarship.

NOTES

1. Much of the following discussion is drawn from the findings of this research, particularly as presented in "Special Issue on Dispute Processing and Civil Litigation," *Law and Society Review,* Vol. 15, No. 3–4 (1980–1981).
2. The instant presentation has relied heavily on Marc Galanter's research and analysis of the issue of American litigiousness. See particularly 1983: 4–71; 1986: 3–39.
3. This article is an especially useful summary and analysis of the major research findings on small-claims courts and is frequently referred to in this narrative.

REFERENCES

Abel, Richard L., ed. 1982. *The Politics of Informal Justice,* 2 vols. New York: Academic Press.
Administrative Office of the U.S. Courts. 1980, 1988. *Annual Report of the Administrative Office of the U.S. Courts.* Washington, DC: U.S. Government Printing Office.
Auerbach, Jerold S. 1976. "A Plague of Lawyers." 253 *Harpers* 37.
"Beyond Tort Reform." 1987. 257 *Journal of the American Medical Association* 827.
Blumberg, Abraham. 1967. "The Practice of Law as a Confidence Game: Organizational Co-option of a Profession." 1 *Law and Society Review* 15.
Broder, Ivy E. 1986. "Characteristics of Million Dollar Awards: Jury Verdicts and Final Disbursements." 11 *Justice System Journal* 349.

Burger, Warren E. 1977. May 27. "Remarks at the American Bar Association Minor Dispute Resolution Conference (cited in Galanter, 1983).

Caplovitz, David. 1971. "Debtors in Default," in Bureau of Applied Social Research, *Report*. New York: Columbia University.

Council on the Rule of Courts. 1984. *The Role of Courts in American Society*. St. Paul, MN: West Publishing.

Curtis, George B. 1977. "The Colonial County Court, Social Forum and Legislative Precedent." 85 *Virginia Magazine of History and Biography* 274.

Daniels, Stephen, and Lori Andrews. 1989. "The Shadow of the Law: Jury Decisions in Obstetrics and Gynecology Cases." In Victoria P. Rostow and Roger J. Bulger, eds., *Medical Professional Liability and the Delivery of Obstetrical Care: An Interdisciplinary Review,* Vol. II. Washington, DC: National Academy Press.

Daniels, Stephen, and Joanne Martin. 1986. "Jury Verdicts and the 'Crisis' in Civil Justice." 11 *Justice System Journal* 321.

Felstiner, William L. F., Richard L. Abel, and Austin Sarat. 1980–1981. "The Emergence and Transformation of Disputes: Naming, Blaming, Claiming. . . ." 15 *Law and Society Review* 631.

FitzGerald, Jeffrey. 1983. "Grievances, Disputes and Outcomes: A Comparison of Australia and the United States." 1 *Law in Context* 15.

Friedman, Lawrence M., and Robert V. Percival. 1976. "A Tale of Two Courts: Litigation in Alameda and San Benito Counties." 10 *Law and Society Review* 267.

Galanter, Marc. 1974. "Why the 'Haves' Come Out Ahead: Speculations on the Limits of legal Change." 9 *Law and Society Review* 95.

Galanter, Marc. 1981. "Justice in Many Rooms: Courts, Private Ordering, and Indigenous Law." *Journal of Legal Pluralism* 1.

Galanter, Marc. 1983. "Reading the Landscape of Disputes: What We Know and Don't Know (and Think We Know) About Our Allegedly Contentious and Litigious Society." 31 *UCLA Law Review* 4.

Galanter, Marc. 1986. "The Day After the Litigation Explosion." 46 *Maryland Law Review* 3.

Galanter, Marc. 1988. "Beyond the Litigation Panic." In Walter Olson, ed., *New Directions in Liability Law*. New York: Academy of Political Science.

Haley, John O. 1978. "The Myth of the Reluctant Litigant." 4 *Journal of Japanese Studies* 359.

Hollingsworth, Robert J., William B. Feldman, and David C. Clark. 1973. "The Ohio Small Claims Court: An Empirical Study." 42 *University of Cincinnati Law Review* 479.

Jacob, Herbert. 1984. *Justice in America: Courts, Lawyers and the Judicial Process*. Boston: Little, Brown.

"Jurisdiction of Small Claims Coiurts." 1923. 11 *California Law Review* 276.

Kawashima, Takeyoshi. 1963. "Dispute Resolution in Contemporary Japan." In Arthur Taylor VonMehren, ed., *Law in Japan: The Legal Order in a Changing Society*. Cambridge, MA: Harvard University Press.

Koenig, David Thomas. 1979. *Law and Society in Puritan Massachusetts: Exxex County, 1629–1692*. Chapel Hill: University of North Carolina Press.

Kritzer, Herbert M. 1984. "Formal and Informal Theories of Negotiations: Paths to Understanding the Settlement Process in Ordinary Litigation." Paper presented at the meeting of the Law and Society Association, Boston.

McIntosh, Wayne. 1980–81. "150 Years of Litigation and Dispute Settlement: A Court Tale." 15 *Law and Society Review* 823.

Manning, Bayless. 1977. "Hyperlexis: Our National Disease," 71 *Northwestern University Law Review* 767.

Mather, Lynn, and Barbara Yngvesson. 1980–1981 "Language, Audience and the Transformation of Disputes," 15 *Law and Society Review* 775.

Miller, Richard E., and Austin Sarat. 1980–81. "Grievances, Claims, and Disputes: Assessing the Adversary Culture," 15 *Law and Society Review* 525.

Mnookin, Robert H., and Lewis Kornhauser. 1979. "Bargaining in the Shadow of the Law: The Case of Divorce." 88 *Yale Law Journal* 950.

Moulton, Beatrice A. 1969. "Note: The Persecution and Intimidation of Low-Income Litigants as Performed by the Small Claims Court in California," 21 *Stanford Law Review* 1657.

Nader, Laura, ed. 1980. *No Access to Law: Alternatives to the American Judicial System.* New York: Academic Press.

National Center for State Courts. 1986. *A Preliminary Examination of Available Civil and Criminal Trend Data in State Trial Courts for 1978, 1981, and 1984.* Williamsburg, VA: National Center for State Courts.

National Center for State Courts. 1989–1990. *State Court Caseload Statistics: Annual Report, 1987–1988.* Williamsburg, VA: National Center for State Courts.

National Institute for Consumer Justice. 1972. *Staff Studies on Small Claims Courts.* Boston, MA: National Institute for Consumer Justice.

National Law Journal. 1987, February 16.

Ostrom, Brian J. 1990. Data from the National Center for State Courts, supplied to authors.

Ross, H. Laurence. 1970. *Settled Out of Court: The Social Process of Insurance Claims Adjustment.* New York: Aldine.

Sarat, Austin. 1987. "Alternatives to the Formal Judicial System." In Robert J. Janosik, ed., *Encyclopedia of the American Judicial System,* Vol. II. New York: Scribner.

Sarat, Austin, and Joel B. Grossman. 1975. "Courts and Conflict Resolution: Problems in the Mobilization of Adjudication." 69 *American Political Science Review* 1200.

Shapiro, Martin. 1978, February 13. Personal letter to author.

Shapiro, Martin. 1981. *Courts: A Comparative and Political Analysis.* Chicago: University of Chicago Press.

Sherman, Herbert L., Jr. 1987. "Torts." In Robert J. Janosik, ed. *Encyclopedia of the American Judicial System,* Vol. II. New York: Scribner.

"Small Claims Courts and the Poor." 1969. 42 *Southern California Law Review* 493.

Steele, Eric H. 1981. "The Historical Context of Small Claims Courts." 1981 *American Bar Foundation Research Journal* 293.

USA Today, June 6, 1986: 12A.

Vander Kolk, Kenneth J. 1985. "Is That All There Is?" 152 *American Journal of Obstetrics and Gynecology* 139.

Yngvesson, Barbara, and Patricia Hennessey. 1975. "Small Claims, Complex Disputes: A Review of the Small Claims Literature." 9 *Law and Society Review* 219.

CHAPTER 6

The Criminal Judicial Process

Probably no other function of the legal system has come under as much public criticism as the courts' handling of criminal matters. Such criticisms are understandable given the dramatic increase in crime over the past three decades. If the fear of crime were not sufficient to make many citizens double-bolt their doors, the many allegations that suspected criminals are set free on legal technicalities (or receive exceedingly lenient sentences for serious crimes) have caused some liberals to join with conservatives in questioning whether or not the criminal justice system has broken down entirely.

THE DILEMMA OF CRIME IN THE UNITED STATES

Although the United States has never enjoyed a crime-free period, there have been times when the increase in crime seems inexplicable. Two crime-related issues have been especially troubling in the last 15 years. First, despite the overall affluence that characterizes American society, violent crime is substantially higher in the United States than in other Western nations. A woman is 7 times more likely to be a victim of rape in the United States than in European countries. Murder rates in the United States are 10 times higher than in Japan and 5 times higher than in Canada (Kalish, 1988). Homicide is the leading cause of death for black males between 15 and 24 years old and the third leading cause of death among white males in that age category in the United States (Fingerhut and Kleinman, 1990: 3292). Second, the level of deliberately violent crimes committed by youthful offenders in the United States is disturbing. How does one explain why a 24-year-old enters an elementary school playground, randomly kills 5 students and wounds 29 others, as occurred in Stockton, California, in 1989? That tragedy propelled the California legislature to ban the sale and unlicensed possession of assault rifles; yet most legislators acknowledged that this law would not have much of an impact on crime in the state. Several months after the Stockton incident, a 29-year-old woman banker was brutally assaulted while jogging in Central Park in New York. Her assailants, ranging in age from 14 to 19, attributed their attack to boredom!

An estimated 3 million crimes were committed on public school grounds in 1989. In response to the number of students carrying guns to school, 15 New York City public schools have installed metal detectors through which all students must pass (Gest, 1989). In some schools in Los Angeles, Long Beach, and Oakland, students conduct "yellow-code alert" drills as a response to gunfire on public school grounds. Pupils are instructed to lie on the floor with their hands over their heads until a teacher gives the all-clear signal.

Several factors are linked to violent criminal activity—race, sex, economic status, self-esteem, and age. Part of the problem, according to liberals, rests with the lack of educational and employment opportunities for the impoverished, particularly black, male teenagers in the urban areas. Unable to obtain meaningful employment because of inadequate schooling and a lack of marketable skills, some youths turn to crime as a way to support themselves. Often these individuals grow up in an environment that is a constant reminder of social injustice. However, because most poverty-stricken residents do not resort to crime, according to conservatives, those who choose deliberately to violate society's order do so because they think they will not be apprehended and not punished if caught. They willfully make the decision to assault and steal from victims who are likely to be economically disadvantaged as well. A third line of reasoning, one that is more apolitical, connects criminal motives to the thrill of illicit action (Katz, 1988). Although one cannot attribute any one motive for criminal behavior, the prevalence of drugs has compounded the crime problem.

The Impact of Drugs

The surge in the use of drugs in the 1980s created additional problems for the criminal justice system. Federal law enforcement officials were ill prepared to slow the flow of narcotics into the country, and local police were unable to counter the gang turf wars over the distribution of drugs in urban neighborhoods. Lawmakers have been frustrated over their inability to halt drug usage by simply passing laws increasing penalties for drug offenses. In particular, cocaine has become the nemesis of state and federal officials involved in the war against drugs. In 1985, drug enforcement officers seized over 100,000 pounds of cocaine. Three years later, cocaine seizures amounted to almost 300,000 pounds. There were 186 drug-related murders in Washington, DC, in 1983. Five years later, this number soared to 372. Drug prosecutions represent about 45 percent of the felony caseload for prosecutors in Baltimore. Juveniles involved in drug sales can earn thousands of dollars a week. Civil litigation has been delayed so that judges can devote more time to drug trials. Says one judge, "From a judge's point of view you don't think you're making a dent. You can delude yourself with the view that you're helping stamp out crime. But it makes no difference what you do with them or where you send them" (Strasser et al., 1988).

Despite the clamor of a federal "war on drugs," illegal drug actions most directly affect state courts. According to one study, drug-related cases constitute at least one-quarter, and most likely more, of the felony court cases in the states (Goerdt and Martin, 1989). Some 97 percent of all drug prosecutions are handled in state courts. Nationwide, the drug caseload increased by 56 percent between 1983 and 1987. This surge in drug prosecutions has affected the normal business of the state trial courts. As Goerdt and Martin note, "the increase in and the magnitude of drug caseloads appear likely to contribute to delay in processing other felony cases in those courts particularly burdened by drug cases. The result tends to be further court delays in nondrug cases" (7).

Although society as a whole has to contend with the results of crime, the issue of reducing crime necessarily rests with lawmakers, law enforcement officers, and the criminal justice system. For some critics, a harsher system of justice is necessary, one that brings the full brunt of the law down on violators. According to one Texas legislator, a stiffening of criminal penalties is needed, although his proposal to remove the fingers of convicted drug dealers was killed in the legislature in 1989. A former Colorado lawmaker proposed that lobotomies be performed on prison inmates. Lobotomies would make them "forget who they were and whatever they've done" in addition to serving as a deterrent to others contemplating criminal actions (Sanko, 1989). No legislators responded favorably to this suggestion. Other critics believe that crime will decrease only when major systemic changes in society are implemented.

Understanding the Criminal Justice System

The problems associated with the operation of the criminal justice system are far more complex than the public realizes and politicians acknowledge. Although the U.S. Supreme Court has held the states responsible for respecting certain rights of the accused, there are considerable variations among the states over how broad these rights should be.

The ease in making generalizations about the operations of the federal courts disappears when one enters the judiciary at the state and local levels, especially when discussing the criminal justice system. As Sam Walker (1989) says in his book on criminal justice policies, "The beginning of wisdom in any discussion of criminal justice is sensitivity to the special quality of the particular jurisdiction you happen to be discussing" (34). The "special quality" that Walker refers to is a combination of factors that give states and cities their own peculiar identity, including the history of the area, demographics, traditions, political leadership, and other features unique to the region, state, or community.

Four concepts help to explain the operation of the criminal justice system across the states and communities.

1. The criminal justice system is characterized by great *discretion* at all levels. Law enforcement officers, prosecutors, and judges have a variety of options at their disposal. Arrests can be made (or not made), charges can be filed (or dismissed), and judges can levy a variety of sentences to different individuals convicted of similar criminal offenses. This discretion, in part, is influenced by local and regional politics and, in turn, affects how smoothly the system operates.

2. The criminal justice system operates under *conflicting goals*. Police officers, for example, perceive their jobs in terms of arresting suspected criminals. In contrast, the role of judges is to ensure that the constitutional rights of all suspects are respected (Packer, 1968: Ch. 8).

3. The criminal justice system is *not as much a system as it is an assemblage of institutions and legal personnel who are involved in the common enterprise of*

dealing with those who violate the law. In a biological sense, a system implies an interconnectedness of related components. In reality, the components of the criminal justice system do not "operate in concert to produce an agreed upon social outcome. If anything, objectives of individual agencies create tensions among these bodies" (Zedlewski, 1979: 490–491).

4. The criminal justice system is *responsive to the demands of others* such as legislators, public citizens, local politicians, the press, and crime victims (Cook and Johnson, 1982: 47). These demands vary depending on state and local situations.

LAW ENFORCEMENT IN THE STATES

Collectively, there are more than 750,000 federal, state, and local law enforcement personnel in the nation. Some 77 percent work at the county and municipal level, 14 percent are employed at the state level, and 9 percent are federal officers who have jurisdiction over certain illegal activities in the states. Citizens have more contact with law enforcement officers than with any other members of the criminal justice system. Because of the discretion and power police officers wield, they have been dubbed by one scholar as "streetcorner politicians" (Muir, 1977). As with politicians in general, much of what the police do involves negotiating as well as determining the consensus of the community over the scope of their actions. Police departments reflect the communities they serve. They are local in nature and very different from one another. Muir attributes this difference to the nature of the demographics in the communities, the political structure of the community, the attitudes and values of the police chief, and the history of the municipalities and their law enforcement programs.

TV Police

Hollywood movies and television shows have shaped the public image of the police for over a half century. Probably no other occupational field has been so publicized, celebrated, and examined on the screen as that of law enforcement. In part, these shows and movies have mirrored the public's concern with security, domestic as well as international. From the 1950s into the 1970s, the police on television were portrayed as efficient, dedicated, and professional crime fighters.

Two messages were conveyed to an interested viewing public. First, police officers were a stabilizing force in a troubled society. The emphasis was on action, firepower, and the frustrations encountered by the police in apprehending criminals. A major source of their frustration was attributable to Supreme Court decisions, particularly in the 1960s to mid-1970s, which made the job of the crime fighters more difficult. Second, the dramas deemphasized the role of the ordinary citizen in sharing some responsibility for community crime. Either because of a lack of civic-mindedness or courage, only the police, not the citizen, could combat lawlessness. Undoubtedly, many viewers were disappointed that their own local police officers could not solve crimes as rapidly and efficiently as the TV police. By the mid-1970s and into the 1980s, a new genre of cop shows began to depict the police as mortals faced with a job they could never perform to the public's satisfaction.

In reality, of course, the police evoke a number of images, some contradictory. For many, police officers are the guardians of public safety, whereas for others they symbolize the oppressive power of the ruling elite, who advocate only selective enforcement of the law. The police, probably more than others in the legal system, reflect the predominant values of middle-class America as well as the local norms in the communities they serve.

Styles of Policing

Political scientist James Q. Wilson (1968) developed a three-part typology of police orientations based on his study of law enforcement in eight communities. Some communities, where major crimes were not a serious problem, employed what Wilson labeled the "watchman style." The emphasis of this style is on the maintenance of order in the community rather than on the strict enforcement of all laws. Hence, minor violations of the law are tolerated as long as nobody objects and the actions are not especially serious. In contrast, police departments that adhere to a "legalistic style" enforce the letter of the law. A legalistic department will issue traffic tickets at a high rate, detain and arrest a high proportion of juvenile offenders, act vigorously against illicit enterprises, and make a larger number of misdemeanor arrests even when, as with petty larceny, the public order has not been breached. The third Wilson typology is the "service style," in which police officers will respond to the public's call for law enforcement or order maintenance but not with the heavy-handedness characteristic of the legalistic style. Communities that encourage a service style are usually middle class, homogeneous, and more likely to worry about disruptions caused by outsiders than by community residents.

Wilson's (1968) study was done in the 1960s, when police departments and communities were experiencing dramatic changes. Although one may question the utility of his typologies today, they do serve to point out that the police can take on a variety of roles. These roles, or orientations, are a result of how the police chief sees his or her job in terms of what the community residents want or will tolerate.

Contemporary Background

During the postwar years until the early 1960s, the police and the country were experiencing changes along a number of fronts. Cops who once walked neighborhood beats were now given greater mobility in police cars with two-way radios. This change, which enabled city cops to respond to calls more quickly and efficiently, was not without cost since it also made the police more remote from the citizens. The police also assumed a greater responsibility for traffic enforcement. Most important, however, was the beginning of the migration of white, middle-class residents from the cities into the suburbs. The cumulative effects of the suburbanization of the country was to be felt in the mid-1960s, when major sections of the urban areas, especially the inner core, were simply relegated to the poor, minorities, and the elderly.

The 1960s were particularly difficult years for law enforcement officers. The civil rights struggle in the South pitted black demonstrators against police and state troopers, who sought to protect the old, segregationist order. Similarly, as the "long, hot summers" in the mid-1960s saw cities across the country racked by urban rebellion, city cops were portrayed by white and black radicals as the enemy of the people. In all too many black neighborhoods, resentment against the police had been festering for years. In the turbulence of the 1960s the racial factor combined with the anti-Vietnam War and student protests in many metropolitan areas. Cops who aspired to middle-class status for themselves and their families could not identify with youthful college protesters, who were openly rejecting those very values. As two observers noted, "A growing and open resentment was created between the police and a whole generation of young minorities and antiwar college students. Ill-equipped and poorly trained to deal with these social problems, the late 1960s were marked by a number of bloody confrontations between the police and the public" (Senna and Siegal, 1984: 150).

The turmoil of the 1960s did produce a number of positive changes in law enforcement that have become firmly rooted. Most urban police departments now have community relations programs designed to encourage neighborhood-police contact. And most police departments and other state law enforcement agencies emphasize the recruitment of blacks, Latinos, and women. However, affirmative action programs have come to many departments only because of court order; in others, racial discrimination and sexual harassment appear to be commonplace. Still, the changes are real. In 1976, only Newark (New Jersey) had a chief of police who was black. By 1990, over 10 major cities had black chiefs of police, and the number of black officers in the country's 50 largest cities is roughly equivalent to the percentage of blacks in the cities' population (Malcolm, 1990).

Community Policing

Academicians who have studied law enforcement for some time agree that the traditional police approach to fighting crime does not work. However, a study of innovative programs in six cities concluded that increased police interaction and identification with the community would produce results. Innovations that work are increased police contact with the public, more police substations and foot patrols so that cops can focus on particular areas within communities, and the hiring of civilians to assume some of the routine tasks (Skolnick and Bayley, 1986: 210–219). Essential to this concept of "community policing" is the establishment of mutual legitimacy and respect between citizens and law enforcement officers. Quite simply, citizens cannot be ignored. They give police officers the legitimacy and assistance they need to perform their jobs.

Ironically, community policing represents a return to the old beat system before World War II, when officers were deployed on foot patrols. By walking the beat, the police were able to know merchants and to identify with the problems in their respective areas. The move to squad cars in the 1950s sacrificed this personal contact between officers and neighborhood residents. In 1990, the New York City Police Department initiated an ambitious plan to have over half of its officers involved in community policing within three years.

Corruption

Corruption, long the bane of law enforcement agencies, has its roots in nineteenth-century America, in the political corruption of local constables, sheriffs, and the urban police. The most prevalent form of police corruption involves officers breaking the law, or being paid not to enforce the law, for their own financial benefit. Five occupational aspects of policing make it tempting for law enforcement officers to engage in corruption: (1) the discretion an officer has in determining whether to enforce the law or not; (2) an environment in which most officers operate free from the direct control of their supervisors; (3) the absence of public involvement in what the police do; (4) the "police fraternity," which promotes isolation from civilian life and reinforces acceptance of what the police do; and (5) the historically low status and low pay given to law enforcement officers (Sherman, 1974: 12–14).

Corruption scandals periodically strike police departments in Denver, Chicago, and New York City, whereas other departments, such as in Seattle and Los Angeles, have remained relatively clean since reform-minded police chiefs cleaned house decades earlier. The increase in the drug market since the 1960s has proved too profitable for some cops to resist temptation. The Miami Police Department, sensationalized in "Miami Vice," was wracked by a drug-related scandal in 1987. Several officers were involved in a $15 million drug ring that murdered four drug dealers and terrorized others. The officers would seize the cocaine from dealers and then sell it themselves. According to Miami police officials, their rush to hire new officers in the late 1970s to mid-1980s to cope with the surge of crime in Dade County resulted in insufficient screening of many new applicants, some of whom later turned bad.

Minorities and the Police

The situation in Miami illustrates another problem as well, one long associated with the relationship between the police and the minority communities in urban areas. Although most urban police departments have made efforts to recruit women and minorities into their ranks, often under court order, minority group members are more critical of the police than are Anglos. One concern expressed by minorities is that the police seem to employ excessive force on nonwhites, without fear of punishment. Racial tensions are particularly acute between Hispanics and blacks in Miami. With the growth of the Hispanic community in Dade County, many blacks feel the new Hispanic residents are getting the jobs blacks should have. Miami's population is now 60 percent Hispanic.

In 1980, several days of rioting in a black section of Miami were touched off after an all-white jury acquitted four Dade County sheriffs in the beating death of a black insurance agent. More rioting followed in 1982 when an Hispanic city police officer was found not guilty in the shooting death of a young black man. Most recently, the trial of an Hispanic police officer accused of the deaths of two young, black males sparked fears of another episode of racial strife. The deaths set off three days of rioting in the black areas of Miami. Unlike past trials, however, the multiracial, six-member jury returned a guilty verdict against the officer. But the feeling in the Hispanic community was that the officer was found guilty simply to avoid an outburst from black residents had he been acquitted (Resnick, 1989: 8).

For years members of the black community in Los Angeles complained that city police officers and county sheriffs used excessive force against blacks. Traditionally, such charges were dismissed by law enforcement officials because evidence of excessive force was lacking. Also, some groups, such as the Black Muslims, who charged brutality, had no credibility with white residents or city officials. However, a dramatic example of police brutality against a black male was captured on videotape by a white resident in 1991. The two-minute tape, which was replayed on national TV news, showed four Los Angeles police officers beating a black man who had been stopped for a traffic citation. The man, who offered no resistence and lay on the ground, was repeatedly kicked and hit with batons by the officers while a number of other officers stood by and watched. The startling footage seemed to document what many had long suspected. The police chief promised disciplinary action against those officers who observed the beating and criminal sanctions against those who participated in it. This sort of behavior is not only offensive, counterproductive, and unprofessional but often expensive as well. The previous year, baseball star Joe Morgan was roughed up by a Los Angeles officer who thought Morgan was a drug courier. Morgan was awarded $540,000 by a jury. Other complaints of police misconduct cost the city $8 million in settlements in 1990 ("The Investigation of a Videotaped Beating," 1991).

Change

Law enforcement has changed dramatically over the past 150 years. In contrast to the old, volunteer, night-watch system, in which town citizens patrolled the streets at night primarily to look for fires, today the nation spends more than $20 billion annually on policing. In particular, two major trends are apparent. First, the police have become more preoccupied with crime over the years, especially since the 1930s, when the Uniform Crime Report (UCR) was developed. The UCR represents the crime reports from some 15,000 law enforcement agencies in the United States for eight criminal offenses: murder and nonnegligent manslaughter, forcible rape, robbery, aggravated assault, burglary, larceny-theft, motor vehicle theft, and (added in 1978) arson. The statistics that appear in the UCR are used to gauge the increases and decreases in crime for the country, specific regions, and states. For the police, the UCR has become the measure of their success—was crime going up or down in their areas (Walker, 1984: 77)? However, as the police have long been aware, there is really little they can do to prevent crime from occurring.

The image of the cop as a crime fighter may be appealing for police, but it can also be exasperating given their lack of success in reducing crime rates. Most of the police officer's day is spent assisting the public and simply being visible; less than 20 percent of their time is spent on crime-related matters (Kelling, 1988). Second, the police have become more professional over time, especially since the 1950s. Many law enforcement agencies are very selective in whom they recruit, some require college degrees before promotion to the supervisory level, training has become more comprehensive, and salaries have increased as well.

THE JUDICIAL PROCESS IN CRIMINAL CASES

From the 1960s on, public opinion polls demonstrated clearly that most citizens blame the courts for being too lenient in dealing with criminals (Jamieson and Flanagan, 1987: 82). This criticism is not directed at how cases are tried but rather with the perception that the courts are overly concerned with the rights of criminals and too lenient when handing down sentences on those convicted of criminal offenses. Variations in sentencing will be discussed later in this section, but for now attention is directed to how cases proceed through the criminal courts.

The basic premise underlying the operation of the criminal courts is that there will be "equal justice under the law." This means that all defendants are entitled to certain procedural and substantive constitutional guarantees as well as the presumption of innocence. Words that underscore the ideal of equality of justice are etched in the facades of courthouses throughout the states. However, most participants in the system agree that there is a Grand-Canyon-sized gap between the theory of equal justice and how the criminal justice process operates in reality. There are two major parts of the criminal justice process in the courts, the pretrial stage and the trial itself, which includes sentencing. A third component, appeals, lies beyond the jurisdiction of the trial courts and is discussed in Chapter 7.

Pretrial Process

The person who is arrested for a felony offense is usually arraigned in a court of limited jurisdiction. It is at this point that the defendant is formally notified of the charges, bail is set, and the date for a preliminary hearing is established. If the accused in indigent (unable to afford an attorney), the court will appoint counsel. At the arraignment, the defendant will plead guilty or not guilty.

Bail.   The idea behind bail is that no one should be punished by being kept in jail until the trial court has determined the guilt of the accused. Bail is a sum of money given to the court as security to ensure that the accused will show up for trial. If the defendant shows up for trial, as most do, the bail money is returned regardless of the guilt or innocence of the defendant. The amount of bail a defendant has to post to be released from jail is a function of the person's employment and residence history as well as the likelihood that the accused will appear in court for trial. The Eighth Amendment prohibits "excessive bail," and all of the states can refuse bail to an individual charged with a capital crime (i.e., premeditated murder). Under normal circumstances, a middle-class person who is arrested will be able to pay the bail and thus avoid pretrial incarceration. A low-income individual who is arrested may have to go through a bail bondsman to secure release, and an indigent will probably remain in jail until the conclusion of the trial. Use of a bail bondsman means that the accused will normally pay 10 percent of the actual bail and the bondsman guarantees the remainder. This 10 percent fee is not returned to the defendant regardless of the outcome.

The bail a suspect has to pay is established by local officials—judges, prosecutors, and law enforcement officials. Cities maintain a bail schedule that specifies what the amount of bail should be for specific offenses. At the arraignment, the judge may increase or decrease the bail, depending on the circumstances of the offense and the background of the alleged offender.

In 1966, Congress enacted the Bail Reform Act to alleviate the inequities associated with the practice of bail. The intent was to make it easier for low-income suspects to be released from custody before trial. In a number of states and communities, this meant the adoption of Release on Recognizance (ROR) programs, whereby poor defendants could be released without posting bail, assuming they were found to be unlikely to flee. But when Congress passed the Federal Bail Reform Act of 1984, it had another goal in mind. Under the more recent act, individuals who are thought to pose a danger to the community, if they were to be released on bail, can be held in "preventive detention." In spite of bail reform measures, local jails continue to hold a substantial number of individuals accused of relatively low-grade felonies who are unable to make bail or qualify for ROR. These suspects are more likely to be convicted than those free on bail (Neubauer, 1984: 225–228).

Preventive detention obviously rejects the notion of innocence until guilt is determined. By the mid-1980s, over 37 states had adopted similar provisions. In Indiana, a person charged with "forcible felonies" while out on bail for a previous offense can be denied bail. In Georgia, a long list of crimes, including burglary, arson, and drug-related offenses are sufficient to keep a person in jail until trial (see Goldkamp, 1985). Both state supreme courts and the U.S. Supreme Court have upheld the constitutionality of preventive detention laws. Undoubtedly, these laws would be used more often if local jails throughout the country were not already overcrowded with suspects unable to make bail while awaiting trial or serving short sentences for criminal convictions.

In some cities, jail overcrowding has led to the release of some suspects who probably do constitute a threat to the public's safety. Currently, 130 cities are under federal court orders to free some suspects to prevent overcrowding. The alternative is to build more jails, although both time and finances are obstacles. Houston jails house 8,000 prisoners, although they were built to handle half that number. As a result, those sentenced to jail serve only one-thirteenth of their court sentence on the average. Chicago has to release about 100 suspects a day without bail or much screening of their past offenses. Suspects in Los Angeles and New York City are released without bail if the charges would not warrant a bail of more than $2,500.

One result of the early releases of some suspects without screening is their failure to show up in court for trial. Victims and witnesses may be there, but trials cannot proceed without the defendants. An estimated 30 percent of defendants in Chicago fail to appear for their initial trial date, and Houston has over 25,000 outstanding warrants for suspects who have been released from jail without bail but have not appeared for trial (Hinds, 1990).

Preliminary Hearing.   Before the accused goes to trial, a preliminary hearing is conducted, although it can be waived by the defendant. The purpose of the preliminary hearing is to determine whether or not there is probable cause to proceed to a trial. At this stage, the defendant can challenge evidence that might be introduced at the actual trial. Often the defense agrees to forego the preliminary hearing, especially if a plea bargain has been agreed to by both sides.

During the time between arraignment and trial, the defense can introduce a variety of motions to challenge the evidence, witnesses, or other aspects of the case to be presented against the accused. Often such motions will contest the legality of the arrest, denying that the police had probable cause to arrest or to seize the incriminating evidence.

Plea Bargaining.   As Lois Forer (1980), a Court of Common Pleas judge in Philadelphia, notes, "The majority of criminal prosecutions have non-trial dispositions." She adds, "This is a polite euphemism for plea bargaining" (109). Plea bargaining involves an agreement between the defense and prosecution whereby the defendant will plead guilty to a charge (or charges) in exchange for not being prosecuted on all charges or the most serious charge, as well as agreement on the recommended sentence. Whether or not plea bargaining actually works to the benefit of defendants is unclear since suspects are routinely overcharged in criminal cases. However, a number of "organizational incentives" make plea bargaining attractive to both sides. The uncertainty of a trial outcome is eliminated, delay is avoided, money is saved, and defendants usually think they are better off than going to trial. As Scheingold (1984) summarizes, "Plea bargaining, in short, allows cases to be handled more predictably, expeditiously, and harmoniously" (159).

The role of the judge in plea bargaining is to ensure that defendants are aware of what their plea means and that they get what they bargained for. Moreover, judges are to reject those plea bargains that are overly lenient or overly severe. The available evidence suggests that only rarely do judges object to the agreed-upon plea between the defendant and the prosecution. Judges are anxious to find plea bargains acceptable to avoid the time-consuming process of formal trials. A jury trial in a theft case may average several hours, and a more serious charge of rape may require two or more days of the court's time. In contrast, a study of plea bargaining in six cities found that the average plea bargain in a felony case consumed 10 minutes and misdemeanor offenses averaged about 5 minutes (McDonald, 1987: 204).

The importance of plea bargaining for the criminal justice process cannot be overstated. Roughly 80 to 90 percent of all felony criminal cases are resolved in this fashion in the metropolitan courts across the country. In a four-city study, guilty pleas were the norm in 81 percent of the criminal cases in Miami, 82 percent in Detroit, 83 percent in Pittsburgh, and 85 percent in the Bronx (Church, 1982: 49).

Alaska abolished plea bargaining in 1975 with surprising results. According to one study, explicit plea bargaining almost vanished and more convicted felons were sent to prison than before. Contrary to expectations, the judicial system did not bog down but worked more efficiently (Rubinstein and White, 1979). Such successes in rural Alaska are unlikely to be replicated in the more populous states or large urban centers. Indeed, when several El Paso, Texas, judges attempted to end plea bargaining in their courts, the result was a doubling of trial rates. Two years later plea bargaining was once again the norm (Weninger, 1987). Plea bargaining is also widely used to settle misdemeanor criminal actions (Mendes and Wold, 1976).

The Trial—Process and Actors

Most of us are familiar with the adversarial process in criminal cases as portrayed in Hollywood movies and TV shows. If such dramas have a common theme, it revolves around the notion that justice will out—the innocent go free, the guilty are discovered, and justice prevails—as a result of the verbal combat between the attorneys for the two sides. As in its treatment of law enforcement, Hollywood's depiction of the criminal justice process is usually simplistic, often legally inaccurate, but mainly distorted. Although most criminal cases do not go to trial because of plea bargaining, the trial nonetheless represents the standard public image of the way serious criminal matters are resolved.

Process.   The process one encounters in the handling of criminal cases at the trial stage in both federal and state courts is quite similar. In minor criminal cases, the trial is usually held before a judge, whereas in the serious criminal matters the defendant can choose to go before a judge or have the case decided by a jury. The prosecution begins with an opening statement summarizing the evidence against the defendant. The defense then responds, most often by citing the weaknesses of the prosecutor's arguments and calling the court's attention to whatever evidence works to the advantage of the accused. As the case proceeds, both the prosecution and the defense may ask the judge to strike certain testimony as being immaterial to the case. The judge can address questions to the witnesses. After both sides have presented their cases, closing arguments may be made by the prosecutor and defense. However, since closing arguments are usually for the benefit of a jury, often they are not made when the judge is the trier of the case.

With the completion of this aspect of the formal trial, the judge can then deliberate the decision or, more likely, issue an immediate decision about the guilt of the accused. If the verdict is not guilty, the accused is dismissed and set free. If the verdict is guilty, the now-convicted felon may be released on bail or kept in custody to await sentencing. By the time of the sentencing, the judge, who presumably has examined the overall record of the defendant (presentence report), hands down a criminal sentence that can vary greatly in terms of severity. After sentencing has been passed, the defense may request that the client be released on an appeal bond pending a decision by a higher court on the decision reached by the trial court.

Judges.   The key players in the criminal trial, in addition to the defendant, are the attorneys prosecuting and defending the accused, the judge, and the jury (if the case if tried before a jury). The main order of business for trial court judges is to process cases as quickly and efficiently as the system allows. They do not have the luxury of engaging in policy making to the extent of their brethren at the appellate levels.

There are more than 8,500 state trial court judges in the country. There are some 1,500 trial court judges combined in California, Texas, and Florida but less than a total of 70 in Delaware, Wyoming, and Rhode Island. The size of the community where the judges serve has an influence on the adjudicative function. Thus, according to the authors of one study of trial judges, "In larger courts, judges are much more likely to hear jury trials; in smaller courts, nonjury trials. This reflects, in part, the more highly adversarial character of larger urban courts, where attorneys are more combative and standard jury trials consume more time" (Ryan et al., 1980: 229).

In some states, newly appointed or selected trial court judges are encouraged to attend "judicial colleges," where veteran judges host seminars on recent developments in the law and the administrative aspects of the job. This socialization process for most new judges, however, comes from the older judges and other judicial personnel in the courthouse where he or she is assigned (Alpert, 1981). In this respect, the young judge, like the recently sworn-in law enforcement officer, gains a working knowledge of what is expected by the veterans in the same organizational environment.

Prosecution.   The person in charge of prosecuting a criminal case on behalf of the state is the district attorney (DA) or other attorney from the DA's office. The power of the prosecutor is considerable and is put into action well before a trial commences. The prosecutor decides whether an individual should be tried and on what charges. An individual arrested and charged by the police with the commission of several crimes can be set free if the prosecutor feels that the case is weak or other uncertainties lessen the likelihood of a conviction. Prosecutors like to boast of a high conviction rate. Two ways to keep the rates high are to engage in plea bargaining and to prosecute only on those charges for which a guilty verdict is most certain. The prosecutor who does not have a favorable conviction:acquittal ratio is at a disadvantage politically (Albonetti, 1987: 311).

The power of the prosecution is visible in several ways. Most obviously, prosecutors moderate the flow of cases in the courthouse. Less visible to outsiders is the prosecutor's ability to build a power base within the local political party or independently of it. This power can be employed to advance to higher political office, the bench, or simply to get one's way in the courthouse. Prosecutors arrive in office with different ambitions. They may want to initiate reforms in office policy, increase the status of the office, or become accepted by the status quo (Flemming, 1990).

Counsel.   Defendants who can afford to hire their own attorneys usually do so. Indigents may be represented in court by a public defender, a court-appointed attorney, or one who is on contract to the county. Most counties more often use assigned counsel to represent indigents, although the use of public defenders is increasing. About 11 percent of the counties contract with private attorneys to serve the poor. The provision of legal services to the poor in criminal cases costs the counties over $1 billion annually. Overall, the amount spent on behalf of indigent criminal defendants increased by 60 percent between 1982 and 1986. Fees paid to attorneys to represent the poor vary considerably among the states. In 1986, the average cost to defend an indigent was $540 in New Jersey but only $63 in Arkansas (Spangenberg et al., 1988).

Public defenders are generally available only in the urban areas. Just as district attorneys are paid by taxpayers to prosecute, public defenders receive their salaries from the state (or local government) to defend indigents. This financial arrangement means that many of the poor accused of criminal acts see their public defenders as working for the government, not for them (Casper, 1971). The public defender is usually an overworked individual with little time and resources to defend the accused in the manner of an attorney who is being paid by the defendant. Lawyers appointed by the courts to defend indigents when there is no public defender are most often selected from a list of attorneys who volunteer for such appointments. They, too, are compensated by the state for the time they spend defending their clients.

The difficulties faced by public defenders are illustrated in Fulton County, Georgia, where competent attorneys are struggling in a system on the brink of collapse. The problems are the same as those faced by other public defenders—too many cases and not enough resources—only worse, according to a recent report. In Fulton County, which includes Atlanta, felony arrests have more than doubled between 1985 and 1990, in part because of drug offenses. An estimated 70 to 80 percent of those arrested cannot afford a lawyer. The result? Some 1,500 defendants, unable to make bail, sit in jail for months until their arraignment; most will see their public defender for only 5 to 10 minutes before they enter a plea; and public defenders have over 500 clients each to represent, although a national criminal justice commission has set 150 clients a year as a recommended caseload. As the head of the public defender system in Fulton County said, "Indigent defense just doesn't have a high priority. The fact is, everything is 'law and order, let's lock everybody up,' and it's law enforcement that's getting the money" (Applebome, 1990).

Juries.   Jury trials are employed in criminal cases more frequently on television than in reality, and only a small percentage of cases end up with jury verdicts (Roper, 1986: 5). The use of jurors to decide criminal (and civil) cases really is quite remarkable. Judges, of course, are regarded as professional decision makers who are trained in the law. Jurors, in contrast, are lay members of communities where trials occur. They do not have legal backgrounds, they deliberate their verdicts in secrecy, and they do not have to justify their decisions (Loh, 1984: 353). The juror's duty is a testimonial to the common sense of the average person. An alternative view was offered by Mark Twain: "A jury consists of twelve persons of average ignorance."

The decision to have a criminal case heard by a judge or a jury is left to the defendant. Defense lawyers usually try to avoid a jury trial if the charge involves child abuse, torture, or other particularly heinous actions and if the case is especially complex (Sipes et al., 1988: 21). Additionally, the age and background of the judge are important. A younger judge may be perceived as more liberal than an older one, and a judge who was a former prosecutor may be considered, from the defendant's standpoint, more favorable to the prosecution. The characteristics of the community where the trial is scheduled can also have a bearing on opting for a judge or jury. This aspect is illustrated by the comment of one New Jersey prosecutor that his community was "primarily a 'conservative' ethnic population of 'Italian, Irish, and Jewish' people who are more inclined to 'believe anything a police officer might say in court, unlike people in California' " (62).

By tradition, it was assumed that 12 individuals would constitute a jury in criminal cases. However, in 1970, the U.S. Supreme Court upheld a Florida law that provided for only 6 members in criminal jury trials. But when Georgia began using 5-member juries, the Supreme Court said that it was not acceptable (*Ballew v. Georgia*, 1978). In 1972, the Supreme Court upheld provisions in two states that allowed for less than a unanimous verdict (*Johnson v. Louisiana; Apodaca et al. v. Oregon,* 1972). Only in capital cases is a unanimous verdict by 12 jurors required. If the jurors are unable to arrive at a verdict in a criminal case after a reasonable period of deliberation, the jury is considered to be "deadlocked" (or "hung") and the judge can dismiss the jurors. Then it is up to the district attorney to decide whether to attempt a second prosecution before a new group of jurors.

One of the more perplexing issues involving jurors rests with how representative of the community they really are or should be. It is unconstitutional of course, for states to prohibit individuals from serving on juries because of their sex, race, ethnicity, or religion. However, this does not mean that lawyers for both sides cannot attempt to arrive at a jury that they feel is most inclined to deliver the verdict they want. Jurors for a case are selected randomly from the venire, the large pool of potential jurors who may be called to serve. Each side, prosecution and defense, is allowed a certain number of preemptory challenges, which can be used to dismiss an individual from the jury. This practice presumably ensures that both sides will arrive at an impartial jury. However, not very subtle prejudices and stereotypes can play a role in who is accepted for, and dismissed from, jury duty. For example, a district attorney who is prosecuting a black man on a charge of assault and battery may not want any black jurors on the assumption that they will feel sympathetic to the defendant. The defense may want black jurors for exactly that reason. Or if a man is being charged with child molesting, the prosecutor may want several young mothers on the jury. The defense, knowing the fears of mothers about child molesters, would like such women to be excluded. Both prosecution and defense lawyers can also dismiss jurors for cause. This type of dismissal recognizes that impartiality can be jeopardized because of a juror's situation (e.g., married to a law enforcement officer or recent experience as a crime victim).

Because jurors are to be representative of the community and since they do not have legal training, lawyers use courtroom tactics to influence their consideration of nonlegal issues. Defense attorneys take pains to make sure their clients dress for a jury. If the defendant is charged with the sale of narcotics, a defense lawyer does not want the client to appear in court as if he or she just portrayed a drug dealer on an episode of "Miami Vice." Similarly, the prosecutor in a rape case will instruct the victim not to appear before the jury in a low-cut blouse or miniskirt, which suggests a low moral standard to some. Lawyers for both sides also recognize the importance of their image on jurors. The prosecutor who berates witnesses unmercifully or the defense attorney who comes across as a hired gun will feel the sting of the jury.

A unique experiment in more than 100 courts in 36 states may provide jurors with a new role in the courtroom. The experiment, conducted under the auspices of the American Judicature Society and the State Justice Institute, allows jurors to ask questions of the witnesses, a function traditionally relegated to attorneys. The jurors do not ask questions directly; rather questions are submitted in writing to the judge, who then directs the question to a witness. Ideally, this procedure will improve jurors' attentiveness and enable them to get answers to questions neither the prosecution nor defense has asked. At the same time, this practice could encourage some jurors to make up their minds before all the evidence has been presented. Additionally, the extent of juror questioning could be grounds for an appeal. The results of this experiment will most likely lead to an expanded role for jurors as well as action by state legislatures to establish limits on the scope of its use.

The function of the jury in deciding criminal cases is well established. However, less well known is the ability of the jury to determine sentences in noncapital cases in six states (Arkansas, Kentucky, Missouri, Oklahoma, Texas, and Virginia). The American Bar Association, among other groups, has criticized jury sentencing on the grounds that sentencing is a judicial function, that it can lead to sentencing disparities, and that jurors are less likely to think of rehabilitation than punishment in deciding on a sentence. But according to one Texas prosecutor, juror sentencing is preferable to judge sentencing: "Judges get jaundiced and fail to treat each case individually. For them it's just another murder, another rape, and then they focus on the defendant." Moreover, the prosecutor acknowledges the influence of local values: "The punishment phase is when you can open up full throttle. The community speaks through the jury and it's just more fun to prosecute with it" (Taylor, 1987: 277).

Sentencing

Before the judge passes a sentence, a background report on the individual has been prepared. This report reveals the defendant's employment history, previous convictions, and other details that can help the judge decide the appropriate sentence. The latitude judges have in sentencing depends on the state where the crime was committed and the applicable laws prescribing minimum and maximum sentences for various crimes. Judges are also influenced by the remorse, or lack of remorse, of the defendant for what he or she did.

Five options are available to a judge when sentencing someone who has been convicted of a felony criminal offense—prison, jail, probation, fine, or alternative sentence such as compensation to the victim or community work. Often a sentence will include two or more of the options—two years in prison, five years' probation, and a $5,000 fine, for example. The person who is convicted of a federal crime will be sent to a federal or state prison, if incarceration is part of the sentence, and a person convicted of a state offense will serve time in a state prison or a county jail, if confinement is part of the sentence.

Historically, judges have had considerable discretion in sentencing. However, the many abuses and discriminatory aspects of this practice led to reforms in sentencing laws in the states and the federal government. Today, states employ *indeterminate sentencing* (i.e., 1 to 20 years in prison), which provides a minimum and a maximum term in prison, or *determinate sentencing,* in which the defendant is given a specific period to serve (i.e., 5 to 7 years). But under either system, a felon can have the prison time reduced for good behavior.

Additionally, almost all of the states have enacted *mandatory sentencing laws,* which require a specific sentence upon conviction of certain crimes. The majority of these laws apply to individuals who are convicted of particularly violent crimes, narcotic violations, and the use of guns in the commission of crimes, as well as those who are designated habitual offenders.

The victims' rights movement has persuaded the legislatures in 30 states to pass bills enabling victims of violent crimes (or their survivors) to address the court before a sentence is handed down. This right of *allocution* also allows victims to speak before parole boards when a convict is eligible for release. Although few persons actually take advantage of it, it is a victory for victims, who often feel that the criminal justice system is insensitive to their losses (Wiehl, 1989).

Sentences for criminal convictions vary greatly among the states as well as among different jurisdictions within the states. Such intrastate sentencing disparities have led to legislative enactment of sentencing guidelines. For instance, Minnesota adopted sentencing guidelines in 1980 that emphasized punishment. Under the guidelines, the severity of the crime is the primary concern, and the criminal record of the defendant is given less importance. Before the guidelines were passed, the defendant's past criminal behavior was more important. As a result of the change, the incarceration rate for persons convicted of serious offenses who had the least serious criminal backgrounds increased from 47.4 percent to 79.0 percent. Conversely, for those with "moderately serious criminal histories" who were convicted of least severe offenses, the decision to sentence to prison dropped from 38.4 percent to just under 10.0 percent (Koppel, 1984: 3). According to a report by the Committee on Sentencing Guidelines in New Mexico, persons convicted of serious violent crimes were given more lenient prison sentences than those convicted of less violent crimes. The report urged adoption of sentencing guidelines to bring an element of uniformity to felony sentencing practices (Burks, 1985).

The data in Tables 6.1 and 6.2 illustrate how sentencing varies in a study of 28 different felony courts across the country (Cunniff, 1987: 9, 13). The figures in Table 6.1 do not indicate differences in sentences for specific offenses but rather the aggregate sentences to prison and jail for felony convictions in jurisdictions that use determinate or indeterminate sentences. In the eight jurisdictions that employ determinate sentences, 87 percent of the convicted defendants spend some time in jail or prison. In contrast, 65 percent are confined in the 20 jurisdictions that employ indeterminate sentencing. The decision to sentence to jail or prison varies dramatically. In Denver, only 1 percent of the convicted defendants served time in jail whereas felons in other jurisdictions received a

TABLE 6.1   Percentage of Convicted Defendents Sentenced to Jail or Prison in 28 Jurisdictions, 1985

Jurisdiction	Percent of All Sentences to		
	Incarceration *(Jail and Prison)*	*Prison*	*Jail*
Overall average	75%	45%	30%
Determinate	87%	42%	45%
Dade County	89	58	31
Denver	44	43	1
Hennepin County	76	26	50
Kane County	82	40	43
King County	81	24	57
Los Angeles County	90	41	49
Mecklenburg County	60	55	5
San Diego County	93	41	52
Indeterminate	65%	48%	17%
Baltimore City	59	56	3
Baltimore County	57	36	21
Dallas County	65	63	1
Davidson County	84	41	43
Erie County	69	40	30
Essex County	63	41	22
Harris County	61	59	1
Jefferson County	65	56	9
Jefferson Parish	59	27	31
Lucas County	79	51	28
Manhattan	78	53	25
Maricopa County	60	36	24
Milwaukee County	61	34	27
Multnomah County	63	39	25
Oklahoma County	38	32	6
Orleans Parish	53	39	14
Philadelphia	71	33	38
St. Louis	57	42	15
Suffolk County	77	39	38

Note: Percents may not add to total due to rounding.
SOURCE: Mark A. Cunniff, "Sentencing Outcomes in 28 Felony Courts, 1985," U.S. Department of Justice, Bureau of Justice Statistics (Washington, D.C.: U.S. Government Printing Office, 1987), p. 9.

jail sentence 45 percent of the time. The disparities are evident in jurisdictions with determinate sentencing. The person who is found guilty of a felony in Oklahoma County is unlikely to be sent to prison or jail. However, the odds of being incarcerated upon conviction in Suffolk County (New York) are high.

The likelihood of being sent to prison for specific offenses is shown in Table 6.2. There is a consistency between the *average* sentences in jurisdictions employing indeterminate and determinate sentencing. But sentencing across jurisdictions for specific offenses varies substantially. Thirty-eight percent of those convicted of rape in Hennepin County, Minnesota (which includes Minneapolis), were sentenced to prison in 1985,

TABLE 6.2 Percentage of Individuals Sentenced to Prison for Selected Criminal Offenses in 28 Jurisdictions, 1985

Jurisdiction	Percent Sentenced to Prison for Conviction Offense of							
	Homicide	Rape	Robbery	Aggravated Assault	Burglary	Larceny	Drug Trafficking	All Cases
Overall average	84%	65%	67%	42%	49%	32%	27%	45%
Determinate	83%	62%	68%	39%	49%	27%	20%	42%
Dade County	88	81	87	48	57	40	50	58
Denver	79	95	75	43	41	34	19	43
Hennepin County	83	38	50	19	23	13	2	26
Kane County	82	81	59	49	38	30	27	40
King County	83	55	97	24	24	3	15	24
Los Angeles County	83	62	65	42	52	30	18	41
Mecklenburg County	79	86	83	44	57	44	28	55
San Diego County	74	66	62	25	51	18	28	41
Indeterminate	85%	68%	66%	44%	48%	34%	34%	48%
Baltimore City	90	61	64	80	59	26	34	56
Baltimore County	100	100	75	74	40	25	15	36
Dallas County	80	74	82	66	64	50	41	63
Davidson County	71	74	80	33	37	23	16	41
Erie Coiunty	80	91	52	31	42	29	15	40
Essex County	87	80	91	38	33	18	20	41
Franklin County	74	91	74	65	64	55	37	58
Harris County	88	69	87	57	62	53	45	59
Jefferson County	77	92	69	50	59	47	43	56
Jefferson Parish	56	82	71	26	36	6	21	27
Lucas County	85	100	83	65	76	32	35	51
Manhattan	98	86	63	39	60	31	41	53
Maricopa County	79	58	63	39	42	26	24	36
Milwaukee County	75	52	52	22	30	16	16	34
Multnomah County	73	43	58	26	44	20	20	39
Oklahoma County	94	77	87	30	22	17	21	32
Orleans Parish	81	93	73	32	43	10	31	39
Philadelphia	92	61	42	32	19	16	12	33
St. Louis	64	80	76	43	37	26	39	42
Suffolk County	91	66	59	29	34	24	36	39

SOURCE: Mark A. Cunniff, "Sentencing Outcomes in 28 Felony Courts, 1985," U.S. Department of Justice, Bureau of Justice Statistics (Washington, D.C.: U.S. Government Printing Office, 1987), p. 42.

whereas the comparable figure for Denver was 95 percent. In Milwaukee County, only 22 percent of those convicted of aggravated assault received prison terms, whereas in the city of Baltimore, 80 percent were sent to prison for aggravated assault.

Another discrepancy in sentencing is based on who determines the guilt of the accused. According to a recent multistate study by the Bureau of Justice Statistics, people convicted of felonies by judges are less likely to be sentenced to prison than those found guilty by juries. The explanation for the sentencing differences rests in large part on plea bargaining, an arrangement that does not involve a jury (Gaskins, 1990: 4).

Often judges try to be creative in sentencing when the offender deserves punishment but not to the extent of prison time. Trial court judges in several states have required individuals convicted of drunk driving, shoplifting, and prostitution to take out ads in local newspapers apologizing for their illegal actions. A far more controversial type of nontraditional sentencing attracted national publicity in 1991, when a California judge ordered a mother who had been convicted of child abuse to have a birth control implant as a condition of her probation. The judge's sentence has been appealed. In other cases, this same judge ordered an illiterate woman to learn how to read, a man to donate his car to a women's shelter, and another to wear a t-shirt that said he was on probation for theft.

Capital Punishment

The use of the death penalty in the states has gone through several phases in the twentieth century. Capital punishment increased from the turn of the century until the 1930s, when 1,523 people were put to death in that decade. From that peak, capital punishment declined over the years. In 1967, only two men were executed. By the mid-1960s, public support for capital punishment declined, and legal challenges resulted in Supreme Court decisions that forced those states with death penalty laws to rewrite them in 1972 (*Furman v. Georgia*) and 1976 (*Gregg v. Georgia; Woodson v. North Carolina*). The following year, the Court held that capital punishment was not a permissible penalty for rape convictions nor for kidnapping unless the victims were killed (*Coker v. Georgia* and *Eberheagt v. Georgia*).

A variety of factors rekindled support for the death penalty during the 1970s. The conservative mood of the electorate, the increase in crime, the problem of drug usage, and the publicity created by radical groups encouraged many citizens to think of capital punishment once again as a means of sending a message to drug pushers, killers, and terrorists. Presidents Richard Nixon, Ronald Reagan, and George Bush were all vocal in support of capital punishment. By 1991, 37 states provided for the death penalty. The vast majority of executions that have occurred in the post-*Furman* era have been in 9 southern states. Although 15 federal offenses are punishable by death, no one has been executed by the federal government since the early 1960s.

Proponents support capital punishment on the grounds that it is fitting retribution for those who commit the most heinous of crimes, that it is less expensive than keeping dangerous felons locked up until their natural death, and that it is a deterrent to others. Sentences in the criminal justice system are predicated on the notion of punishment. As the severity of the offense increases, so does, in theory, the severity of the punishment. At first blush, it seems reasonable to assume that it is less expensive to execute someone than to keep that individual in confinement for several decades. But the costs of appeals for those sentenced to die push the costs of executions up tremendously; since almost all those who are sentenced to death are indigents, the costs of the appeals are paid by the state. Executions in Florida since the *Gregg* decision have averaged about $3.2 million each, or about six times what it would cost to keep someone in prison for life (Spangenberg and Walsh, 1989: 58). However, the question of the death penalty as a deterrent is arguable. Statistical manipulations of data can be used to support as well as refute this point (see Archer et al., 1983; Ehrlich, 1977). Using the deterrent argument, one legislator in Georgia in the early 1980s unsuccessfully proposed a bill that would have provided for an executioner's van. The distinctly marked vehicle would be driven from the site of one execution to another, thereby reminding viewers that the executioner's fate awaits someone.

Opponents of capital punishment counter that it inherently discriminates along racial and economic lines and that there is no way to correct an error should an innocent person be put to death. Pre-*Furman* data on the use of the death penalty support the discrimination argument (Wolfgang, 1974). Post-*Furman* data on individuals who have been executed since 1977 show that most of them were in the lower economic levels. The third argument of death penalty opponents can be accepted without debate.

Process.   States that allow the death penalty follow the bifurcated procedures upheld by the U.S. Supreme Court. That is, a capital case has two main parts. First is the trial stage, wherein the defendant is tried and found guilty, guilty of a lesser offense, or not guilty. If the defendant is found guilty on a charge that qualifies for the death sentence, the second stage of the process, the penalty phase, begins. Jurors are convened to decide the sentence of the defendant—life in prison without possibility of parole or death. It is during the penalty phase of the trial that the prosecution stresses the aggravating factors that justify a death sentence and the defense argues mitigating factors that would encourage the life-in-prison sentence. Typical aggravating factors include a defendant's past criminal conduct and violent tendencies; mitigating factors might include evidence that the defendant had been severely abused as a child, suffered from mental retardation, or experienced some traumatic emotional upheaval as a child. The jurors have the responsibility to consider these aspects of a defendant's past in deciding his or her fate.

The quality of legal representation for capital defendants is a major determinant in the outcome of the case. A skilled attorney can introduce evidence or expert witnesses to persuade a jury that the defendant is not guilty of the charge or, if guilty, not deserving of the death sentence. Skilled legal counsel is expensive, and most of those ultimately sentenced to die have little money and are represented by court-appointed attorneys. According to a *National Law Journal* study of capital cases in six southern states (where the death penalty is most likely to be imposed), court-appointed counsel often lack the resources, training, and legal skills to represent adequately capital case defendants (Coyle et al., 1990). Court-appointed attorneys are compensated by the states, but a cap is established on the maximum they can be paid. For example, the $1,000 ceiling on fees for attorneys in Mississippi is a disincentive for attorneys to spend the necessary time in preparation for a death penalty defendant.

The study cited attorneys who were appointed to represent indigent defendants but had little or no background in criminal law, had been disciplined by state bar associations for various infractions, and had drug abuse problems. In one 1985 capital case in Texas, the defendant's court-appointed attorney opened and closed his defense at the penalty phase of the trial with this statement: "You are an intelligent jury. You've got that man's life in your hands. You can take it or not. That's all I have to say" (Coyle et al., 1990: 34). As the study noted, the issue of what a defendant did is often less important than who the attorney is.

Death penalty opponents were dealt a major setback in 1987 when the Supreme Court upheld Georgia's capital punishment statutes despite statistical evidence that those convicted of killing white people were far more often sentenced to death than those convicted of killing black people (*McCleskey v. Kemp*). Two years later, a divided Court ruled that states could execute murderers who were mentally retarded (*Perry v. Lynaugh*) as well as individuals who were as young as 16 when they committed their crimes (*Stanford v. Kentucky*). Collectively these three decisions have given a clear signal to the states that they can establish their own death penalty policies as long as they adhere to basic constitutional rights for the defendants at the trial and appellate stages. The Supreme Court took a giant step toward reducing death penalty appeals in 1990. In two cases that year, the Court held that a state death penalty conviction was valid despite new rulings by the federal courts that set new standards in capital prosecutions (*Butler v. McKellar; Saffle v. Parks*).

Postconviction appeals in capital cases not only increase the costs associated with implementing the death penalty but also increase the time between the death sentence and the execution. Although some capital defendants may be executed within several years after being sentenced to die, most are not. The average stay on death row for a convict is eight years (Spangenberg and Walsh, 1989: 56). That so much time lapses between the imposition of the death sentence and the actual execution infuriates the public, politicians, and even some legal officials. Former U.S. Supreme Court Justice Lewis Powell, Jr., addressed this issue after he resigned from the Court. According to Powell, this delay was unconscionable; either executions should be prohibited or they should be carried out without excessive delay. The current chief justice, William Rehnquist, has asked Congress to limit death penalty appeals, and it is likely that Congress will respond accordingly in the early 1990s.

Capital Punishment Politics.   Few criminal justice issues are as volatile in state politics as capital punishment. In the New York City Mayoral race in 1989, one candidate was repeatedly questioned by voters about his personal opposition to the death penalty. He patiently explained that citizens in the Big Apple should inquire about his views on more pertinent matters since the mayor's post has absolutely no authority over criminal sentencing policies.

Former California Supreme Court Chief Justice Rose Bird and two of her fellow justices were defeated in 1986 largely because of decisions that were viewed as anti-death penalty by the voters. Several months before the end of his term as governor of New Mexico, Toney Anaya (D) commuted the death sentences to life in prison for five condemned men. Anaya's 1986 Thanksgiving eve action, which applied to all those on death row, was taken despite polls that showed that 75 percent of New Mexicans supported capital punishment for convicted murderers. Governor-elect Garrey Carruthers (R) immediately announced his opposition to what Anaya had done and reaffirmed his support for capital punishment.

The Hawaii legislature defeated an attempt to pass a capital punishment law in 1986, and despite strong conservative support, bills to introduce capital punishment in Alaska have been unsuccessful during the 1980s. Between 1979 and 1986, the Kansas legislature passed capital punishment bills each year, but they were vetoed by anti-capital punishment governors. In 1987, a pro-capital punishment governor was elected, but by that time the Kansas legislature voted against the death penalty on the grounds that it was too expensive to carry out, given the costs to the state in death penalty appeals by defendants (Culver, 1989).

It is unlikely that convincing evidence will surface to prove or disprove the use of capital punishment as a deterrent. Moreover, the U.S. Supreme Court is unlikely to declare the death penalty unconstitutional as long as the states do not violate the procedural rights of the accused in capital cases. Thus, the future of capital punishment is left in the hands of state residents and their legislatures, governors, and courts. Canada and Mexico have abolished the death penalty, as have all the western European countries. The United States is one of the few industrialized nations in the world where executions are still legal.

ASSESSMENT

American criminal justice is characterized by discretion at all stages of the system—police decide whether to arrest; district attorneys choose whether to prosecute, plea bargain, or dismiss charges; and judges can levy a variety of sentences for those found guilty. The legal roots of the discretionary aspects of the system lie in the U.S. Constitution, state constitutions, and landmark state and federal supreme court decisions that have defined the procedural guarantees accorded to defendants in criminal cases.

When most citizens go to court, they enter an environment over which they have little influence. The lawyers engage in conversations with one another, the bailiff, and the judge. Conversations may turn on fine points of the law unfamiliar to the layperson. When the issue is resolved, the citizen leaves the judicial environment, another one enters, and the process is repeated. On any given day in Manhattan's criminal courts, an arraignment judge can expect to handle 100 cases. Numerous guilty pleas are entered, some cases are dismissed, and some are scheduled for trial in other courtrooms. The average case may receive four minutes of the judge's time (Martin, 1987). The judge, attorneys, and other judicial personnel work with one another on a daily basis. The operation of the courtroom does not focus on the individual defendant but rather on maintaining the organizational structure of the court so that a reasonable number of cases can be processed each day (see Blumberg, 1967). The urban courtroom, notes one former public defender, is much like a package express terminal. The defendants are the packages, and the judges and attorneys decide when and where they will be shipped (Kunen, 1983: 5).

Particularly in the large metropolitan areas the local criminal justice system appears on the verge of a breakdown as a result of too many cases, various degrees of ineptitude among court officials, and general bureaucratic inefficiency. Attorney Steven Brill's (1989) critical account of operations in the Manhattan criminal courts brought howls of protest from some attorneys and judges. They did not counter his pessimistic account as much as they objected to his candor. According to Brill, the system was overloaded to be sure, but the haphazard manner in which cases were processed defied logic. There were too many judges who shortened courtroom hours (the average time court was in session was just four and one-half hours), too few police to contend with the 200,000 arrest warrants that are issued each year, and too many victims and witnesses who were summoned to court repeatedly only to have the hearings canceled because defense lawyers and/or defendants were not present. To Brill, the urgency of dealing with crime and restoring a sense of justice in the system requires a new mind set:

> The people who run these urban justice systems—mayors, governors, chief judges, prosecutors, defense lawyers—should stop "understanding" the problem and start screaming from the rooftops that we need more resources, more taxes, hard-nosed management, better people, and, above all, a new mind-set to achieve criminal justice.
> We can't continue to operate our law enforcement system like a third-rate motor vehicles bureau. We can't continue to process cases rather than redeem the rule of law.

The adversary process creates an inherent conflict between truth and the will of both parties to win. Ideally, justice is the desired product of the judicial process in criminal cases. For justice to be done, the important events in a criminal matter have to be revealed. Yet the revelation of such events may compromise the chance each side has of winning. The key players in the game have their own goals. The judge wants truth (and not to be overturned on appeal), the prosecutor wants a guilty verdict, and the defense and defendant seek an acquittal. The jurors, in the experience of one judge, "who should leave the courthouse more appreciative than they were of themselves and the laws they helped to vindicate, too often receive an unedifying demonstration that trickery and low cunning may be permitted to defeat the ends of justice" (Frankel, 1985: 53).

The judiciary, and particularly the criminal courts, have been criticized from all sides for years. Conservatives rail against liberal Supreme Court decisions and trial court judges who are perceived as prodefendant. There are, of course, some judges whose actions upset local police and prosecutors. But popular opinion aside, Supreme Court decisions such as *Mapp* and *Miranda* have not adversely affected crime control. A recent study by an American Bar Association committee found that only .60 percent to 2.35 percent of all adult felony arrests are not prosecuted because of illegal searches. According to this report, "The police, prosecutors and others surveyed do not believe that the Miranda requirements significantly inhibit effective interrogation or prosecution" (Raven, 1988: 8). Liberals maintain that the criminal justice system discriminates against the poor, the uneducated, the unpopular, and minorities. No doubt there is some truth to these allegations, perhaps more so in some jurisdictions than in others. At the same time, our prisons are not filled with innocent defendants who were wrongfully convicted by a repressive system.

Criminal laws are constantly being revised, usually as a result of legislators reading the will of their constituents. Thus, many states in the 1960s and 1970s lessened penalties for possession of small amounts of marijuana on the grounds that marijuana smoking was not as dangerous as originally thought when stringent laws were enacted in the 1930s. But "new" drugs such as crack and cocaine have led lawmakers to increase penalties for their use and distribution. As justified as this might be, the impact of such laws is less clear. For example, a Minnesota judge declared an anticrack law unconstitutional in 1991 on the grounds that it was racially discriminatory. The new law required first-time offenders who were convicted of possessing more than three grams of crack cocaine to be given a four-year prison term. However, possession of the same amount of cocaine in powder form required probation. The judge found no rational basis for the different sentences for the same amount of the same illegal drug. But she did note that black youths were much more likely to use crack cocaine, whereas white youths favored the powder form (London, 1991).

From the 1940s to the 1980s, the California Supreme Court broadened the rights, beyond what the U.S. Supreme Court established, for the accused in criminal law. This practice was reversed by the California electorate in 1990, when voters approved an initiative that amended the state constitution so that suspected criminals in California would have no greater rights than afforded by the federal Constitution. But in a surprise ruling several months after the election, the state supreme court struck down the heart of the initiative on the grounds that it unfairly limited the power of the judiciary under the California constitution.

CONCLUSION

For all of its faults, the criminal courts have become more professional over the years. Because of Supreme Court decisions, defendants have easier access to lawyers. Moreover, the increase in the number of female and minority attorneys has resulted in a more representative bench than was the case a decade ago. Meanwhile, the criminal courts have not been able to keep pace with the increase in the number of those arrested. In many urban areas, judicial gridlock is a daily reality for the criminal courts. The states and cities do not have the funds to upgrade the courts and increase the number of judges to speed the processing of cases. But neither the criminal courts nor trial judges can have much of an impact on crime. They become involved after crimes have been committed and suspects arrested. Although they decide the fate of the guilty, they are not responsible for rehabilitating the offenders nor ensuring that those on probation do not commit additional crimes.

American society is at a crossroads in trying to reduce crime rates. Since the 1960s, the political response has been to build more prisons, enact new laws, and pass mandatory sentencing legislation. The widespread availability of guns and drugs, unemployment, overcrowded schools, and a host of other social and economic ills affect crime rates. If we return to the past, when prisons were expected to be spiteful institutions where guards dispensed their own form of justice, judges will be reluctant to send all but the most predatory criminals to prison.

REFERENCES

Albonetti, Celesta A. 1987. "Prosecutioral Discretion: The Effects of Uncertainty." 21 *Law & Society Review* 291–313.

Alpert, Lenore. 1981. "Learning About Trial Judging: The Socialization of State Trial Judges." In James Crammer, ed. *Courts and Judges,* pp. 105–147. Beverly Hills, CA: Sage.

Applebome, Peter. 1990, November 30. "Study Faults Atlanta's System of Defending Poor." *New York Times,* p. B14.

Archer, D., R. Gartner, and M. Beittel. 1983. "Homicide and the Death Penalty: A Cross-National Test of a Deterrence Hypothesis." 74 *Journal of Criminal Law and Criminology* 991–1013.

Blumberg, Abraham S. 1967, June. "The Practice of Law as a Confidence Game: Organization Cooptation of a Profession." 1 *Law & Society Review* 15–39.

Brill, Stephen. 1989, July/August. "Fighting Crime in a Crumbling System." *The American Lawyer.*

Burks, Susanne. 1985, August 17. "Serious Crimes Get Light Time, Report Reveals." *Albuquerque Journal.*

Casper, Jonathan D. 1971, Spring. "Did You Have a Lawyer When You Went to Court? No, I had a Public Defender." 1 *Law and Social Action* 4–9.

Church, Thomas W., Jr. 1982. *Examining Local Legal Culture.* Washington, DC: National Institute of Justice.

Cook, Thomas J., and Ronald W. Johnson. 1982. "Basic Issues in Court Performance." U.S. Department of Justice, National Institute of Justice. Washington, DC: U.S. Government Printing Office.

Coyle, Marcia, Fred Strasser, and Marianne Lavelle. 1990, June 11. "Fatal Defense." *National Law Journal.*

Culver, John H. 1989. "State Politics and The Death Penalty." 12 *Journal of Crime & Justice* 1–19.

Cunniff, Mark A. 1987. "Sentencing Outcomes in 28 Felony Courts, 1985." U.S. Department of Justice, Bureau of Justice Statistics. Washington, DC: U.S. Government Printing Office.

Ehrlich, Isaac. 1977. "Capital Punishment and Deterrence: Some Further Thoughts and Additional Evidence." 85 *Journal of Political Economy* 741–788.

Fingerhut, Lois A., and Joel C. Kleinman. 1990, June 27. "International and Interstate Comparisons of Homicide Among Young Males." 263 *Journal of the American Medical Association* 3292–3295.

Flemming, Roy B. 1990, January. "The Political Styles and Organizational Strategies of American Prosecutors: Examples from Nine Courthouse Communities." 12 *Law & Policy* 25–50.

Forer, Lois G. 1980. *Criminals and Victims.* New York: W. W. Norton.

Frankel, Marvin E. 1985. "The Adversary Judge: The Experience of the Trial Judge." In Mark W. Cannon and David O'Brien, eds., *Views from the Bench,* pp. 47–54. Chatham, NJ: Chatham House.

Gaskins, Carla K. 1990, February. "Felony Case Processing in State Courts, 1986." Bureau of Justice Statistics Special Report. Washington, DC: U.S. Department of Justice.

Gest, Ted. 1989, March 13. "These Perilous Halls of Learning." *U.S. News & World Report,* pp. 68–69.

Goerdt, John A., and John A. Martin. 1989, Fall. "The Impact of Drug Cases on Case Processing in Urban Trial Courts." 13 *State Court Journal* 5–12.

Goldkamp, John S. 1985, Spring. "Danger and Detention: A Second Generation of Bail Reform." 76 *Journal of Criminal Law and Criminology* 1–74.

Hinds, Michael. 1990, August 15. "Philadelphia Justice System Overwhelmed." *New York Times,* p. A1.

"The Investigation of a Videotaped Beating." 1991, March 7. *Los Angeles Times,* p. B6.

Jamieson, Katherine M., and Timothy J. Flanagan, eds. 1987. *Sourcebook of Criminal Justice Statistics—1986.* U.S. Department of Justice, Bureau of Justice Statistics. Washington, DC: U.S. Government Printing Office.

Kalish, Carol B. 1988. "International Crime Rates." Bureau of Justice Statistics, U.S. Department of Justice. Washington, DC: U.S. Government Printing Office.

Katz, Jack. 1988. *Seductions of Crime: Moral and Sensual Attractions in Doing Evil.* New York: Basic Books.

Kelling, George L. 1988. "What Works—Research and the Police." U.S. Department of Justice, National Institute of Justice. Washington, DC: U.S. Government Printing Office.

Koppel, Herbert. 1984, October. "Sentencing Practices in 13 States." Bureau of Justice Statistics Special Report. Washington, DC: U.S. Department of Justice.

Kunen, James S. 1983. *How Can You Defend Those People?* New York: Random House.

Loh, Wallace D. 1984. *Social Research in the Judicial Process.* New York: Russell Sage Foundation.

London, Robb. 1991, January 11. "Judge's Overruling of Crack Law Brings Turmoil." *New York Times,* p. B9.

McDonald, William F. 1987, December–January. "Judicial Supervision of the Guilty Plea Process: A Study of Six Jurisdictions." 70 *Judicature* 203–215.

Malcolm, Andrew. 1990, April 23. "Police Chief's Objective: Greater Responsiveness." *New York Times,* p. A11.

Martin, Douglas. 1987, February 16. "The Rising Pressure in Criminal Court: The View from the Bench." *New York Times,* p. A29.

Muir, William Ken, Jr. 1977. *Police: Streetcorner Politicians.* Chicago: University of Chicago Press.

National Center for State Courts. 1987. *State Court Caseloads Statistics: Annual Report, 1985.* Williamsburg, VA: National Center for State Courts.

Neubauer, David W. 1984. *America's Courts and the Criminal Justice System,* 2nd ed. Monterey, CA: Brooks/ Cole.

Packer, Herbert L. 1968. *The Limits of the Criminal Sanction.* Stanford, CA: Stanford University Press.

Raven, Robert D. 1988. "Crime and the Bill of Rights: Separating Myth from Reality." *American Bar Association Journal* (1): 8.

Resnick, Rosalind. 1989, November 27. "Miami Officer's Case: Symbol of City's Ills?" *The National Law Journal,* p. 8.

Roper, Robert T. 1986, Spring. "A Typology of Jury Research and Discussion of the Structural Correlates of Jury Decision Making." 11 *The Justice System Journal* 5–15.

Rubinstein, Michael L., and Teresa J. White, Winter, 1979. "Alaska's Ban on Plea Bargaining." 13 *Law & Society Review* 367–384.

Ryan, John Paul, Allan Ashman, Bruce D. Sales, and Sandra Shane Du-Bow. 1980. *American Trial Judges.* New York: Free Press.

Sanko, John. 1989, September 13. "Lobotomy Urged on Inmates." *Rocky Mountain* (CO) *News,* p. 8.

Scheingold, Stuart A. 1984. *The Politics of Law and Order.* White Plains, NY: Longman.

Senna, Joseph J., and Larry J. Siegal. 1984. *Introduction to Criminal Justice,* 3rd ed. St. Paul MN: West Publishing.

Sherman, Lawrence W., ed. 1974. *Police Corruption.* Garden City, NY: Anchor Books.

Skolnick, Jerome, and David Bayley. 1986. *The New Blue Line: Police Innovation in Six American Cities.* New York: Free Press.

Sipes, Dale A., Mary E. Oram, Marlene A. Thorton, Daniel J. Valluzzi, and Richard V. Duizend. 1988. *On Trial: The Length of Civil and Criminal Trials.* Williamsburg, VA: National Center for State Courts.

Spangenberg, Robert L., Judy Kapuscinski, and Patricia A. Smith. 1988. "Criminal Defense for the Poor, 1986." Washington, DC: U.S. Department of Justice, Bureau of Justice Statistics.

Spangenberg, Robert L., and Elizabeth R. Walsh. 1989, November. "Capital Punishment or Life Imprisonment? Some Cost Considerations." 23 *Loyola* (Los Angeles) *Law Review,* pp. 45–58.

Strasser, Fred, Marianne Lavelle, and Terry Carter. 1988, August 8. "Baltimore: A City Under Seige." *National Law Journal.*

Taylor, Gary. 1987, January 19. "Jury Sentencing: A Last Stand in Six States." *National Law Journal*.

Walker, Samuel. 1984, March 1984. "'Broken Windows' and Fractured History: The Use and Misuse of History in Recent Police Patrol Analysis." 1 *Justice Quarterly* 75–90.

Walker, Samuel. 1989. *Sense and Nonsense About Crime: A Policy Guide,* 2nd ed. Pacific Grove, CA: Brooks/Cole.

Weinger, Robert A. 1987, December. "The Abolition of Plea Bargaining: A Case Study of El Paso County, Texas." 35 *UCLA Law Review* 265–313.

Wiehl, Lis. 1989, September 29. "Victim and Sentence: Resetting Justice's Scales." *New York Times,* p. B5.

Wilson, James Q. 1968. *Varieties of Police Behavior*. New York: Atheneum.

Wolfgang, M. E. 1974. "Racial Discrimination in the Death Sentences for Rape." In W. J. Bowers, ed., *Executions in America*. Lexington, MA: Lexington Books.

Zedlewski, Edwin W. 1979, September/October. "Performance Measurement in Public Agencies: The Law Enforcement Evaluation." 39 *Public Administration Review* 484–493.

CHAPTER 7

State Appellate Courts

Appellate courts, whether at the state or national level, have long been of central interest to political scientists, and for good reason. Although these rather familiar tribunals do not engage in the routine business of community dispute processing, as do trial courts, their work is in a sense even more political. In addition to their role in sorting out and correcting errors of lower courts (thereby bringing some degree of consistency to legal rules within the system), they serve an even more important function: maintenance and enhancement of the political regime. To correct errors, intermediate appellate courts would be adequate. They provide the loser at a trial with something of a face-saving "out," reasserting a claim in a new arena; and for the government there is the opportunity to clear up any glitches in the application of legal rules (Shapiro, 1981: 49). But in addition, a court of final resort exists in all states (and of course, at the national level) to assist the central government in what one scholar called "hierarchical political management":

> . . . The extension of judicial services outward and downward is a device for wedding the countryside to the regime . . . for keeping the strings of legitimacy tied directly between the ruled and the person of the ruler or the highest institutions of government. . . . The ability to reach down occasionally into the most particular affairs of the countryside provides an important means of reminding the rank and file that the rulers are everywhere, that no one may . . . hide from [the] central authority. . . . Thus, appellate institutions are more fundamentally related to the political purposes of central regimes than to the doing of individual justice. That this is true is evidenced by the nearly universal existence of appellate mechanisms in politically developed societies. . . . (52)

Appellate courts carry out these functions largely through the device of policy-making, incremental or otherwise, and it is on these grounds that their significance is usually asserted. The role of state appellate courts in this regard is often eclipsed by the relatively recent surge of federal judicial power. But it should be recalled that state courts antedate federal courts, and at one time state supreme court justices represented the finest legal minds of the nation and were accorded the respect now customarily reserved for justices of the U.S. Court. Chancellor James Kent of New York, Lemuel Shaw and Joseph Story of Massachusetts, John Gibson of Pennsylvania, and George Wythe and Spencer Roane of Virginia were among the leading judges and legal scholars of their day who graced the state appellate bench at the beginning of nationhood (Friedman, 1985: 134–138). Although the conversion of the colonies to states occurred at a time of rising state legislative dominance, state courts soon made good their claim to a leading role in state policy-making.

The enunciation of the doctrine of judicial review by Chief Justice John Marshall in *Marbury v. Madison* in 1803 (1 Cranch 137) was warmly embraced by state appellate judges, who used the doctrine to enhance their own stature against the growing power of the state legislature. But even before Marshall's celebrated edict, state courts had held void legislative enactments in a number of instances. Although there was understandable judicial reluctance to use this power to excess (it was not unknown for state legislatures to impeach judges for the "crime" of invoking judicial review), the doctrine came to be employed as a powerful symbol, enhancing the image of state supreme courts as apolitical agencies with the solemn duty of upholding the great principle of constitutionalism in the workings of state government (Haines, 1932).

The conception of judicial review in this early period was what legal historian Kermit Hall called "departmental," the power being used primarily as a protective measure against legislative and executive encroachments on the province of the judicial department. Thus, although legislative supremacy was generally honored, state supreme courts tended to focus on issues of separation of powers in which judicial territory was being threatened (Sheldon, 1987: 72).[1] However circumspect state courts were in this period of legislative dominance, they nonetheless were quite willing to assert their traditional role as creative interpreters of the common law. As legislative supremacy began to wane in the mid-nineteenth century, state supreme court justices "embraced common law decision-making with impassioned enthusiasm, and judge-made law began to fill the law reports." (74). In pointing to this second, more expansionist era of state judicial activism in the interpretation of the common law, one commentator noted.

> Two facts are basic. The first is that, in the complex system of government we adopted, most questions of private law were left to the states. The national government had almost no part in establishing or developing the law of property, contracts, wills, personal injury, or damages. The second is that within the states it was often the courts rather than the legislatures that actually formulated such law. (Rosenblum, 1967: 406).

One example of such common law development by state courts in the mid-nineteenth century was set forth by Benjamin Cardozo (1924) in his classic work, *The Growth of the Law*. There, he discusses the progressive demise of the old doctrine of "privity" through decisions rendered by the New York Court of Appeals in the 1850s. Literally, privity means a connection or bond between two parties in a transaction. In our early industrial period it had come to mean that unless there was a contractual relationship between a manufacturer and a customer, say, the latter had no claim to damages from faulty merchandise. This interpretation created virtual immunity for commercial interests from suits for damages suffered by purchasers of their products, a doctrine befitting the laissez-faire, caveat emptor thinking of nineteenth- and early twentieth-century America.

Through a series of decisions beginning with *Thomas v. Winchester* (6 N.Y. 397) in 1852, the New York Court of Appeals gradually expanded the categories of defective products for which American manufacturers could be found liable. Later, other state appellate courts broadened the newer doctrines; in Connecticut, for example, in 1961 that state's highest court held that by marketing products in sealed containers, the manufacturer implicitly warrants the item to be suitable and safe for its intended and advertised use (Rosenblum, 1967: 407). The growth of the law in such a fashion often escapes our attention, thereby leading the student of American law to ignore the important legal pioneering undertaken by state appellate courts (see also Baum and Canon, 1982: 83–108).

Thus, throughout much of the nineteenth century state supreme courts were probably a good deal more creative in the use of their own powers than were the federal courts, many launching out to fashion bold, new legal doctrine. With the unwillingness of state legislatures to address the needs of a growing America, especially in the last half of that century, state courts stepped into the breach through their common law decisions, transforming whole areas of law, such as the law of property, contracts, and negligence, and in doing so laying the groundwork for the industrial revolution (Tarr and Porter, 1988: 51).

Roughly around the turn of the century, state legislatures began to reassert themselves, leading to a more restrained period of state judicial policy-making. As one commentator put it, quoting Roscoe Pound,

> "The '. . . cautious eking out of the traditional law' by interstitial law-making lost favor in '. . . an impatient age accustomed to instant communication, super-rapid transportation and governmental activities of the first moment. . . .' " (Aumann, 1940: 215)

Other developments, too, augured for a reduced role for state appellate courts. The expansion of federal court jurisdiction through various congressional acts in the 1875–1925 period raised the specter of competition from federal courts (Bator et al., 1988: Ch. 1). Moreover, the nation was moving to a more formalistic model of jurisprudence and judicial decision making, a view that depreciated the social creativity of common law decisions and replaced it with the deception of mechanical jurisprudence—the notion that judges decided cases strictly in accordance with *the law* as written (Sheldon, 1987: 75–78; Stumpf, 1988: 8–11). The ever-increasing pace of social and economic change as we moved into the twentieth century continued to leave state courts in a noncompetitive position, with legislatures and their offshoots, boards, agencies, and commissions, at both the national and state level taking center stage in policy-making.

As this is being written there is considerable evidence that state appellate courts are entering a fourth era of their history, with greater attention now being given to developments in state constitutional law as the leading edge of national judicial policy-making (Friedelbaum, 1988; Galie, 1982; "The Interpretation of State Constitutional Rights," 1982; "State Constitutions in a Federal System," 1988; Tarr and Porter, 1988). As with previous shifts in the fortunes of state judicial power, there is probably no single explanation for this important development. The current national trend toward decentralization of political power throughout our federal system, as seen in the administrations of Ronald Reagan and George Bush, is usually cited as a leading factor, although the historic swings of the pendulum of American federalism make this anything but a novel development.

An important, indeed crucial aspect of this general trend has been the propensity of the Burger-Rehnquist Supreme Courts to move away from the major policy thrusts characteristic of the Warren Court. In its increasing deference to lower (especially state) courts, the Supreme Court is literally inviting an increased activism in state judicial policy-making, and in many instances state supreme courts have displayed their willingness, if not at times their eagerness, to move into the vacuum ("New Developments in State Constitutional Law," 1987). These developments will be more fully discussed below as part of our assessment of a newly emerging state appellate judiciary. But it should be clear from this brief overview that despite the ebb and flow of state power, state appellate courts remain major players in the overall growth of American law.

One further factor may be suggested as a reason for the renaissance of state judicial power in the late twentieth century—the evolution of state supreme courts, as a group, from rather passive, inefficient agencies of government to more modern adjudicative bodies reminiscent of the U.S. Supreme Court. By the 1980s they thus found themselves in a much better position to assume leadership roles in state and national policy-making. Robert Kagan and his associates (1978) have documented this development along a number of dimensions. A 16-state supreme court study spanning the years 1870 to 1970 revealed that in the late nineteenth and early twentieth centuries, the workloads of these courts had grown to such levels as to make them virtual slaves to a mundane, error-correcting appellate role. Thus, as populations grew and state legislatures shrank from the task of reforming their judicial systems along more modern lines, the number of written opinions of some of these courts rose to as high as 400 to 500 per year (e.g., California and Michigan); for other state supreme courts (North Carolina, Alabama, and Minnesota), this figure hovered around 300 to 400 per year (968). Such figures may be contrasted with the number of written opinions currently handed down by the U.S. Supreme Court, which is about 130 per term. As a rule, this figure means less legal research undertaken in the writing of opinions, fewer dissents, shorter opinions, and an overall lower quality of output than these state courts had produced in earlier periods. Their capacity to articulate carefully legal policy for the state, and nation, was thus seriously impaired.

Although these trends continued in some states even up to the current era, a general movement toward relief occurred in the mid-twentieth century when legislatures gave a number of state supreme courts much greater discretion in determining their own case-loads. As expected, this power usually enabled state supreme courts to focus on fewer legal issues per year; compose longer, more scholarly opinions; issue more dissents; and generally improve their ability to develop legal doctrine more thoughtfully for their states. Whereas the 1915 average number of written opinions for these 16 state supreme courts was 219, that figure dropped to 167 by 1970, with the reduction in opinion load in some states being even more dramatic—North Carolina from 440 opinions rendered in 1910–1915 to 118 in 1970; Michigan with 413 opinions in 1885 to only 96 in 1970 (Kagan et al., 1978: 965–983).

These sometimes dramatic changes in the workings of state supreme courts were accomplished by a variety of reforms, usually directed toward eliminating excessive case demand on the courts or providing the justices with tools to cope with large workloads or both. The creation of an intermediate appellate court was perhaps the most common reform. State legislators, jealous of their primacy in state policy-making, were not always ready to provide such relief for their judicial counterparts. But as pressures mounted on the legislators themselves because of the rising demands of a changing and growing America, and as the legal profession marshalled its organizational and political clout in state and nation, states began to move to a more modern, efficient model of appellate review. As Robert Kagan and his associates (1978) wrote, these developments pointed to

> . . . an emerging societal consensus that state supreme courts should not be passive, reactive bodies, which simply applied "the law" to correct "errors" or miscarriages of justice, in individual cases, but that these courts should be policy-makers and, at least in some cases, legal innovators. (1983)

THE APPELLATE PROCESS

Inasmuch as most of our previous discussion of the judicial process has emphasized the work of trial courts, it might be useful to indicate briefly the chief differences in court processes when cases reach the appellate level. First, appellate courts spend much more time focusing on the *law* as opposed to the *facts*. It is not true that appellate courts never engage in fact determination, but that important and difficult task (see Frank, 1949: 111) is primarily in the hands of trial courts and judges.

Second, in focusing mainly on the issues of law, appellate courts are document- rather than people-oriented. With no witnesses, no juries, and often no oral argument, appellate judges work much more in a closeted, rarified atmosphere akin to the "Ivory Tower" of scholarship. It is a world of ideas, theories, and principles, in contrast to the "real world" of the bargaining pit characteristic of trial courts.

Third, in the move to the appellate level, the issues in the case are likely to be transformed completely. For example, in a criminal trial, the focus may be on the *what* of the case: What did the defendant do? Was the law violated? What is the punishment to be? But in the appellate court, questions are more likely to have to do with *how* the lower court arrived at these determinations. Hence, issues of the judicial process itself or of broad application of the law per se are more often the grist for the appellate mill.

Finally, these differences lead to a broader policy role for appellate courts. Even when engaged in the seemingly narrow business of correcting errors, appellate judges render decisions that affect a larger number of people, creating legal rules applicable to potentially large numbers of cases in the future. As Henry Glick (1988) explains,

> When lawyers appeal cases, they usually concentrate on larger, more general issues of law and policy in addition to the details of the particular case. . . . Lawyers try to persuade appellate judges that . . . the law itself should be changed, and this usually requires greater attention to the meaning of the law, what legislators or judges intended when rules were developed, and the consequences of law. (225–226)

This last point, of course, underscores the obvious significance of the work of appellate courts, notwithstanding our earlier discussion of the de facto "finality" of trial court determinations because of the very low incidence of appeal. Although caseload growth, as we shall see, constitutes perhaps the single most pressing problem for state appellate court administration, the *percentage* of cases appealed in the states remains quite small, as is the case in the federal judicial system. The contrast between the disposition of cases in state trial courts of general jurisdiction (from which the vast bulk of appeals come) and the filing of cases in state intermediate appellate courts affords a rough idea of the incidence of state appeal. As seen in Table 7.1, the ratio is, on the average, about 1:168.

Although there is a dearth of empirical research on the point (Lawrence, 1989), scholars have nonetheless set forth several possible explanations for why cases are appealed. At the outset it must be recalled that with some exceptions, the vast majority of state trial court determinations are not appealable at all because they were bargained, out-of-court settlements. Thus, as suggested in our earlier coverage of the civil and criminal judicial process, only about 8 to 10 percent of filings in each category are usually processed by trial courts in such a way that the decisions are appealable. The actual trial rate (percentage of case dispositions in trial courts of general jurisdiction by jury and

TABLE 7.1 State Appeals from General Trial Court Dispositions 1988

State	Case Dispositions of Trial Courts of General Jurisdiction	Filings in State Intermediate Appellate Courts
Alaska	17,268	497
Arizona	134,379	3,962
Arkansas	126,809	899
California	788,607	17,959
Colorado	142,310	1,946
Connecticut	479,464	1,093
Florida	635,377	16,480
Georgia	221,564	3,023
Hawaii	43,814	120
Idaho	352,587	227
Illinois	5,105,400	8,119
Indiana	541,979	1,222
Iowa	925,748	728
Kansas	415,172	1,176
Kentucky	74,741	2,757
Maryland	180,963	1,974
Massachusetts	1,776,401	2,280
Michigan	243,374	8,559
Minnesota	1,975,887	2,396
Missouri	791,544	3,315
New Mexico	71,342	712
North Carolina	182,047	1,797
Ohio	635,377	10,005
Oregon	101,741	3,739
South Carolina	105,769	307
Utah	26,565	741
Virginia	169,557	1,746
Washington	160,608	3,529
Wisconsin	1,000,889	2,375

SOURCE: National Center for State Courts, *State Court Caseload Statistics: Annual Report 1988* (Williamsburg, VA: National Center for State Courts, 1990), Tables 2 and 8. Reprinted with permission.

nonjury trials combined in 1988) was 6.1 percent for criminal cases and 9.2 percent for civil cases (National Center for State Courts, 1990: 55–60). Further, it is clear that courts themselves, by the content and manner of their decision making, emit signals encouraging or discouraging appeals. Lengthy delays in disposing of appeals, narrowing legal doctrine on substantive points of law, and similar judicial actions can significantly affect the propensity to appeal.

Moreover, Baum (1990: 278–280) has suggested three other factors that help to explain the decision to appeal: the cost of the procedure, the degree of satisfaction with the trial court decision, and the calculation of one's chance of success on appeal. First, in civil cases, it is usually only the relatively prosperous litigant, most commonly Galanter's "Repeat Players" (Wheeler et al., 1987), who can afford the several thousand dollars usually required for appellate expenditures. Trial transcripts, filing fees, briefs arguing points of law not raised at trial—all of this is quite costly, discouraging large numbers of otherwise meritorious appeals. The reverse of this outcome is revealed in the high number of criminal appeals, encouraged by rulings in federal courts that indigents have a right to counsel and free trial transcripts, at least on their first appeal (*Griffin v. Illinois*, 351 U.S. 12, 1956).

Second, and rather obviously, those most dissatisfied with their trial outcome are most likely to appeal. For example, Davies (1982: 558–559) found that jury trial convictions constituted over 70 percent of all criminal appeals to California's First District Intermediate Appellate Court in the late 1970s, such convictions being appealed at the rate of 46.5 percent. This figure may be contrasted to the less than 1 percent of guilty plea convictions being appealed. The two factors most prominent in explaining this difference are the imposition of jail terms (obviously leading to a rather high level of dissatisfaction) and the law itself, which with a few exceptions, prevents appeals of guilty pleas.

Finally, the potential appellant must calculate the probability of success. Even if money is no object in a case in which the outcome is extremely unsatisfactory to the loser, no appeal may be forthcoming if the chances of success are seen as dismal. In some types of cases the advice of appellate attorneys may be crucial. They are likely to be highly knowledgeable in predicting appellate outcomes. Of course, an appeal may be brought as a bargaining tool—to persuade the opposition to settle out of court on terms more favorable than the trial court's award. But in general, these seem to be the factors most likely to affect the decision to appeal.

Except in a small percentage of cases in which state law provides for automatic appeal, one of the parties must initiate the action. Since it is the (sometimes unwritten) rule that all litigants have the opportunity of appellate review, at least at the first level, the first appeal brought is almost always granted. Normally a verbatim record of the trial transcript is required, along with several copies of a written brief covering the issues of fact and law, setting forth arguments about why the decision of the lower court should be reversed. State law usually provides a time deadline by which appeals must be filed. Afterward, the opposing party is given a limited time to file a response.

The case may then be processed by clerks of the appellate court in a number of ways. As seen below, with the dramatic expansion of workloads of state appellate courts, there has been an increasing reliance on "staff processing," whereby attorneys hired by the court screen cases, routing those they regard as truly significant into a category for "full consideration," probably with formal oral argument, leading to a full written opinion.

However, it is likely that the great majority of cases will be reviewed by the clerks or the attorney court staff and decided (usually with affirmations of lower court rulings or, for state supreme courts, an outright denial of review), the judges themselves doing little more than providing general guidelines for screening and overseeing this administrative process (Bird, 1978; Carrington, 1980). In addition to staff screening, a number of other shortcuts to the appellate process are currently practiced by state courts (discussed below).

Some indication of the winnowing process of state supreme courts is suggested by the data in Table 7.2. In the 15 states with intermediate appellate courts and a full set of data available for 1988, we have presented the number of petitions (both mandatory and discretionary) filed with the court for the year, the number granted, and the number of signed opinions. On the average, signed opinions represent only 12 percent of the total cases filed and 29 percent of the petitions granted. The difference in the latter two figures is explained largely by the various shortcut methods these courts now use (in this case, primarily per curium, or abbreviated, opinions) to reduce the number of full opinions their justices write in a given term. Again, figures in the last column may be compared with the 130 to 140 or so full written opinions issued by the U.S. Supreme Court in recent terms.

Less is known about the internal operating procedures of state appellate courts than of federal appellate court procedures. For what could be called "full dress treatment" by state supreme courts, oral argument (an average of 40 minutes in 1984) is usually scheduled, followed by a discussion and vote of the justices in conference, either in person or by phone. Although oral argument has been somewhat reduced in these courts over the past several years, some 7 out of 10 cases considered on the merits are still accompanied by this important procedure (Marvell, 1989: 290).

Following (though sometimes preceding) the conference discussion and vote, the task of drafting the court's opinion is assigned to one of the justices. In a few states the

TABLE 7.2 Disposition of State Supreme Court Filings 1988

State	Petitions Filed	Petitions Granted	Signed Opinions
Alaska	607	392	193
California	4,670	541	122
Georgia	1,637	785	348
Hawaii	760	725	320
Louisiana	2,781	519	149
Maryland	924	382	112
Massachusetts	659	292	253
Michigan	2,666	83	79
Minnesota	922	408	165
Missouri	1,119	177	133
New Jersy	1,711	483	68
New Mexico	1,328	1,116	220
North Carolina	783	204	188
Oregon	1,049	313	128
Wisconsin	915	181	98

SOURCE: National Center for State Courts, *State Court Caseload Statistics: Annual Report 1988* (Williamsburg, VA: National Center for State Courts, 1990), Tables 2 and 6. Reprinted with permission.

chief justice has the prerogative of assigning the opinion, but much more commonly it is determined by lot or by rotation (M. L. Hall, 1990). The drafting, circulating, and bargaining involved at this stage can be important in determining the outcome of the case.

Justices unable to agree fully with the emergent majority opinion are at liberty to draft and submit a concurring or dissenting opinion. Although very common on the U.S. Supreme Court, such open disagreement is relatively rare on state supreme courts. For example, in a study of six such courts in 1975 (Arizona, California, Kentucky, Michigan, Nebraska, and Rhode Island), an average of about 72 percent of their *en banc* (full court) decisions were unanimous, that is, without either concurring or dissenting opinions. Dissent alone occurred in an average of only about 17 percent of the opinions (Fino, 1987: 72). This frequency of dissent would be closer to 10 percent were it not for three rather high-profile, "lighthouse" supreme courts in this sample (California, Michigan, and New Jersey), which are close to the Kagan profile of high-discretion, low-caseload courts— tribunals usually registering dissent rates higher than the national average. State supreme courts frequently report dissent rates below 10 percent, with only about a dozen or so courts above 25 percent (Glick, 1988: 235). As already noted, however, rates of dissent appear to be rising.

For some time political scientists have been intrigued with the question of what factors influence judicial decision making. Research in this vein has tended to be focused on the U.S. Supreme Court, although state appellate courts, especially courts of last resort, have also been the targets of such judicial "behavioral" studies. Background factors (e.g., political party affiliations of the judge, race, religion, and education), conceptions of their judicial role, factors relating to the structure of state courts, and similar variables have been studied in an attempt to predict (explain) appellate and some-times trial court decision making. The findings of this research are much too voluminous to report in detail here (see Baum, 1990: 296–312; Fino, 1987: Ch. 1; Glick, 1990, Chs. 10–11; Goldman and Lamb, 1986; Goldman and Sarat, 1989), but scholars tend to agree that three general clusters of factors can explain most of judicial decision making on state and federal appellate courts. These categories include the values or attitudes of the judges or justices, the internal dynamics of collegial decision making, and sociopolitical environ-mental factors of various kinds. A few examples in each category will be cited to illustrate this strain of research.

It is far too late in the day to argue that the classic or traditional model of decision making by judges explains very much. This model suggests that the judge applies the relevant legal precedent to the instant case (stare decisis), the decision emerging more or less automatically by force of logic. The classic statement of this position, growing directly out of Austinian-Langdellian jurisprudence (Stumpf, 1988: Chs. 1, 2, 7) is that of Justice Owen Roberts in *U.S. v. Butler* (297 U.S. 1, 193) in 1936. In response to continued criticisms for the economically conservative policy-making tendencies on the Court, which led to a number of New Deal measures being held unconstitutional, Justice Roberts, in a somewhat defensive tone, explained the work of the justices thusly:

> There should be no misunderstanding as to the function of this court. . . . It is sometimes said that the court assumes a power to overrule or control the action of the people's representatives. This is a misconception. The Constitution is the supreme law of the land ordained and established by the people. All legislation must conform to the principles it

lays down. When an act of Congress is appropriately challenged in the courts as not conforming to the constitutional mandate, the judicial branch of the Government has only one duty—to lay the article of the Constitution which is invoked beside the statute which is challenged to decide whether the latter squares with the former. All the court does, or can do, is to announce its considered judgment on the question. The only power it has, if such it may be called, is the power of judgment. This court neither approves nor condemns any legislative policy. Its delicate and difficult office is to ascertain and declare whether the legislation is in accordance with or in contravention of, the provisions of the Constitution; and having done that, its duty ends. . . .

Presented in this way, it is easy to see why Roscoe Pound denounced such conceptions of judicial decision making as the "slot machine" theory of law, or what others called "mechanical jurisprudence."

In place of this model of the judicial function modern political scientists, following the general notions of sociological-realist jurisprudence, have substituted an empirically based conception grounded in the values or attitudes of judges. One could argue that casual observation is all that is needed to confirm the apparent validity of this view— judges *are* human and rather obviously decide cases, at least in part, in accordance with their own notions of right and wrong. But political researchers such as Harold Spaeth (1979) and many others have empirically demonstrated this fact through techniques such as cumulative scaling, showing that Supreme Court justices' attachment to certain values common in contemporary society (e.g., freedom, equality, and New Deal economics) can explain some 85 percent of their decisions (Spaeth, 1979).

This is not to deny that stare decisis can be at least the starting point in the complex task of judicial decision making or that *the law* is not a variable to be taken into account in understanding the work of appellate courts. But on balance, we can now say, with Baum (1990), that "policy preferences are the most important of the factors that affect Supreme Court decisions" (136). And what is true of the U.S. Supreme Court is also true, with only minor modifications, of state supreme courts. Although the latter function within a significantly different political and legal context, the very wide range of creativity of state supreme court decision making leaves no doubt that state justices are following the lead of their federal appellate colleagues in reading their own notions of "good" public policy into their decisions.

Too much can be claimed for the value-attitudinal model, however, and no thoughtful scholar of the modern period would argue that it explains all appellate judicial decision making. There are simply too many constraints on judges, including those internal to the judicial decisional framework as well as many to be found in the external political environment in which courts function, to suggest that they are completely free to read their own values into their decisions.

External forces are many, particularly as they operate on state courts. Federalism itself, with the important supremacy clause of the Constitution, means that state judicial action is always subject to review by federal courts. Also, the judiciary of each state functions within a certain political-legal culture, which imposes a number of limits on the range of choices realistically available to the state judge (Tarr and Porter, 1988). More proximate forces of public opinion and political pressures—say, surrounding such issues as the death penalty, crime control, abortion, and the like—can also limit if not at times virtually determine judicial choice in state appellate court decision making. Such environmental factors are too numerous and complex to detail here, but the point seems clear: State courts are far from unchecked in the imposition of the policy choices of their judges.

Finally, most state appellate court determinations are made in a collegial context, either of the court sitting as a whole (*en banc,* as it is called) or at least in panels, usually of three judges. Small-group theory suggests, as has been demonstrated empirically, that such decisional settings can and do impose additional constraints on the "free will" of the judges. The personalities, including leadership qualities, of fellow judges may at times explain voting on collegial courts. Certain justices of state supreme courts (e.g., Alabama, New Jersey, and California) have, by dint of personality, exerted a strong influence on the general direction of state judicial policy (Tarr and Porter, 1988). Increasingly, state supreme courts are given the luxury of controlling their own caseloads, leading, as we saw, to courts with increasing numbers of dissents and more free time for the justices to bargain over drafts of opinion. In such bargaining, personal and collegial variables can often influence the outcome. Also, conflictful relations on the courts can influence the alignment of votes (Baum, 1990: 308). In sum, as Murphy and Pritchett (1961) wrote some time ago,

> Judges . . . are influenced in their judging by personal predilections, by their commitments to ethical norms, and by their understanding of the realities of political life. But . . . the freedom of a judge is limited by the institutional ethos and by the traditions of his calling. A judicial decision is an amalgam of personal judgment and institutional control.

STATE INTERMEDIATE APPELLATE COURTS

For a number of reasons, our attention in this chapter falls primarily on the work of state supreme courts. But as state judicial systems move to the "federal" mode of high-discretion, low-caseload supreme courts, and as caseloads throughout the American judicial system expand, the institution of the state intermediate appellate court (IAC) increases in importance. Our coverage of state appellate processes would thus not be complete without some attention to these "first-level" institutions.

As suggested, these intermediate appeals courts were not common in the nineteenth century (only 7 had been created by 1891), and even by the late 1960s only 9 more states had used this device to relieve their supreme courts of the heavy caseloads, previously discussed. Between 1968 and 1984, however, 15 additional states joined the IAC movement, with 7 more IACs being created since 1984. Thus, today only 12 (mostly small or sparsely populated states) are without these courts (National Center for State Courts, 1990: 18).

As shown in Figure 7.1, the states have developed four basic models of appellate court structure. The most common arrangement, that found in 32 of our states, is of one court of last resort (usually called the supreme court) and one IAC. However, in a number of these (usually populous) states, the IAC is subdivided into geographic districts, as opposed to hearing appeals statewide, as in California and Florida. A second basic plan is to have two courts of last resort (the Texas and Oklahoma model), one each for civil and criminal appeals, combined with one IAC. Third is an arrangement in four states of

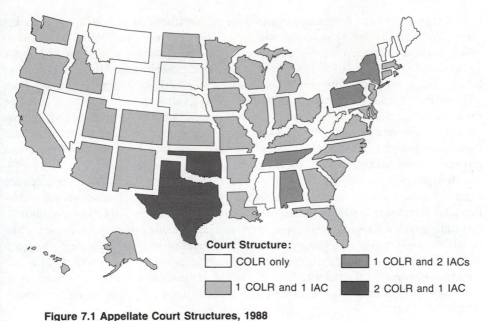

Court Structure:

☐ COLR only   ▨ 1 COLR and 2 IACs

▧ 1 COLR and 1 IAC   ■ 2 COLR and 1 IAC

Figure 7.1 Appellate Court Structures, 1988

SOURCE: National Center for State Courts, *State Court Caseload Statistics: Annual Report, 1988*
(Williamsburg, VA: National Center for State Courts, 1990). Reprinted with permission.

multiple (two) IACs combined with one court of last resort at the apex of the structure.
Alabama, New York, Pennsylvania, and Tennessee have created such systems, although
they vary in the jurisdiction of their IACs. Pennsylvania's two IACs are called The
Commonwealth Court and the Superior Court, with jurisdiction divided along subject
matter. The two Alabama and Tennessee intermediate courts are completely separated
between civil and criminal cases, and New York divides the work of its two IACs in
accordance with the trial court originating the appeal (National Center for State Courts,
1990: 18–19). Finally, as noted, 12 states and the District of Columbia have only one
appellate court, their court of last resort.

By definition, the vast majority of cases heard on appeal in the states are disposed of
by state IACs. As we saw, this was the primary, although not exclusive, purpose for which
they were usually created—to act as screening devices so that state courts of last resort
could concentrate on the important policy issues in the law. Data supplied by the National
Center for State Courts (1990: Table 6) indicate that of the 221,794 cases filed in all state
appellate courts in 1988, some 70 percent, or about 154,500, were IAC filings. These
courts account for about 87 percent of all signed opinions issued by state appellate courts
in states in which they are found. Moreover, their workload is even heavier if measured by
per-judge output. Figures for 1988 indicate that in the 25 states for which we have
complete data, the average written opinion per judge for justices of state courts of last
resort was 4,984, whereas for judges of the state IACs the figure was 34,384.

In a study of the workloads of all state appellate courts from 1968 to 1984, Marvell
(1989: 285) reports that as measured either by case filings or decisions on the merits, the

rate of growth has been dramatic. Decisions on the merits issued by both levels of courts grew 252 percent in the 39 states for which complete data were available. The extent to which IACs have become the draft animals of state appellate review is suggested by the astounding fact, reported by Marvell, that as measured either by case filings, decisions on the merits, or numbers of judges, 98 percent of this overall state appellate growth from 1974 to 1984 occurred at the intermediate appellate level. Although allowances must be made for different methods of reporting as well as how opinions are reached (whether by the entire court or by panels of judges) in the various states, the excessive workloads of these intermediate appellate bodies, however measured, have become one of the major problems in the smooth functioning of the process of state appellate review.

It is for this reason that the lion's share of research and administrative attention regarding state IACs has been focused on the caseload problem. Researchers have catalogued at least seven techniques, some quasi-experimental, others rather well established, that state judges and legislatures have developed to handle this massive case demand. The first is the basic step of establishing, or if already established, then expanding, the reach of the IAC. We have already noted the incidence of this approach. From 1968 to the present, nearly half of the states (22) have established these courts anew, and a dozen or so other state legislatures have significantly increased the jurisdiction of the previously established court.

One of the most important questions concerning IACs is whether, in fact, they lead to a significant reduction in the workload of the state supreme court, and more generally, what the impact of their creation is on the overall operation of state appellate processes. This is a difficult question to answer because outcomes depend on the jurisdictional share each level of court is assigned when the IAC is created. Given a rather sharp jurisdictional separation between the two courts (the error-correcting function left to the IAC, and lawmaking to the court of last resort), combined with a high level of discretion accorded to the state supreme court justices in what cases they take, it is possible to create a situation in which over 90 percent of all appellate cases are handled by state IACs (e.g., California, 99 percent; Florida, 95 percent; New Jersey, 98 percent; Marvell, 1989: 286). However, with relatively large numbers of cases qualifying for mandatory review by the state's court of last resort, combined perhaps with legislation providing for double review of major categories of cases (see Marvell, 1989), one may find only limited relief to the state's supreme court, with the IACs processing much smaller percentages of the state's total appellate load (e.g., 46 percent in Connecticut, 54 percent in Iowa, and 68 percent in New Mexico in 1984). The point is, of course, that creation of an IAC does not automatically decrease the supreme court's workload.

It should also be noted that the creation of an intermediate appellate court of review, unless accompanied by a seriously restricted grant of jurisdiction, does not guarantee an overall reduction in appellate case filings in the state. In fact, it is not uncommon for the establishment of such courts to coincide with, if not help bring about, a rise in appellate demand, resulting in a shift of the "caseload crisis" from the supreme court to the new IAC. For instance, between 1977 and 1981 four states created new IACs: Alaska, Arkansas, Hawaii, and Wisconsin. In all four states overall appellate filings increased significantly, an average of about 150 percent (Stumpf, 1988: 365).

Second, states have used the simple device of increasing the number of judges on their IACs as a means of handling the burgeoning caseloads. The number of state IAC judges increased 73 percent in the decade 1974–1984, and the growth continues unabated. The average number of authorized judgeships on these 37 courts (omitting North Dakota) is now about 21 (National Center for State Courts, 1990: Table 3). These judges usually work in panels of three (the third time-saving device), although at least two states use somewhat larger panels. This arrangement, of course, permits a reduction in the number of arguments heard for the court as a whole as well as fewer briefs to read per judge and less work in preparing and reading drafts of opinions. The panel system, also used in the U.S. courts of appeal, is often cited as one of the reasons for the low incidence of dissent on these courts. With this smaller group of decision makers, dissent is by definition a one-person game. In explaining this phenomenon for the federal appellate courts, Richardson and Vines (1970) remarked,

> Since there are only three judges to a panel . . . the objective probability of dissent is much less than on a court with nine [or 5 or 7] judges. Furthermore, a judge, when he dissents, always dissents alone. The intrinsic loneliness of dissent . . . may well act as a deterrent. . . . (139)

These considerations, combined with the general press of time, make dissents a luxury usually bypassed by judges of these courts. As one California judge confessed, "I hate to say this, but just the workload alone may encourage one judge to agree with the others, because otherwise he or she would have to write a dissenting opinion" (Wold, 1978: 64).

Abbreviated practices relating to oral argument, the handling of opinions, and summary judgments are three further devices used on state IACs (as well as some state supreme courts) to help handle large caseloads. Since the drafting, circulation, and preparation of opinions for publication constitute the most time-consuming steps in the work of appellate judges, it is in these areas that IACs can gain the most ground in keeping up with their caseloads. Deciding cases with no opinion is practiced in at least some cases by about half of all state appellate courts. Even more common is the practice of not publishing opinions, one observer concluding that unpublished opinions take about half the time of fully published ones (Marvell, 1989: 288). Wold and Caldeira (1980: 343) report that the California Court of Appeals published only 15.7 percent of its opinions in 1977. At present, well over half of the decisions issued by state IACs nationwide are unpublished, and the practice is definitely growing—in California and elsewhere.

Oral argument, too, seems to be passing from the scene in a growing number of state appellate courts. In 1984, only 30 percent of cases heard before state IACs were accompanied by oral argument, and over the past 20 years the time limit for oral argument has been reduced by nearly half. When one adds the growth in the practice of summary judgment—a procedure permitting decisions quite early in the appeals process, even before the filing of case records or briefs—one can hardly avoid the conclusion that American state appellate procedure may well have been curtailed to the point of seriously endangering its value from the point of view of error correcting, aside from the important function of developing new law. This conclusion is buttressed by the incidence of the seventh technique frequently employed by state IACs as well as a growing number of supreme courts—the use of law clerks and screening personnel in the form of staff attorneys.

Law clerks, of course, are used in all appellate courts in the land, and staff attorneys, too, are becoming increasingly common. But it is the pace of growth, combined with the significantly enhanced role of these additional court personnel, that is causing increased concern in a number of observers. The most frequent criticism is that our appellate courts, state IACs being perhaps the best (or worst) examples, are becoming little more than faceless (or judgeless) bureaucracies, these various shortcuts to genuine appellate adjudication increasingly devaluing the supervisory role of legal appeal (Bird, 1978; Davies, 1981; Howard, 1981: 277–279; McCree, 1981). A particularly telling study pointing to this conclusion is that of Thomas Davies in his research on California's Intermediate Appellate Court for the First Appellate District, sitting in San Francisco.

California's IAC was created in 1905 and now addresses some 99 percent of all appellate cases in the state. Its caseload in 1977 was about 11,000 filings per year, the work at that time being divided among 51 appellate judges throughout the state. This number, of course, has helped to provide that state's supreme court with the freedom to pick and choose its own cases, resulting in a high-discretion, low-caseload supreme court, which has moved to first rank as perhaps the most creative policy-making state judicial body in the nation. At the same time, California's IAC has shouldered an immense caseload in that state of 30 million population. In 1988 it handled some 18,000 filings among 88 judges, or about 124 per judge, and it issued over 8,600 opinions, the largest output of any appellate court in the nation (National Center for State Courts, 1990: Tables 2, 6).

Early in its history this court, especially its First District, moved to abbreviated procedures in processing its cases. Shortened opinions, the panel approach, reduction in the number of written opinions, an increasing use of clerks, and a central staff of attorneys to screen cases became the principal means to handle its ballooning caseload. But as Davies (1981) studied the work of this court, he found something of a Gresham's Law at work. That is, these shortcuts to full appellate review were not applied to all cases equally. Rather, as one might expect based on extant organizational theory, this court distributed its scarce resources in a manner appropriate to its central concerns of political survival and the enhancement of values shared by its most significant political constituents.

Thus, with the criminal bar having low status (Heinz and Laumann, 1978), criminal defendants having little or no political influence, and with criminal cases affording little opportunity for creative lawmaking leading to the enhancement of the careers of IAC judges, criminal appeals are given short shrift as contrasted to civil cases. Lawyers involved in civil litigation, especially those representing corporate interests, enjoy much higher prestige in the practicing bar. Such attorneys are more likely to be active participants in the politics of their communities and in the local bar, and being highly paid counsel, they have a much greater interest in the development of full and complete court processes as a demonstration to their clients of the results of their often expensive handiwork (Davies, 1981: 379). Moreover, in part because of the greater resources usually invested in the civil appeal, the briefs are more likely to contain interesting, even novel legal claims more attractive to appellate judges.

For these and other reasons the organizational imperative of this IAC led to a highly disproportionate amount of resources expended on civil as opposed to criminal appeals. Research findings indicate a rather remarkable bias, even in the planning stages of court operations. Thus, when California's Administrative Office of the Courts undertook to estimate the resources required to process various types of cases, civil appeals were assigned a weight of 20, criminal appeals only 10. Similarly, civil writ petitions were given a weight of 2 units, habeas corpus petitions 1 unit.

Criminal appeals much more frequently led to nonpublished or, if published, brief, opinions (civil opinions were, in fact, three times more likely to be published). Further, criminal appeals were two and one-half times as likely to be processed by the attorney staff of the court as opposed to receiving the full attention of the judges. Even among civil cases, Davies (1981: 396) found that the more prestigious (commercial/corporate money claims and the like) were over three times as likely to receive full judicial attention as were lower status civil appeals such as divorce or personal injury cases. Thus, in the business of allocating scarce resources to the important issues of legal appeal, all parties are not equal, with the criminal cases, theoretically involving the most significant issues for society as a whole, receiving only minimal attention. As Davies concludes, the danger is that

> . . . expedited processes might divert the Court of Appeal's attention away from criminal appeals to such an extent as virtually to preclude meaningful appellate supervision over the quality of criminal justice proceedings. What supervision is possible when staff attorneys write two-thirds of the court's criminal opinions with the expectation that they are dealing with only "routine" or "frivolous" cases? (399)

Although the findings from one court do not conclusively demonstrate a serious decline in the quality of state appellate review, such case studies, along with ancillary commentary (e.g., Carrington, 1980; Howard, 1981; McCree, 1981; Wold and Caldeira, 1980), suggest that this may be happening in a number of jurisdictions. Given the continued, and increasing, pressure of caseloads on these courts, we probably cannot avoid a deterioration of meaningful review of state trial court decision making, a development that also appears rather well advanced at the federal level.

STATE SUPREME COURTS: THE EMERGENCE OF THE "NEW" JUDICIAL FEDERALISM

If one doubts the reemergence of state supreme courts as major policy-making institutions in our political-legal system, one has only to consider the recent events surrounding the California Supreme Court. In perhaps the most intense, celebrated, and expensive judicial "election" in American history, three members of that court were, as one activist put it, "slam dunked out of business," giving then Governor George Deukmejian an opportunity to replace them with justices more sympathetic to a conservative, "law and order" orientation. Although retention elections under merit selection plans usually produce little voter interest, this referendum was probably the hottest issue in the 1986 California elections (see Chapter 3 and Culver and Wold, 1986–1987). In excess of $6 million was spent in the campaign to defeat these three justices—Chief Justice Rose Elizabeth Bird and Justices Cruz Reynoso and Joseph Grodin—and some $2 million dollars were expended on behalf of these justices in their unsuccessful fight for retention.

By all accounts, the record of these "liberal" justices in death penalty cases was the prime issue in the campaign. In 56 cases in which the California Supreme Court was asked to review death penalties imposed by California trial courts, the justices overturned the sentence in 95 percent of the cases. Chief Justice Bird became the lightening rod of the whole campaign, in part because of her record of voting to overturn death penalty cases *100 percent* of the time. With the replacement of these justices by those having a greater willingness to please the voters, the sustaining of death penalty sentences rose dramatically, 58 of 83 such sentences being upheld between 1986 and 1989.

Although few expect a frequent replay of these dramatic events in other states, the California election graphically demonstrates the intense interest of voters, interest groups (including bar associations), political parties, and of course other politicians in the outcome of state appellate court decisions, all of which underscore the political character of the work of these tribunals. Indeed, by 1990, in California and elsewhere political candidates considered it political suicide to run for office without announcing that they stood foursquare behind capital punishment.

As suggested, the historic swing in our federal system of government signaled by the Reagan presidency portends a significantly enhanced role for state supreme courts. With the increased modernization of these tribunals at the apex of state adjudicatory systems, we now find ourselves in an exciting new era of state appellate court activism. Indeed, whereas only a decade or two ago American constitutional law was almost exclusively the province of the federal courts, it is now impossible to understand the leading edge of American legal doctrine without serious attention to developments in state constitutional law.

To highlight the renaissance of state constitutional law it is necessary to take a quick look backward to an earlier, more familiar era of judicial policy-making. Since the early 1950s an entire generation of scholars, teachers, and commentators have become accustomed to stating American constitutional law almost entirely in terms of the evolution of federal, especially Supreme Court, doctrine. An examination of current scholarly texts and treatises on the subject will quickly reveal the almost total exclusion of state constitutional law (Friedman, 1988: 34; Galie, 1987). This bypassing of state court activity grew out of the dramatic judicial activism of the Warren Court, particularly in the civil liberties field. Although the "nationalization" of the federal Bill of Rights began in the 1920s with decisions such as *Meyer v. Nebraska* (262 U.S. 390, 1923) and, more pointedly, *Gitlow v. New York* (268 U.S. 652, 1925), the Warren Court decisions in the 1960s greatly accelerated this important constitutional development, causing observer and practitioner alike to look to the U.S. Supreme Court for the protection and enhancement of basic rights.[2]

Decisions applying the Bill of Rights to the states in the areas of right to counsel, protection against unreasonable searches and seizures (the exclusionary rule), prohibition against cruel and unusual punishment, the right to trial by jury, and so on virtually transformed American criminal law from a two-level system of national (federal) versus state criminal law to a set of standards universally applied to all courts and police activities in the nation. When one adds the startling Warren Court doctrines in the areas of racial segregation, separation of church and state (e.g., prayer in public schools), legislative reapportionment, and a newly created national right of privacy, it is easy to understand why American constitutional law came to be defined as national or federal in nature, state supreme courts being brought into the picture largely as examples of evasion of federal legal doctrine (see, e.g., Johnson and Canon, 1984).

Beginning in the early 1970s, however, the thrust of liberal judicial activism began to wane under the more conservative orientation of the Burger Court. Although the somewhat realigned Court did not engage in outright reversal of important Warren Court decisions, the broadening of civil rights slowed considerably, and the Burger Court justices began to chip away at a number of Warren Court doctrines (Blasi, 1983). More important for our discussion, the Burger and Rehnquist Courts have shown signs of actually inviting a larger role for state appellate courts, either by refusing to hear cases (thereby allowing state courts to make these final determinations) or by setting forth doctrine rather clearly intended to encourage a larger role for state supreme courts (see, e.g., Savage, 1990).

In 1972, for example, Justice Lewis Powell wrote for the Supreme Court in the watershed case of *San Antonio Independent School District v. Rodriguez* (411 U.S. 1). The Court was faced with the question of whether or not wide disparities in state funding of public schools between richer and poorer school districts violated the equal protection clause of the U.S. Constitution. Earlier, in August 1971, the California Supreme Court had made national headlines in its decision in *Serrano v. Priest* (5 Cal. 3rd 584), by holding that the state's school-funding formula violated the equal protection clause of both the state and federal constitutions. And about the same time, a three-judge federal district court in Texas had ruled that the gross inequalities in the funding of education between the wealthier and poorer school districts in that state stood in violation of the federal equal protection clause (*Rodriguez v. San Antonio Independent School District,* 337 F. Supp. 280, W.D. Texas, 1971).

Although Justice Powell declined to declare education a fundamental right and poverty a "suspect classification," he was not content simply with reversing the federal district court decision in Texas. Rather, in a wide-ranging essay on American education and American federalism, he shunned "judicial intrusion into otherwise legitimate state activities," denounced a too long and heavy reliance by states on local property taxes for the funding of education, and in general encouraged innovative and creative policy-making at the state level to handle the problem (Friedelbaum, 1987: 39–42). Few who read the decision could doubt the strong encouragement it gave for state action, and a number of states responded positively.

As seen, the California Supreme Court, as it often does, led the nation in using its own state constitution's equal protection clause to reorder public school financing in that state. Under what observers have called the influence of "horizontal federalism," a number of other states followed suit. In New Jersey, for example, the supreme court held, in *Robinson v. Cahill* (62 N.J. 473, 1973), that the state's constitutional provision requiring the legislature to provide a "thorough and efficient system of free public schools" mandated an abandonment of public school financing strictly on the basis of property taxes. The court subsequently forced the state legislature to adopt an income tax law to help bring about a more equitable distribution of school funds (see Lehne, 1978). Since then, about a dozen additional states have moved in a similar direction, either by state supreme court decision or by legislative enactment or both (Briffault, 1988: 119–120; Flanigan, 1990; Mosk, 1988: 56).

In another key decision of the U.S. Supreme Court, the invitation to state judicial creativity was stated more explicitly. In *Robins v. Pruneyard Shopping Center* (592 P.2d 341, 1979), the California Supreme Court (Justice Frank Newman) held that in spite of U.S. Supreme Court rulings to the contrary, private shopping centers, under California's constitution, could not ban student appearances on the premises to circulate political petitions. In an earlier decision, *Lloyd Corp. v. Tanner* (407 U.S. 551) in 1972, the U.S. Supreme Court had ruled that private shopping centers were not required to permit such free speech.

Although many observers expected the Burger Court to reverse California's *Pruneyard* ruling, the exact opposite occurred. In a unanimous decision written by Justice Rehnquist, the high court emphasized the doctrine of independent state grounds in upholding, "the State's asserted interest in promoting more expansive rights of free speech than conferred by the Federal Constitution" (*Pruneyard Shopping Center v. Robins, 447 U.S. 74, 85, 1980*). As one scholar noted,

> If there is any unifying element that permeates the opinions in *Pruneyard* [several justices wrote concurrent opinions] it is adherence to the principle of state-created rights independently derived. . . . Justice Rehnquist's sweeping prose . . . def[ies] any meaningful rationale except for this dedication to a "new" judicial federalism. . . . [The Court's unanimity] was grounded upon the untapped and largely untried resources of the state courts. (Friedelbaum, 1987: 38)

If there remains any doubt about the leanings of the U.S. Supreme Court on this matter, we may refer to the remarks of Associate Justice William Brennan (1987), who in a speech at Harvard Law School argued that the "dimunition of federal scrutiny and protection [of civil rights] mandates the assumption of a more responsible state court role." He added that he was certain that the Court's recent retreat on civil rights "should be interpreted as a plain invitation to state courts to step into the breach." And step into the breach they did!

Before surveying recent state court policy developments, it might be well to describe briefly the tools available to state appellate courts to enter into their new policy activism. Although the doctrine of supremacy of federal law significantly limits the range of policy-making available to these courts, there is nothing preventing states from either breaking new ground in state constitutional law or extending rights and liberties beyond those minimally guaranteed under the national Constitution as interpreted by the U.S. Supreme Court. The constitutions of the 50 states are rich in detail and novel provisions, affording state appellate court judges fertile soil for the nurturing of unique if not exotic legal doctrine. For example, 17 state constitutions contain "little ERAs"; 10 embody specific provisions protecting the right to privacy; and a number of others provide, in varying language, for the protection of the environment (Tarr and Porter, 1987: 4). As long as state constitutional doctrine does not minimize federal guarantees and/or where the state courts explicitly stake out their decisions on "bona fide separate, adequate, and independent [state] grounds. . ." (*Michigan v. Long, 463 U.S. 1041, 1983*), state court rulings may be presumed to be valid (see Abrahamson and Gutmann, 1987: 96–99).

Additionally, state judges enjoy several advantages of flexibility usually denied their federal brethren. First, states are the recipients of inherent, plenary power rather than specific, delegated powers. In these circumstances, state courts are not required to search for constitutional provisions *supporting* state policies; rather, they have only to satisfy themselves that there are no specific federal or state constitutional provisions *prohibiting* the action in question (Galie, 1985: 3).

Second, federal courts, as they themselves have interpreted the Constitution, are limited in their work by the "cases and controversies" rule. Historically, this rule has narrowed the types of cases federal courts will hear as well as the nature of decisions they render. Taxpayer suits, for example, have generally been ruled out of federal adjudication on grounds that the parties lack sufficient standing (e.g., *Frothingham v. Mellon,* 262 U.S. 447, 1923). On similar grounds, federal courts have usually declined to hear cases in which there is no real, live dispute. Moot or hypothetical issues are thus nonjusticiable, placing advisory opinions out of bounds (*Hayburn's Case,* 2. Dall. 409, 1792). On both counts, state courts are at an advantage. At least 10 states specifically permit advisory opinions, and in Massachusetts, for example, "the advisory opinion is used regularly and in connection with matters of major constitutional significance" (Galie, 1985: 4). Likewise, taxpayer suits are allowed in a number of states concerning a wide variety of public issues.

Another difference between the exercise of state and federal judicial power lies in the Fourteenth Amendment. As a basis for the application of federal constitutional standards to state law, this amendment is specifically limited to *state action:* "No *state* may make or enforce any law which shall abridge the. . . ." Although federal court rulings have sometimes circumvented this language, the doctrine of state action unquestionably limits the ability of federal courts to scrutinize the private activities of citizens within the states. The Supreme Court's *Pruneyard* ruling, discussed above, is only one example of this limitation in operation. But whatever constraints this amendment places on federal courts, it operates on state judicial policy-making not at all, leading to a much broader range of activity subject to state judicial cognizance.

Finally, considerations of federalism per se can often interfere with federal judicial policy-making, whereas by definition state courts have no such restriction. The holding of the U.S. Supreme Court in the landmark case of *San Antonio Independent School District v. Rodriguez* (411 U.S. 1, 1973), discussed more fully above, is a prime example. The fact that we have a federal system of government, with powers divided between the two levels, means in law as well as in practice that federal courts are reluctant to play a hands-on role in many state and local policy disputes. State supreme courts, on the other hand, have been known to mention specifically this absence of federalism's restraints in moving ahead with important policy pronouncements (Galie, 1985: 6–7).

Clearly, additional factors work to the advantage of state courts in fashioning public policy or in helping to determine the policy agenda for other state agencies. But this discussion should suffice to suggest the broad legal base these courts enjoy as they launch into the current era of increased judicial activism. It is now appropriate to set forth a few examples of extant judicial policies that are being developed at the state level.

The field of state constitutional law is currently characterized by a richness and variety unknown since the aggressive development of the common law in the late nineteenth century. Although it is impossible to cover the entire terrain in this brief discussion (for overviews, see Abrahamson and Gutmann, 1987; Friedelbaum, 1988; Galie, 1987; "The Interpretation of State Constitutional Rights," 1982; "New Development in State Constitutional Law," 1987; "State Constitution in a Federal System," 1988), we may begin by noting that in the field of civil liberties alone, scholars have catalogued over 450 instances in which state courts of last resort have interpreted their own constitutions as providing rights broader than those contained in U.S. Supreme Court rulings (Sullivan, 1990; Wermiel, 1988). Indeed, this new "judicial federalism," as it is called, is probably the most noteworthy development in American constitutional law in the present era. A few examples will illustrate this ground swell of state judicial policy-making.

In addition to the school-funding revolution noted above, freedom of speech and press, as in the *Pruneyard* case, has been a subject of considerable activity. One of the most notable departures of state supreme courts has been in the area of public access to judicial proceedings. In *Gannett v. DePasquale* (443 U.S. 368) in 1979, the U.S. Supreme Court upheld the exclusion of the press from a pretrial court hearing. Although the Court later seemed to retreat a bit from that position, *DePasquale* caused considerable concern in the states, not to mention in the press. In North Dakota, for example, the supreme court there interpreted the state constitution to the contrary, that is, as guaranteeing public and press access to virtually all judicial proceedings. Similar rulings came from the Oregon and West Virginia supreme courts. In other states, restrictions on press access to court sessions have been severely curtailed, the overall impact being a more liberal view of the freedom of the press in such matters relative to the doctrine set forth in *DePasquale* (Tarr, 1988b: 33–36).

Since California's *Pruneyard* ruling, other state appellate courts have been careful to stake out independent state positions on the right of free speech on private property. Although few states have followed the California lead in toto, some state supreme courts (e.g., New Jersey, Pennsylvania, and Washington) have upheld petition drives or the distribution of leaflets on private property, in seeming contradiction to federal court interpretations of the First Amendment (Davies and Banks, 1987: 16–21; Tarr, 1988a: 9).

In part because the U.S. Supreme Court has been unable to develop uniform, clear-cut guidelines on what types of expression (e.g., alleged obscenity) are protected by the First Amendment, state supreme courts are developing their own approaches, often taking into consideration the political culture and history of their state. Thus, in a rather remarkable opinion striking down the conviction of an adult book store owner in 1987, the Oregon Supreme Court rejected the strictures of the federal doctrine in holdings such as *Miller v. California* (413 U.S. 15, 1973), reasoning that the Oregon constitution was written by "rugged and robust individuals" who did not look kindly on "governmental imposition of some people's views of morality on the free expression of others." The court then held that "In this state any person can write, print, read, say, show or sell anything to a consenting adult even though that expression may be generally or universally considered 'obscene' " (732 P.2d 9, 18, Ore. 1987).

Indeed, Oregon's Supreme Court, under the leadership of Justice Hans Linde, has become a national beacon in the development of a body of state constitutional law on freedom of expression (Tarr, 1988b; 46, n. 74). However, a number of other states have also been quite active in the field, prime examples being New York, California, and New Jersey.

Criminal procedures issues have also provided a fruitful arena for state judicial policy-making in this era of the new judicial federalism. In the area of search and seizure, particularly the application and interpretation of the exclusionary rule, states have always been at some variance with federal judicial doctrine. A number of state supreme courts had instituted the exclusionary rule well before the U.S. Supreme Court did so in 1961 in *Mapp v. Ohio* (367 U.S. 643). And when the Supreme Court, in *U.S. v. Leon* (468 U.S. 897, 1984) and *Maryland v. Garrison* (480 U.S. 79, 1987), began to chew away at the requirements of that rule (that evidence illegally seized in violation of the Fourth Amendment may not be admitted in court), a number of state courts refused to go along. Again on independent state grounds of their own constitutions, states such as New Jersey, New

York, Michigan, Mississippi, and Massachusetts struck out in other directions, generally hewing to a fairly strict exclusion of tainted evidence (Mosk, 1988: 60–61). Additionally, the supreme courts of Washington and Oregon have given advance notice that their states' exclusionary rules rest on independent state ground, should the U.S. Supreme Court further water down this right (Tarr, 1988a: 9).

In a similar vein, as the current Supreme Court shows signs of moving away from the requirements of *Miranda v. Arizona* (384 U.S. 436, 1966)—criminal suspects must be warned of their rights, including the right to remain silent and to request the assistance of an attorney—a number of states have not been willing to follow that lead, preferring a closer observance of these rights. The California and Hawaii supreme courts are only two examples (Mosk, 1988: 58).

In a wide-ranging set of other civil liberties issues, state supreme courts are making new law at a surprising rate. The rights to privacy, issues of gender discrimination, further issues having to do with search and seizure, variations of federal rights in jury trials, right to counsel, state aid to religion, and so on—these and other areas suggest the spread of current policy-making by state supreme courts (Davis and Banks, 1987; Friedelbaum, 1988; Mosk, 1988). But it is not only in the field of civil rights that state supreme courts are breaking new ground. Property and economic rights are also being reexamined by these tribunals.

Whereas students of constitutional law are familiar with the abandonment of the substantive due process doctrine of liberty of contract in federal courts, state courts, under long-established interpretations of state constitutions, continue to use such concepts as due process and equal protection to judge the reasonableness of public incursions into private property rights. After a detailed study of such adjudication at the state level, Galie (1988) concluded,

> State supreme courts continue to . . . grant greater protection to economic rights than would be forthcoming from the federal judiciary. All but three states have refused to follow the lead of the U.S. Supreme Court in its rejection of substantive due process and equal protection in the area of economic regulation. There is no doubt about the continued solicitude for economic rights on the part of state supreme courts; there are doubts about the justification for such activism. (81–82)

At the same time, supreme courts in other states are developing new doctrines to move public policy in an opposite direction, so to speak. In New Jersey, for example, the state's highest court held in 1975, and again in 1983, that municipalities must provide their fair share of low-cost housing. These widely heralded rulings, dubbed *Mt. Laurel I and II (Southern Burlington County NAACP v. Township of Mt. Laurel*, 336 A. 2d 713, N.J. 1975; and 456 A. 2d 390, N.J. 1983), were based on the doctrine of "regional general welfare"—that states may be required to use their powers to promote the general welfare, particularly in economically deprived areas. This was probably the most far-reaching judicial decision on exclusionary zoning in the nation (Galie, 1988: 109). The impact of these rulings on the state's economic and political system was profound. Said one observer, the court "irrevocably changed the name of the political game in New Jersey" (Witt, 1988: 33). The main result of these decisions, as it was in a number of other state supreme court policy forays, was to create a policy agenda item for the state legislature:

> Of lasting benefit [of Mt. Laurel] is the conversation that it set off. What the court did was to force upon the legislature consideration of an issue that the legislature did not want to think about and would not have done anything about but for the litigation. The problem was brought into the sunlight by litigation. (35)

Land use cases in general have helped to change the face of cities and towns in a number of states. State courts are increasingly showing their willingness to limit private land development in the interest of the community as a whole. An example recently cited was the Fairfax County (Virginia) Board of Supervisors, which replated a housing development from 40,000 to 8,000 homes on the basis of earlier Virginia Supreme Court holdings indicating support for such action. Faced with voter initiatives and doctrines, such as regional general welfare and/or environmental protection clauses in state constitutions, private land developers are being forced to curtail their activities in favor of long-dormant environmental concerns. Thus, joined either by the grassroots sentiments of citizens or the legislature or both, state supreme courts are increasing their relevance across a broad terrain of state and local policy-making.

As one observer noted, "The realm of state constitutional law is a beehive of activity," with state supreme courts for the first time in over 50 years beginning to experiment in policy areas previously thought to be exclusive federal domain. "Truly," as Justice William Brennan (1987) has said, "state courts have responded with marvelous enthusiasm to many not-so-subtle invitations to fill the constitutional gaps left by the decisions of the Supreme Court." As the U.S. Supreme Court continues to move in the direction of a lower level of policy creativity, it may be expected that state supreme courts will increasingly "define the quality of life" in American states and communities (Witt, 1988: 30).

CONCLUSION

With the preponderance of appellate judicial policy-making taking place in the states, combined with the swing toward decentralization within the American federal system, a whole new (or actually, renewed) chapter in the study of the American judiciary is opening up for scholar and practitioner alike. Not only may American constitutional doctrine (the substance of the law) no longer be stated purely in terms of the work of federal courts, but also important new lessons having to do with the process or politics of our judicial system are being written at the state level. Surely the case has been made that in our teaching and research, state courts can no longer be ignored as stepchildren of our judicial system. And nowhere is the evidence supporting this proposition more convincing than in the current work of state appellate tribunals.

NOTES

1. The authors are indebted to Charles Sheldon (1987) for his discussion of the development of state judicial review. Also insightful is Charles Grove Haines (1932).
2. For readers unfamiliar with the meaning of the "nationalization" of the Bill of Rights, see any standard constitutional law casebook, such as Alpheus T. Mason and Donald Grier Stephenson,

Jr., *American Constitutional Law,* 9th ed. (Englewood Cliffs, NJ: Prentice Hall, 1990), especially Ch. 9. *Nationalization* essentially means the application of the guarantees in the Bill of Rights of the national Constitution to the states, largely through a broadening of the due process clause of the Fourteenth Amendment.

REFERENCES

Abrahamson, Shirley S., and Diane S. Gutman. 1987. "The New Federalism: State Constitutions and State Courts." 71 *Judicature* 88.

Aumann, Francis R. 1940. *The Changing American Legal System: Some Selected Phases.* Columbus: Ohio State University Press.

Bator, Paul M., Paul J. Mishkin, Daniel J. Meltzer, and David L. Shapiro. 1988. *Hart and Wechsler's the Federal Courts and the Federal System,* 3rd ed. Westbury, NY: Foundation Press.

Baum, Lawrence. 1990. *American Courts: Process and Policy,* 2nd ed. Boston: Houghton Mifflin.

Baum, Lawrence, and Bradley C. Canon. 1982. "State Supreme Courts as Activists: New Doctrines in the Law of Torts." In Mary Cornelia Porter and G. Alan Tarr, eds., *State Supreme Courts: Policymakers in the Federal System.* Westport, CT: Greenwood Press.

Bird, Rose Elizabeth. 1978. "The Hidden Judiciary." 17 *Judges Journal* 4.

Blasi, Vincent, ed. 1983. *The Burger Court: The Counter-Revolution That Wasn't.* New Haven, CT: Yale University Press.

Brennan, Justice William J., Jr., 1987, April 11. "Remarks of William J. Brennan, Jr. 100th Anniversary Dinner." *Harvard Law Review.*

Briffault, Richard. 1988. "Localism in State Constitutional Law." 496 *Annals* 117.

Cardozo, Benjamin N. 1924. *The Growth of the Law.* New Haven, CT: Yale University Press.

Carrington, Paul D. 1980. "Ceremony and Realism: Demise of Appellate Procedure." 66 *American Bar Association Journal* 860.

Culver, John H., and John T. Wold. 1986–1987. "Rose Bird and the Politics of Judicial Accountability in California" and "The Defeat of the California Justices: The Campaign, the Electorate, and the Issue of Judicial Accountability." 70 *Judicature* 81, 348.

Davies, Thomas Y. 1981. "Gresham's Law Revisited: Expedited Processing Techniques and the Allocation of Appellate Resources." 6 *Justice System Journal* 372.

Davies, Thomas Y. 1982. "Affirmed: A Study of Criminal Appeals and Decision-Making Norms in a California Court of Appeals." 1982 *American Bar Foundation Research Journal* 543.

Davis, Sue, and Taunya L. Banks. 1987. "State Constitutions, Freedom of Expression, and Search and Seizure: Prospects for State Court Reincarnation." 17 *Publius* 13.

Fino, Susan P. 1987. *The Role of State Supreme Courts in the New Judicial Federalism.* Westport, CT: Greenwood Press.

Flanigan, James. 1990, June 3. "Taxing for Schools, Investing in the Future." *Los Angeles Times,* p. D1.

Frank, Jerome E. 1949. *Courts on Trial: Myth and Reality in American Jurisprudence.* Princeton, NJ: Princeton University Press.

Friedelbaum, Stanley H. 1987. "Reactive Responses: The Complementary Role of Federal and State Courts." 17 *Publius* 51.

Friedelbaum, Stanley H., ed. 1988. *Human Rights in the States: New Directions in Constitutional Policy-Making.* Westport, CT: Greenwood Press.

Friedman, Lawrence. 1985. *A History of American Law,* 2nd ed. New York: Simon & Schuster.

Friedman, Lawrence M. 1988. "State Constitutions in Historical Perspective." 496 *Annals* 33.

Galie, Peter J. 1982. "The Other Supreme Courts: Judicial Activism Among State Supreme Courts." 33 *Syracuse Law Review* 731.

Galie, Peter J. 1985, August 29–September 1. "Why Does He Write It Twice? The Role of State Supreme Courts in State Political Systems." Paper presented at the meeting of the American Political Science Association, New Orleans.

Galie, Peter J. 1987, April 2–3. "Teaching About Civil Liberties: The Missing Dimension." Paper presented at the meeting of the New York State Political Science Association, New York City.

Galie, Peter J. 1988. "Social Services and Egalitarian Activitism." In Stanley H. Friedelbaum, ed., *Human Rights in the States: New Directions in Constitutional Policy-Making*. Westport, CT: Greenwood Press.

Glick, Henry R. 1988. *Courts, Politics and Justice*, 2nd ed. New York: McGraw-Hill.

Glick, Henry R. 1990. *Courts in American Politics: Readings and Introductory Essays*. New York: McGraw-Hill.

Goldman, Sheldon, and Charles N. Lamb, eds. 1986. *Judicial Conflict and Consensus: Behavioral Studies of American Appellate Courts*. Lexington: University of Kentucky Press.

Goldman, Sheldon, and Austin Sarat, eds. 1988. *American Court Systems: Readings in Judicial Politics and Behavior*, 2nd ed. White Plains, NY: Longman.

Haines, Charles Grove. 1932. *The American Doctrine of Judicial Supremacy*, 2nd ed. Berkeley: University of California Press.

Hall, Melinda Gann. 1990. "Opinion Assignment Procedures and Conference Practices in State Supreme Courts." 73 *Judicature* 209.

Heinz, John P., and Edward O. Laumann. 1978. "The Legal Profession: Client Interests, Professional Roles and Social Hierarchies." 76 *Michigan Law Review* 1111.

Howard, J. Woodford. 1981. *Courts of Appeals in the Federal Judicial System: A Study of the Second, Fifth and District of Columbia Circuits*. Princeton, NJ: Princeton University Press.

"The Interpretation of State Constitutional Rights." 1982. 95 *Harvard Law Review* 1384.

Johnson, Charles A., and Bradley C. Canon. 1984. *Judicial Policies: Implementation and Impact*. Washington, DC: Congressional Quarterly.

Kagan, Robert A., Bliss Cartwright, Lawrence M. Friedman, and Stanton Wheeler. 1978. "The Evolution of State Supreme Courts." 76 *Michigan Law Review* 961.

Lawrence, Susan E. 1989. "Appealing: Who and What." 6 *Law, Courts and Judicial Process Newsletter, American Political Science Association* 52.

Lehne, Richard 1978. *The Quest for Justice: The Politics of School Finance Reform*. White Plains, NY: Longman.

McCree, Wade H., Jr. 1981. "Bureaucratic Justice: An Early Warning." 129 *University of Pennsylvania Law Review* 777.

Marvell, Thomas B. 1989. "State Appellate Responses to Caseload Growth." 72 *Judicature* 282.

Mosk, Stanley. 1988. "The Emerging Agenda in State Constitutional Rights Law." 496 *Annals* 54.

Murphy, Walter F. and C. Herman Pritchett, eds. 1961. *Courts, Judges, and Politics: An Introduction to the Judicial Process*. New York: Random House.

National Center for State Courts. 1990. *State Court Caseload Statistics: Annual Report, 1988*. Williamsburg, VA: National Center for State Courts.

"New Developments in State Constitutional Law." 1987. 17 *Publius* 1.

Richardson, Richard J., and Kenneth N. Vines. 1970. *The Politics of Federal Courts: Lower Courts in the United States*. Boston: Little, Brown.

Rosenblum, Victor G. 1967. "Courts and Judges: Power and Politics." In James W. Fesler, ed., *The 50 States and Their Local Governments*. New York: Knopf.

Savage, David G. 1990, July 1. "High Court Puts Its Faith in 'Laboratory of the States.' " *Los Angeles Times*, p. A1.

Shapiro, Martin. 1981. *Courts: A Comparative and Political Analysis*. Chicago: University of Chicago Press.

Sheldon, Charles H. 1987. "Judicial Review and the Supreme Court of Washington, 1890–1986." 17 *Publius* 69.

Spaeth, Harold. 1979. *Supreme Court Policy Making: Explanations and Predictions*. San Francisco: W. H. Freeman.

"State Constitutions in a Federal System." 1988. 496 *Annals* 10.

Stumpf, Harry P. 1988. *American Judicial Politics*. San Diego: Harcourt Brace Jovanovich.

Sullivan, Joseph F. 1990, July 18. "New Jersey Court Seen as a Leader in the Expansion of Individual Rights," *New York Times,* p. A11.

Tarr, G. Alan. 1988a. "Civil Liberties Under State Constitutions." 1 *The Political Science Teacher* 8.

Tarr, G. Alan. 1988b. "State Constitutionalism and 'First Amendment' Rights." In Stanley H. Friedelbaum, ed., *Human Rights in the States: New Directions in Constitutional Policymaking*. Westport, CT: Greenwood Press.

Tarr, G. Alan, and Mary Cornelia Aldis Porter. 1987. "State Constitutions and State Constitutional Law." 17 *Publius* 1.

Tarr, G. Alan, and Mary Cornelia Aldis Porter. 1988. *State Supreme Courts in State and Nation*. New Haven, CT: Yale University Press.

Wermiel, Stephen. 1988, June 5. "State Supreme Courts Are Feeling Their Oats About Civil Liberties." *Wall Street Journal,* p. A1.

Wheeler, Stanton, Bliss Cartwright, Robert A. Kagan, and Lawrence M. Friedman. 1987. "Do the 'Haves' Come Out Ahead? Winning and Losing in State Supreme Courts, 1870–1970." 21 *Law and Society Review* 403.

Witt, Elder. 1988, August. "State Supreme Courts: Tilting the Balance Toward Change." 1 *Governing* 30.

Wold, John T. 1978. "Going Through the Motions: The Monotony of Appellate Court Decision-making." 62 *Judicature* 58.

Wold, John T., and Greg A. Caldeira. 1980. "Perceptions of 'Routine' Decision-Making in Five California Courts of Appeal." 13 *Polity* 334.

CHAPTER 8

The Judiciary in State and Community: An Assessment

State and local courts have matured over the years, transformed from fledgling structures with uncertain and limited functions to quasi-powerful institutions today. Oliver Wendell Holmes's much-cited aphorism "The life of the law is not logic, but experience" applies to the judiciary as well. Throughout this book various examples have been used to illustrate how experience has shaped the state courts. These experiences are the result of social, economic, and political changes that have occurred nationally as well as within the particular states.

In this analysis of the state judiciary we have emphasized the three major components of the judicial system: the courts as *institutions,* the *process* of how business is conducted in them, and *judges* as political actors who help to determine how the courts are run and what judicial policies are enacted for the larger sociopolitical system. Moreover, we have stressed how external influences—political, social, economic—affect the judiciary. These influences affect the state courts in different degrees and at different times, much as an economic recession affects some businesses more than others. The concept of legal culture assists in understanding the differences in the operations and policy-making orientations of the state courts. The state judiciary does not operate with complete independence, of course. State courts are what they are and decide cases as they do in large measure because they function within the federal system of government.

This concluding chapter examines the state of the judiciary today. This assessment addresses four topics: (1) how we conceptualize court processes and the implications therein, (2) alternative means to resolve civil disputes outside of the traditional courtroom environment, (3) the costly and largely ineffective anticrime policies of the past several decades, and (4) some trends and developments that will affect state courts in the future. Central to all of these topics is the dilemma the judiciary faces in attempting to cope with an increase in civil and criminal cases during a period of limited financial resources.

HOW COURTS PROCESS DISPUTES

Providing a succinct account of how the courts process disputes is like trying to herd cats. It is a difficult task at best, especially when one acknowledges, as we have throughout this text, how discretion and other unpredictable elements of human behavior affect the many aspects of the judicial process. Consider, for example, two recent cases from New York (Wise, 1990: 25):

- The first case involved three defendants who sought to suppress the evidence (drugs) that police seized in an apartment house raid. The three were convicted in large part because the evidence was a key element in the prosecution's case at their trial. The defendants appealed, citing as their grounds the issue of whether the evidence had been lawfully confiscated by the police. Two of the defendants appealed jointly and the third separately. The two defendants had their appeal rejected by a panel of appellate judges that ruled the police acted properly. But the third defendant was successful in his appeal before a different panel of appellate judges, and his conviction was reversed.

- In the second case, two suspects in a robbery and kidnapping case were handcuffed together when the victim identified them as his assailants. They were convicted. Both men appealed their convictions independently but on the same grounds, that the victim's identification of each of them was tainted by the fact that they were handcuffed together. One man's appeal was denied. A month later, the same judge granted the second man's appeal and ordered a new trial for him.

How is one to explain how two identical cases could result in two totally different outcomes? First, there is considerable unevenness in how the criminal justice process operates. Second, different attorneys can realize different results when dealing with different judges (or the same one) even though the facts of the case are the same.

Both of these reasons, obvious as they may be, suggest important ways in which we conceptualize the judiciary. Up to the 1940s, the standard academic view of judicial decision making was based on a traditional model, whereby judges squared the facts of a case with the appropriate law in question and rendered a decision. As noted in the previous chapter, this traditional, or mechanistic, focus is rejected by most legal scholars today since it presupposes a professional neutrality in judicial behavior that is unrealistic; there are too many examples to the contrary to support such a notion.

Consider, for instance, the New Port Richey (Florida) county judge who was asked by a defendant to have her 60-day jail sentence postponed for 10 days so that she could have an abortion. The 26-year-old single woman had been convicted of violating the terms of her probation as a result of a drunk-driving conviction. The woman, a part-time bartender, said she was financially unable to care for a baby. Both the defense and prosecution attorneys agreed to the delay. The judge responded, "Do you want a continuance so you can murder your baby, is that it?" He denied her request. The judge's personal view of abortion is clear.

When the Utah Supreme Court was confronted with a challenge to Salt Lake City's obscenity ordinance, the chief justice wrote the majority opinion upholding the ordinance. He dismissed the federal Court's definition of obscenity and wrote that persons who feel that only material that has no redeeming social value is obscene "are depraved, mentally deficient, mind-warped queers." While the ordinary citizen may well agree with the judge's opinion of obscenity, the jurist's own values certainly entered into his legal ruling.

A third example of the convergence of personal values in legal decisions can be seen in the Pennsylvania county judge who refused to allow white families to adopt black, Vietnamese, or Korean children. According to the judge, it is not proper for white families to do this: "It's great when they've little pickaninnies. They're cute and everybody's a do-gooder. But what about when they're older, when they're 14 or 15?" The judge's actions resulted in a state investigation into his fitness for office.

In the opinion of a former state supreme court justice, judges should consider the norms and standards of the community when resolving policy questions and not mistakenly think their own views are shared by the community. But he also notes that a judge's past experiences inevitably can have an affect on judicial rulings: "If a judge were to maintain that he or she was able to discard all personal experience from judgment, I would be troubled on two grounds: first, because I would doubt the claim, and second, because judgment that is not grounded in experience is not likely to be wise judgment" (Grodin, 1989: 159–60).

Concepts of Judicial Decision Making

No one theory adequately explains judicial decision making. There are too many judges in too many jurisdictions, a phenomenal diversity of cases, and any number of various factors that influence them. Yet several different models do shed some light on the environment within which decision making occurs. Microgroup models, for example, focus on how individual behavior is affected by others in the same working environment. This is a common paradigm for examining the interaction of jurists on collegial courts. Role theorists, as mentioned in Chapter 7, are concerned with how a jurist perceives his or her position and the expected predictability of action that accompanies people in certain roles or positions.

Macrogroup models assume that some groups will find the judiciary more amenable to resolving their conflicts than will other groups, just as in the larger political process in government in the United States. As one scholar said, "Access is the crucial concept for the macro-group model. Those who have access to the courts—when the courts exercise a crucial role—are those who have success. Without access, a group's protestations against the authoritative allocation of values remains outside the judicial process" (Sheldon, 1974: 102–103).

Much of the judicial research cited in this text is based on decision-making models in which the individual characteristics of judges are regarded as having an influence on their decisions. Moreover, the attitudes of judges are a reflection of local and regional factors such as the political, economic, and social traditions and norms of specific areas. Thus, we do not expect the criminal courts to function identically in New York City and Lewiston, Idaho, since those two municipalities are so dissimilar in virtually all respects.

But students of the judiciary can assume that the environments of Lewiston and New York have an impact on the decisions made by judges there.

Problems in Case Processing

Television documentaries, popular and professional articles, and political and legal leaders speak of the "crisis in the courts." Sometimes the reference is to the larger legal system or criminal justice system in which the ills of our prisons become identified as an additional dilemma. As one judge summarizes the situation, the courts do not work very well for people with routine civil matters, people are not satisfied with the way they are treated by the courts, and the courts appear ineffective in coping with criminals (Neeley, 1983: 3).

The problems associated with the state and local judiciary have been mentioned earlier, but it is worth repeating them again: delays in processing cases, the expense of litigation, accessability to lawyers, questions about the integrity of the adversarial process, the bureaucratic nature of achieving justice, disparate sentences in criminal cases, and so forth. Above all, there seems to be the attitude held by many citizens that the courts are no longer a match for the sheer volume of civil and criminal cases they are supposed to handle. The number of criminal cases filed in state courts in 1988 increased by 5 percent from 1987, and civil cases increased by more than 4 percent. This expansion may not seem great, but we are dealing with caseload filings that number in the millions.

Some reforms appear obvious—hire more judges and build new courtrooms. The logic is sound. More judges can process cases more quickly. However, these two suggestions, meritorious though they may be, are expensive. And more judges at the "front end" (trial courts) may mean an increased backlog in cases that are appealed, and thus more judges are needed at the appellate end. In reality, appeal caseloads have been doubling about every decade since the end of World War II (Marvel, 1989: 282). Less costly alternatives are available, but there is a downside to these as well. For instance, whereas appellate courts can increase the number of staff attorneys to help process appeals, it could lead to too much staff responsibility for cases that judges should handle. Some jurisdictions have tried reducing the number of written opinions (the task that takes the most time for appellate jurists) produced by judges, but this is unsettling since it leaves the parties in a suit without an explanation of how the matter was resolved (287).

Other reforms would reduce the number of cases that pile up at the courthouse door—more "no fault" actions in divorce and personal injury suits, especially those that result from automobile accidents. But such proposals are often opposed by state and local bar associations, thus making them politically unattractive to state legislators. Two additional suggestions to reduce caseload demands have been made by the Council on the Role of the Courts. The council members suggest removing some civil matters from the courts, to be handled by an ombudsman. Typical issues include administrative claims such as disputes over the amount of public assistance payments and unemployment compensation. These matters, according to the council, do not need a full judicial hearing. The second proposal was to eliminate those civil cases in which the amount of damages sought were less than the cost of having the dispute resolved in a court hearing (Liberman, 1984).

These matters could be treated by other experts outside of the court, a suggestion that is developed in the second section of this chapter on alternative dispute resolution.

"Speedy trial" legislation can impel local prosecutors to take a good case to court or drop charges if the case is questionable within a specific period of time, but it does nothing to forestall delays by the defense. Supreme Court Chief Justice William Rehnquist has pleaded with Congress to ratify legislation to limit appeals in capital punishment cases. It is likely that Congress will respond favorably to Rehnquist's appeal. Congressional action in this direction would certainly encourage states to do likewise. This is an example of how an administrative reform can have an important policy dimension. Although death penalty cases occupy only a fraction of the caseload of the courts, the almost endless appeals in these matters have become symbolic of the frustration felt by many citizens that justice is never done.

Until the midcentury, numerous civil complaints were never adjudicated for the simple reason that neither the courts nor the legislatures extended the right to sue to consumer groups. The notion of public interest advocacy had little currency 75 years ago. It is unlikely that contemporary legislative bodies would revise state codes to give sellers and manufacturers the legal protection they once had when consumers had no standing to sue over product defects and liability.

Most reform proposals have focused on (1) reducing the number of cases brought to the courts, (2) enhancing the ability of the courts to handle cases by increasing the number of judges, and (3) making the courts more efficient through better management techniques and computer technology. What these reforms share is making the dispute resolution function more productive within the traditional institutional framework. Unfortunately, experience has shown that court reforms that should work in theory may not bring about the desired results. A complicating factor in court reform is the judiciary's dependence on legislative bodies for approval and funds to implement needed reforms. Legislators respond to a variety of constituent demands, particularly those that affect a large number of people. Lawmakers can realize considerable political mileage from sponsoring "tough" anticrime and antidrug measures, but their interest wanes on more pedestrian, and less public, issues such as court delay and caseload congestion. However, one proposal that has demonstrated considerable potential in reducing caseloads is alternative dispute resolution (ADR).

ALTERNATIVE DISPUTE RESOLUTION

For reasons of time and expense, litigants have long found it advantageous to settle their disputes before going to trial. Indeed, the data in Chapter 5 illustrate that most civil disputes never reach the trial stage. However, many disputes are never resolved because formal methods are unsatisfactory or the path to the courthouse is too prolonged, bureaucratic, or costly. Moreover, previous experience with judicial reform proposals led many reformers to question whether the traditional judicial structure could respond in the desired fashion to comprehensive changes. One result of this situation has been experimentation with alternative methods to settle disputes outside the courts but "within the shadow of the law." By the mid-1970s, the ADR movement began to gain increased acceptance by the legal community.

The two main dispute resolution mechanisms regarded as compatible alternatives to the courthouse are mediation and arbitration. Both can be employed with the same legal status as if the outcome resulted from a traditional judicial settlement. Indeed, in a growing number of states, one or the other is now required as a prelude to formal litigation should a settlement be contested. Although alternative dispute resolution shows considerable promise, however, some costs are encountered as well.

Mediation

Almost all of us at one time or another have served as mediators or have had a dispute mediated. Most likely, it was conducted in a very informal manner, and the process of mediation as such was never really thought of. Quite simply, mediation involves the use of a neutral third party to resolve a dispute between two other parties. Parents, for example, might mediate disputes between their teenagers over who will use the family car when both want it at the same time. The essential key to mediation success is that both parties must be willing to make concessions to arrive at a settlement voluntarily.

Mediation services fall into two categories: (1) public and private agencies available to handle disputes on a voluntary basis and (2) court-ordered mediation. Examples of public mediation programs include the Center for Dispute Resolution in Denver, which specializes in working with families, caseworkers, and guardians in child abuse and neglect cases, and the Massachusetts Face-to-Face Consumer Mediation Program, which handles consumer complaints. The Center for Dispute Settlement in Washington, DC, mediates disputes between caseworkers and their clients on public assistance issues.

The range of disputes heard by these public agencies is vast, extending from where a sewage treatment facility should be located (New Jersey) to hazardous waste disposal and long-term health care insurance regulation (Massachusetts). A Minnesota program mediates farmer-lender disputes and in 1985 settled a challenge by environmentalists over the aerial spraying of herbicides in forests. Several years ago, the Hawaii Program on Alternative Dispute Resolution interceded to arrive at an agreement involving the management of the state's surface and groundwater resources (Susskind, 1987).

The state of Washington established five dispute resolution centers in four communities in 1987. The services are offered to the public at little or no cost in landlord-tenant disputes, neighborhood conflicts, and consumer-merchant complaints. In Colorado, the legislature expanded the availability of mediation services in domestic cases. Most of the matters involve issues of custody, visitation, and support. Mediation is required in California in contested divorces involving child custody.

Private mediation services that are structured to resolve non-child custody disputes between divorcing couples are available in virtually all urban centers. Mediators, who typically are not attorneys, employ interpersonal rather than legal skills to arrive at a compromise between disputants as an alternative to the more costly, time-consuming divisiveness associated with a formal, court-handled divorce.

Another form of ADR involves the use of retired judges to hear cases but without the formality of the traditional court procedures. This arrangement (often referred to as "rent a judge") can be expensive, as firms that employ retired judges charge up to $300 an hour for their services. And it is unlikely to be available in those jurisdictions that are not bothered by lengthy delays caused by a backlog of cases. But in places like Los Angeles or New York City, where civil cases may languish for several years before a hearing date is set, the use of retired judges is desirable to save time and expense and to avoid the contentiousness of traditional litigation. This arrangement is especially attractive in cases involving complex or technical issues, matters in which typical trial court judges may lack expertise. The retired judge, available from lists maintained by private ADR firms, will include the names of those judges who are familiar with specialized issues (Thompson, 1988).

Arbitration

Arbitration has a long history in domestic as well as international law. In the United States, it is often associated with labor-management conflicts, wage and benefit disagreements between public employees and city management, and more recently cases involving sports figures who feel they deserve more compensation than team owners are willing to offer. As with mediation, arbitration requires a neutral third party to intervene between the two sides in a conflict. Unlike mediation, however, the arbitrator acts in the manner of a judge and renders a decision after hearing both parties. Arbitration is faster than a court hearing since many of the formalities (i.e., rules of evidence) involved in the judicial process are dispensed with in arbitration proceedings.

Arbitration can be binding or nonbinding. If the process is to be binding, both sides agree at the outset to accept the arbitrator's decision as final. In nonbinding arbitration, the losing party can have the matter adjudicated in court.

When the courts require a dispute to be arbitrated, the losing party can still take the matter to trial. Some 37 states have authorized the use of court-ordered arbitration in over some 100 jurisdictions. In Colorado, for example, civil cases involving damages of less than $50,000 are referred to private arbitration for resolution. Washington has a threshold of $35,000 in claims for mandatory arbitration in several counties that are experimenting with arbitration programs.

As with many new reforms, it is premature to pronounce whether the mediation and arbitration programs are working effectively for litigants and reducing the demands on civil courts. In Colorado over 8,000 civil cases were referred by the courts for mandatory arbitration during a six-month period in the late 1980s. Over three-fourths of the cases turned out to be ineligible for arbitration. Of the cases determined to be eligible, only 30 were actually resolved by arbitration. Admittedly, although the Colorado arbitration program is still in an experimental stage, the fact that only 1.5 percent of the cases assigned to arbitration were disposed of by arbitration is less than impressive (*Annual Report, Colorado Judiciary*, 1988: 58). Obviously, better screening of cases initially would separate those eligible for arbitration from those ineligible.

A Rand Corporation assessment of arbitration programs in five jurisdictions concluded that the programs managed to reduce court congestion and lowered costs and delays for litigants. The report emphasized that program design and implementation decisions and the reaction of lawyers to arbitration were the main ingredients on which successful operations hinged (Hensler, 1986: 273). Other reports on both mediation and arbitration indicate client satisfaction (Ray, 1989).

Given the promise of ADR, one may well ask why it is not being used more often. A main reason appears to be lack of knowledge about it by both the public and lawyers.

Attorneys are in the most pivotal position to steer clients to ADR. Yet because it is not institutionalized and some lawyers fear that it represents a threat to their business, lawyers may be reluctant to direct clients to mediation and arbitration services. According to a member of the ABA's Standing Committee on Dispute Resolution, attitudinal changes are necessary of ADR is to reach its potential:

> A drastic change in attitudes on the part of lawyers, judges and the public may be required. The win-lose philosophy that has dominated the educational system must give way to a broader problem-solving orientation. Those lawyers who fear loss of income because of ADR need to refocus on client satisfaction and the efficient operation of the legal system. (Ray, 1989: 68).

Additionally, lawyers may be skeptical of ADR because they fear the loss of influence over their clients. In the formal litigation process, lawyers are the gatekeepers to the courts. They are the ones who guide cases through the legal thicket. But this influence is dissipated in ADR as other third parties become the integral players (Goldberg et al., 1986: 292). Quite simply, ADR poses a financial and psychological threat to some attorneys.

Some critics of ADR wonder whether the movement is another attempt to encourage lower-income citizens to make do with a "second-class" way of resolving disputes while more affluent citizens continue to use the courts. According to this line of reasoning, lower-income users of ADR will receive second-class justice, and they will lose some legal protections that are available to those who use the courts. Moreover, the resolution of one dispute will not help others who are in a similar situation (Goldberg et al., 1986: 293). For instance, an individual who challenges a company's exorbitant credit charges may receive satisfaction by arbitration or mediation, but that single settlement will not be extended to other customers who are also paying high credit rates. In contrast, a judicial decision can often serve as a precedent that others can rely on in similar situations.

Criticisms aside, proponents of ADR point out that informal resolution by ADR enhances the "fairness" of the settlement process in contrast with experiences associated with the traditional courtroom trial. Satisfaction studies of the courts have focused on the litigants' feelings about the decisions in their cases. It is clear that our attitudes about the judiciary change as a result of experiences with the courts. The assumption of some satisfaction studies has been that litigants will perceive the outcome to be fair if they win and, conversely, unfair if they lose. Yet this may not always be the case for there is considerable evidence that the notion of "procedural justice" is a concern to all parties. Although the outcome is important to both sides, they also want assurance that the outcome was fair (see Tyler, 1984, 1988). An integral aspect of procedural justice is the ability of disputants to have the opportunity to participate in the settlement of the dispute. It is because of this that one can accept an unfavorable outcome as fair, if that person perceived the process by which the outcome was arrived at as fair. In most formal judicial proceedings, litigants may be present in the courtroom, but the lawyers are the ones who, along with the judge, determine the outcome. In contrast, ADR represents an effort to maximize litigant involvement in the settlement process. Especially in mediation, both sides participate, and each has the opportunity to see the perspective of the other.

Pending the findings of new studies on the impact of ADR, one may well conclude that it will be successful in some disputes but not in all civil actions. Run properly, ADR has the characteristics that one expects of our courts—fairness, impartiality, availability, and accessibility (Stumpf, 1988: 455). Needless to say, only the naive optimist could claim that our courts consistently make good on these expectations. To the contrary, any realistic assessment of American courts would find that there is a disturbing gap between the way the judiciary should operate and the way it does on a daily basis.

Critics of the judiciary, such as those associated with the Critical Legal Studies movement, argue that the law (and by implication the judiciary) is deliberately structured so that some litigants are in a favored position relative to others. Supporters of the system would concede that it is not perfect but that it does a remarkably capable job nonetheless and only relatively minor changes are needed to make it better.

The benefits of ADR seem both clear and real. Once litigants and attorneys recognize that many civil disputes can be settled through mediation, arbitration, or the use of retired judges, this system may become institutionalized in the nation's urban centers, where time and expense prohibit many individuals from seeking a judicial settlement to their grievances. As a president of the ABA commented, "I like to see the competition with our court system. I think the day will come when we drop the A out of ADR. Alternative dispute resolution will become part of the system" (Thompson, 1988: 46).

CRIME AND CRIMINAL CASES

Plea bargaining is the collary to mediation and arbitration on the criminal side of the law. As noted in Chapter 6, plea bargaining is employed extensively to settle criminal cases without having the issue decided through the formal courtroom process.

At various times in our history, particularly during the nineteenth century, vigilantism has been practiced, though there are few advocates of it today aside from some who feel "big government" has usurped private property rights. Vigilantism flourished when there was no effective law enforcement. This was the situation when much of the West was settled, and town dwellers banned together to deal with outlaws and Indians. However, vigilantism is also associated with acts of violence against individuals solely because of their race, ethnicity, or religious views (Brown, 1969).

Decriminalizing Offenses

There are two ways to reduce the volume of criminal cases in the judiciary. First, some offenses could be decriminalized or simply made legal. For example, a number of states have decriminalized penalties for possession of small amounts of marijuana. Possession of the substance has not been legalized but reduced to a misdemeanor level, much as a traffic citation. Offenders are ticketed rather than arrested and jailed. The idea of legalizing the use of certain drugs has been advocated by some who see it as the only way of reducing the profit margin connected with drug trafficking. Others, not surprisingly, reject this idea out of hand as an admission that mind-altering substances pose no hazard to society. Prominent black leaders such as the Reverend Jesse Jackson view the legalization of drugs as creating a permanent subclass in society, largely black and poor.

Similarly, some offenses such as prostitution and public intoxication could be decriminalized, legalized (as in the case of prostitution), or dealt with by medical personnel (in the case of public intoxication involving the chronic alcoholic). Both of these acts are illegal because they are contrary to the moral order, not because they pose harm to others. Enforcement of laws dealing with prostitution and public intoxication consume significant costs and time of police agencies. In 1985, the Federal Bureau of Investigation (FBI) reported almost 1 million arrests for drunkenness. Many of those offenders are alcoholics who are arrested repeatedly, and a jail sentence has no deterrent effect on them. That same year, according to one study (Pearl, 1987), each prostitution arrest in the country's 16 largest cities cost an average of $2,000 each. In half of these cities more money was spent on prostitution control than on public welfare or education. Pearl concluded that prostitution control costs were unacceptable financially and that they detracted from time law enforcement officers should have spent on serious criminal matters that jeopardized the public's safety. Although prostitution is often linked to other crimes, it may well be that decriminalization and regulation would be more cost-effective.

Reducing Crime

A second way to lower the number of criminal cases in the state trial courts is to reduce the level of crime in society. However, an effective method to do so through criminal sanctions has not been discovered. As crime rates increased from the 1960s on, states responded in several ways including mandating prison sentences upon conviction of certain crimes, restricting the use of probation and parole, and increasing prison sentences for specific crimes. California has experimented with all three of these measures, with the result that the number of inmates in prison has increased over 280 percent between 1979 and 1990; cities have to spend more for public protection and jails, thus reducing expenditures for social service programs; and civil cases are delayed because by law criminal cases have to be processed first. And crime continues to increase in California.

This book is not about either the causes or the extent of crime in American society. Yet one cannot ignore the impact of criminal cases on the judiciary or the frustration felt by decision makers over their inability to enact policies that would reduce crime rates. Crime is a growth industry, not just for those engaged in it but also for those attempting to cope with it.

According to one social scientist, the current crime wave, which began in the 1960s, is the third crime wave to be felt over the past 140 years. The first, from 1845 to 1876, was in part a result of new immigrants to the United States. The second, from 1900 to 1929, corresponded to a shift in migration patterns, as poor people moved from rural areas into the cities and even more immigrants came to the country. Both crime waves were ended as a result of industrial expansion, which absorbed the poor and less educated into employment. This third wave, attributable in part to poverty, social breakdown and disorganization, and drugs, likewise will be reduced only when the economy expands to provide new employment opportunities (Gurr, 1989).

There are ways to reduce the level of crime in society, ways that stress reducing the levels of discontent and the economic inequality among various groups in the United States. Anticrime measures that go beyond legal factors need to be considered or reemphasized. Political decision makers at all levels of government have to recognize that changes in some major social policies may be necessary if anticrime efforts are to succeed.

Programs to expand employment training, improve basic educational instruction, enlarge the number of affordable housing units, and encourage greater citizen-law enforcement cooperation are necessary if crime is to be reduced. The social and economic decay in most of the nation's urban centers has to be reversed. Neither the courts nor law enforcement agencies can deal with the breakdown of community norms, unemployment, high dropout rates in city schools, and a host of other social ills.

According to one analyst, a two-step assault on crime is required. First, the process of community disintegration has to be reversed. Second, criminal justice agencies have to become responsive to the special characteristics of high-crime neighborhoods. In short, considerable crime is neighborhood-based, and it will not be countered until a semblance of order is restored and a basis for community development is established (Scheingold, 1984: 206). Crime will always exist. The task ahead is to develop new public policies to reduce it to manageable levels.

These points are emphasized even more by Elliott Currie (1985), a university criminologist who has served on several state and federal crime commissions. Like Scheingold, Currie sees the resolution of community life as the key to reducing crime. The courts, he argues, really cannot put a dent in crime, although he does advocate alternative criminal sentences to prison as a means of reducing recidivist criminal behavior. Such alternatives involve integrating the offender back into the community through work programs like rehabilating housing. Overall, the thrust of nonprison sentencing must include the provision of some services geared toward rehabilitation. Currie admits that many past liberal crime policies have failed but that some positive programs were eliminated because of a cutback in state and federal funds and ideological reasons. Although rehabilitation programs are expensive, so is the alternative of incarceration, and the evidence is quite clear that prisons serve little purpose other than to keep certain offenders off the streets for limited periods of time.

"Get Tough" Policies. "Get tough" policies on drunk drivers have resulted in mandatory jail sentences in most states. More than 1.7 million drivers annually are charged with this offense. However, a Maryland sentencing study of convicted drunk drivers revealed that not only did the imposition of a jail sentence have no effect on recidivism but also those who received longer jail time were more likely to recidivate (Boersema and Hardenberg, 1990: 5). This does not mean that drunk drivers should not be punished. Rather, it suggests that states need to be more creative in sentencing policies by considering alternatives to jail or prison for many offenders. This point was emphasized by the chief justice of the Virginia Supreme Court in reference to the dilemmas faced by the courts in sentencing decisions. The public wants stiffer sentences but is reluctant to pay for more prison facilities. These realities will force the courts to "customize sentencing": "The courts must seek creative methods to distinguish violent from nonviolent offenders and must consider as alternatives to prison the possible use of electronic monitoring, drug therapies, and other methods of behavior modification" (Carrico, 1990: 29).

According to Barry Krisberg, president of the National Council on Crime and Delinquency, "no one has ever demonstrated that getting tougher or softer affects crime rates" (Dorgan, 1990). He adds that high crime rates are predictable in areas characterized by high rates of unemployment, school dropouts, and drug abuse. Prison is not much of a deterrent since most criminals figure they will not be caught, and some simply have little to lose.

Opinion polls over the past two decades clearly show that the public wants tougher sentencing. Yet it is difficult to find convincing evidence that longer prison sentences do much other than keep some offenders out of circulation for longer periods of time. Prison time may have a salutary effect for some but not all inmates. Nationally about 50 percent of all inmates released from state prisons will be arrested, convicted of criminal conduct, and sentenced to prison once again (*Report to the Nation,* 1988: 45).

What Price Imprisonment?　The costs of cracking down on criminals by sending them to prison for longer terms are high. Budgets for state prisons have been growing at an unprecedented rate since the late 1970s. Each new prison bed costs a state between $50,000 and $75,000, and then an additional $15,000 to $20,000 is required per prisoner per year (Peirce, 1990). Yet prisons are not rehabilitating, recidivism rates are as high as ever, and crime continues to increase. If nothing else, the financial drain of sentencing many offenders to prison will cause some state legislatures to rethink their anticrime policies.

One of the more disturbing results of the "get tough" measures is the number of black males who are sent to prison. According to a study by Sentencing Project, a nonprofit agency in Washington, DC, that lobbies for alternatives to incarceration, one of four black men in their 20s is in jail, prison, or on parole or probation. Whereas blacks make up only about 12 percent of the nation's population, the state prison population is split almost evenly between blacks and whites (Savage, 1990). Does this mean that blacks, as a group, are more likely to commit crimes than whites, Hispanics, or Asians? The answer is no. But because the poor are more likely to be caught and convicted of committing crimes than those in the middle class, and since there is a disproportionate number of blacks living in poverty, the crime rate for impoverished black males is uncomfortably high.

The Role of Education.　Prison and rehabilitation programs, of course, come into play after a defendant has been found guilty and sentenced. Another way of dealing with criminal behavior is to discourage it early on, through education. The link between education and criminality seems clear, as Wilson and Herrnstein (1985) note: "Virtually every inquiry has concluded that young persons who have difficulty in school—low achievement levels, poor behavior—are much more likely than other children to be delinquent and become criminals" (26). At one time it was possible for young males with few skills to obtain the blue-collar jobs that paid relatively well in industry. Those jobs have rapidly disappeared over the past several generations, lost to automation and overseas competition, particularly in auto manufacturing. As one report remarked on the employment situation today, "Young men with poor credentials, finding themselves facing low-wage job offers and high unemployment rates, frequently abandon the labor force intermittently or completely. Some choose criminal activity as an alternative to the labor market" (Jaynes and Williams, 1989: 8).

The dilemma of inadequate education is especially acute in the central cities. Middle-class families escape to the suburbs, where schools are better and safer and where more property tax money is spent on public education. Inner-city schools do not have the financial resources and staff to provide many students with the educational skills they need to compete in an increasingly complex and technologically oriented employment market. Some 30 percent of high school students nationwide quit at some point without earning a diploma, and the rate increases to 40 percent for nonwhite teenagers (Kozol, 1990: 49). In 1979, just over half of state prison inmates had less than 12 years of education. By the mid-1980s, this figure had increased to over 60 percent (Bureau of Justice Statistics, 1988: 3). Although education alone will not ensure a nation of law abiders, more effective education can reduce the dropout rate and increase job skills and thus offer alternatives for those who are most likely to engage in criminal behavior.

Intergovernment Coordination.   Although both the legislative and judicial branches of state government are concerned about crime, it is surprising how little each branch communicates with the other. According to participants at a conference on legislative-judicial relations, a number of obstacles inhibit communication. For example, neither branch is adequately informed about the other's institutional procedures. Moreover, both branches have negative attitudes about the other. As with the federal government, the basic institutions of state government are designed in such a manner that no one branch is too powerful (checks and balances). However, this does not mean that the legislature, the judiciary, and the governor's office should not be able to address jointly a common problem such as crime control. The authors of the conference report recommended the use of joint study commissions and task forces to improve communication and to illuminate common concerns (Ridge and Friesen, 1990).

An Alternative System.   The cornerstone of American criminal law is the presumption of the innocence of the accused. However, this ideal is stood on its head in countries that rely on the *inquisitorial* system. In an inquisitorial legal system, the emphasis is on the protection of society, not the rights of the accused. In some countries, such as France, Spain, and much of Latin America, the assumption is that the accused are probably guilty. The task for the defendant is to show that he or she did not commit the criminal act at issue. Under the inquisitorial process, a defendant must take the stand to answer questions from the judge and prosecutor. The Fifth Amendment in the Bill of Rights in this country protects the defendant from being compelled to testify. That the inquisitorial system results in more convictions than in U.S. courts seems clear. However, it remains to be demonstrated that it produces the desired results—a free and open society where crime is not much of a problem.

The position of the accused in our criminal justice process is the theoretical opposite of that in an inquisitorial system, though such differences may be diminished significantly in the way our system operates on a daily (rather than theoretical) basis. Yet this basic reality appears lost on many citizens. A Hearst Corporation survey of jurors' knowledge of basic legal concepts revealed that 49.9 percent thought that the person accused of a crime had to prove his or her innocence. That same survey, though of the general public rather than just those who had served on a jury, found that a majority incorrectly thought the state could appeal in a criminal case in which the defendant was found not guilty (Bennack, 1983: 8–9). Responses such as these suggest that the public's understanding of the fundamentals of the legal system is disturbingly inadequate. With this level of false information, it is not surprising that public support for wholesale reforms of the criminal justice system is so low.

THE JUDICIARY AND LEGAL ISSUES: TOWARD THE TWENTY-FIRST CENTURY

The country faces new social issues in the decade of the 1990s. At the same time, it wrestles with the resolution of unfinished problems that detract from the quality of life for many. Invariably, political, economic, and social ills have a legal dimension that involves lawyers and ultimately the judiciary at some point. Although some of these matters may be handled by the federal courts, most will land in the state judiciary. It is in the political milieu of the states where various policies and judicial decisions will indicate the states' responsibilities to take corrective action.

Social Issues and the Judiciary

The link between social issues and the judiciary was underscored in a recent survey conducted by several scholars at Georgetown University (Zweig et al., 1990). The survey of legal experts and practitioners was part of a larger effort that identified trends and issues that will shape the courts over the next several decades. According to the respondents, the following 10 developments, listed in rank order, will have a major impact on the courts in the foreseeable future: (1) illegal drug activity, (2) children in poverty, (3) the aging of Americans, (4) poverty cycles, (5) weakening of the family structure, (6) easy access to handguns, (7) child abuse, (8) environmental issues, (9) the deterioration of public schools, and (10) spousal abuse.

The issues of how to counter drug-related problems is perplexing. Three presidents—Nixon, Reagan, and Bush—declared a "war on drugs," with imperceptible results. Problems abound in developing antidrug policies: Should the attack be mounted by federal, state, or local law enforcement agencies or should each tackle one aspect of the problem? Who should be targeted in the assault: users, dealers, international drug traffickers, growers, or all of these? What should the emphasis of the assault be: to encourage drug abusers to enter detoxification programs, increase the criminal penalties for those convicted of drug-related activities, or engage in preventive educational efforts?

The courts have to depend on other branches of government for guidance and resources in how to deal with drug violators. If substance-abuse clinics are funded sufficiently by state and local governments, perhaps alternative sentencing policies for first-time drug felons can be employed. If drug users are to be dealt with harshly, states must build even more prison cells. Yet state prisons house 25 percent more prisoners than they are equipped to handle and federal prisons are more than 50 percent over capacity (General Accounting Office, 1989).

Moreover, the courts need assistance in processing drug cases. Examples of the impact of drugs on the criminal courts were cited in Chapters 1 and 6. As the chief justice of the California Supreme Court warned state legislators recently, "Drug-related cases are swamping the courts. The system has begun to take on so much water we are close to foundering. Too often, civil cases get drowned" (Hager, 1990). This situation is mirrored in urban trial courts across the country.

The Changing Society

Aside from the issues in the survey involving handguns, the environment, and public schools, the others in the top 10 all involve the changing character of both the American family and U.S. demographics. The courts are almost powerless to rectify those conditions that have led to the breakdown of the traditional family. But the courts do become involved in dealing with the resulting wreckage—child abandonment, child neglect, juvenile delinquency, and divorce. The anticipated increase in domestic relations legal problems will add to the growing caseload.

The American family, along with society in general, has undergone significant changes in the post-World War II era. The divorce rate has doubled since 1965, one out of every four children today is raised by a single parent, and some two-thirds of all mothers are working outside the home (Footlick, 1990: 16). Poverty is exacting a toll on parents and children alike. There are more people living in poverty today than 20 years ago. Some 500,000 children are homeless (Kozol, 1990: 49). Not surprisingly, the problems of poverty are often magnified for members of minority groups, especially those in the central cities: "There is a large and growing urban underclass in America—principally made up of blacks and Hispanics in the central cities. They are more economically isolated, more socially alienated, than ever before" (Harris and Wilkins, 1988: xii). A higher percentage of men in the poverty-stricken country of Bangladesh live past age 65 than do men in Harlem.

There are other indications of the deterioration in the quality of life for young people. Suicide is the second leading cause of death among those aged 15 to 24. Black adolescents between 15 and 19 years old are more likely to die as a result of murder than any other cause. Fewer than 5 percent of tenth-graders in 1950 had experimented with drugs. By 1987, the comparable figure was over 30 percent ("Code Blue," 1990). A county hospital in Los Angeles is used for training by military physicians because of the number of gunshot victims that are brought in on a daily basis. None of these factors—divorce, poverty, and single parents—causes criminal behavior, but they can make it more likely for a teenager to commit crimes when alternative means of achieving personal and economic satisfaction are limited.

The same group involved in the Georgetown survey recommended 12 actions to improve the courts (Zweig et al., 1990):

1. Better Access to the Courts—could be accomplished by a nationwide system of legal insurance for the middle class and wider availability of lawyers to do *pro bono* work for the poor;
2. Move Some Disputes Out of the Courts—this could be done by relegating whole classes of disputes (i.e., domestic relations, medical malpractice) to ADR for settlement;
3. Better Management of Dispute Resolution—establish judicial performance standards and require better management of court calendars;
4. "Re-emphasize the Court's Service Ethos"—which would include judicial concern for client satisfaction as well as a new emphasis on fairness in the resolution of disputes within the community;

5. Better Judicial Education—to allow for training of new judges and sabbaticals for veteran judges to assist other judges;
6. Expand Legal Education—to equip lawyers with the techniques of preventive law and ADR;
7. Diversify the Cultural Context of the Judiciary—to make the courts, and the judicial process, more sensitive to the changing and diverse cultures within the states and their communities;
8. New Procedures for Processing Technically Complex Cases—establish special courts to hear cases revolving disputes that are scientifically-intensive and technologically complex; this could entail revised rules of evidence and perhaps special jurors who have technological expertise;
9. Encourage Judicial Innovativeness—provide means for courts to experiment in all aspects of dispute resolutions including criminal sentencing alternatives;
10. Institutionalize Cooperative Problem Solving—by means of establishing incentives for creative dispute resolution;
11. Establish Judicial-Legislative Partnerships—that would promote more cooperation between the two branches of government; and
12. "Modernize the Courts"—through better communication and computer systems, ADR, and decentralizing justice outlets.

Would the enactment of these reforms cure the ills associated with the judiciary? No, but the reforms would enable the courts to resolve disputes in a more efficient and more community-oriented manner. These reforms are economically reasonable. However, as with any reform proposal, there are political costs that have to be considered since the status quo would be altered by their implementation. At a time when American industry is asked to be more creative, public schools more innovative, and legislative bodies more responsive to public needs, one can also put the challenge to the judiciary.

CONCLUSION

Our courts reflect American traditions and values. As such, the judiciary can represent the best and worst aspects of society. The broad goals of the courts are laudable—justice and equality before the law. At the same time, it would be erroneous to assume that these goals are achieved consistently or that the courts operate with complete impartiality, free from the influences of the dominant political and economic forces in the states and communities.

The crisis that has enveloped the judiciary has been building for several decades. How the states will assist the judiciary in handling the increasing caseload remains to be seen. Alternative dispute resolution is one means that has demonstrated potential to steer some civil matters from the courts. The problems of crime and lawlessness remain to be adequately addressed by the courts and, more important, by state lawmakers. These are not new concerns. In 1838, Abraham Lincoln spoke of the "increasing disregard for law which pervades the country" (quoted in Walker, 1980: 57).

Legislative bodies need to arrive at new anticrime policies that include social programs to reduce the economic disparity between the rich and the poor in the nation. Moreover, there needs to be more communication and cooperation between the institutions of government if social problems are to be resolved.

American legal culture, the federal structure of laws and courts, judicial independence, and the adversarial process are deeply rooted in this country. This does not mean that the judiciary cannot be improved. Efforts to decrease the role of politicians in the judicial appointment process, to increase the availability of lawyers for the poor, and to counter the time and expense of litigation need to continue.

REFERENCES

Annual Report, Colorado Judiciary. 1988. Denver: Office of State Court Administrator.

Bennack, Frank A., Jr., 1983, Fall. "The Public, The Media, and The Judicial System." 7 *State Court Journal* 4–13.

Boersema, Craig, and Don Hardenberg. 1990, Winter. "Initial Results from the Maryland DWI/DUI Sentencing Project." 14 *State Court Journal* 4–15.

Brown, Richard M. 1969. "The American Vigilante Tradition." In Hugh D. Graham and Ted R. Gurr, eds., *Violence in America.* New York: Signet.

Bureau of Justice Statistics. 1988, January. *Profile of State Prison Inmates 1986.* Washington, DC: U.S. Department of Justice.

Carrico, Harry L. 1990, Winter. "State Judiciary News: Virginia." 14 *State Court Journal* 28–31.

"Code Blue: Uniting for Healthier Youth." 1990. Report, National Association of State Boards of Education and the American Medical Association.

Currie, Elliott. 1985. *Confronting Crime.* New York: Pantheon Books.

Dorgan, Michael. 1990, March 25. "Different Statistics Tell Different Story." *San Jose Mercury News,* p. 17A.

Footlick, Jerrold. 1990, Winter/Spring. "What Happened to the Family?" *Newsweek,* special ed., pp. 15–20.

General Accounting Office. 1989, November. *Prison Crowding: Issues Facing the Nation's Prison System.* Washington, DC: U.S. Government Printing Office.

Goldberg, Stephen, Eric Green, and Frank E. A. Sander. 1986, February–March. "ADR Problems and Prospects: Looking to the Future." 69 *Judicature* 291–299.

Grodin, Joseph R. 1989. *In Pursuit of Justice.* Los Angeles: University of California Press.

Gurr, Ted Robert, ed. 1989. *Violence in America,* 3rd ed. Beverly Hills, CA: Sage.

Hager, Philip. 1990, February 13. "Drug Cases Imperil Courts, Lucas Warns." *Los Angeles Times,* p. 1A.

Harris, Fred R., and Roger W. Wilkins, eds. 1988. *Quiet Riots: Race and Poverty in the United States.* New York: Pantheon Books.

Hensler, Deborah R. 1986, February–March. "What We Know and Don't Know About Court-Administered Arbitration." 69 *Judicature* 270–278.

Jaynes, Gerald D., and Robin M. Williams, Jr., eds. 1989. *A Common Destiny: Blacks and American Society.* Washington, DC: National Academy Press.

Kozol, Jonathan. 1990, Winter/Spring. "The New Untouchables." *Newsweek,* special ed., pp. 48–53.

Liberman, Jethro, ed. 1984. *The Role of the Courts in American Society.* St. Paul, MN: West Publishing.

Marvell, Thomas B. 1989, February–March. "State Appellate Court Responses to Caseload Growth." 72 *Judicature* 282–291.

Neeley, Richard. 1983. *Why Courts Don't Work.* New York: McGraw-Hill.

Pearl, Julie. 1987, April. "The Highest Paying Customers: America's Cities and the Costs of Prostitution Control." 38 *Hastings Law Journal* 769–800.

Peirce, Neal R. 1990, February. "Can States Rise to the Challenge of the 90s." 11 *Comparative State Politics* 12–15.

Ray, Larry. 1989, June. "Emerging Options in Dispute Resolution." *American Bar Association Journal* 66–68.

Report to the Nation on Crime and Justice, 2nd ed. 1988. Washington, DC: U.S. Department of Justice, Bureau of Justice Statistics.

Ridge, Linda K., and Carl Friesen. 1990, Winter. "Legislative-Judicial Relations: Selling a New Partnership." 14 *State Court Journal* 19–21.

Savage, David G. 1990, February 27. "1 in 4 Young Blacks in Jail or in Court Control, Study Says." *Los Angeles Times,* p. A1.

Scheingold, Stuart A. 1984. *The Politics of Law and Order*. White Plains, NY: Longman.

Sheldon, Charles H. 1974. *The American Judicial Process: Models and Approaches*. New York: Dodd, Mead.

Stumpf, Harry P. 1988. *American Judicial Politics*. San Diego: Harcourt Brace Jovanovich.

Susskind, Lawrence. 1987, December. "Experiments in Statewide Office Mediation." *Dispute Resolution Forum*.

Thompson, Mark. 1988, March. "Rented Justice." 8 *California Lawyer* 42–46.

Tyler, Tom R. 1984. "The Role of Perceived Injustice in Defendants' Evaluations of Their Courtroom Experience." 18 *Law & Society Review* 51–74.

Tyler, Tom R. 1988. "What Is Procedural Justice?: A Critical Examination of An Empirical Research Tradition." 22 *Law & Society Review* 103–135.

Walker, Samuel. 1980. *Popular Justice*. New York: Oxford University Press.

Wilson, James Q., and Richard J. Herrnstein. 1985. *Crime & Human Nature*. New York: Touchstone.

Wise, Daniel. 1990, May 21. "Some Facts But Opposite Rulings." *National Law Journal,* p. 25.

Zweig, Franklin M., S. T. Thurston, S. D. Turpin, D. C. Judge, C. C. Jernigan, D. Melnick, and C. A. Dougherty. 1990, April–May. "Securing the Future for America's State Courts." 73 *Judicature* 296–306.

Index

9768